Financial Inclusion in India

Policies and Programmes

Financial Inclusion in India

Policies and Programmes

By

N. Mani

Professor and Head,
Post-graduate and Research Department of Economics,
Erode Arts and Science College, Erode, Tamil Nadu

New Century Publications
New Delhi, India

NEW CENTURY PUBLICATIONS
4800/24, Bharat Ram Road,
Ansari Road, Daryaganj,
New Delhi – 110 002 (India)

Tel.: 011-2324 7798, 4358 7398, 6539 6605
Fax: 011-4101 7798
E-mail: indiatax@vsnl.com • info@newcenturypublications.com
www.newcenturypublications.com

Editorial office:
LG–7, Aakarshan Bhawan
4754-57/23, Ansari Road, Daryaganj,
New Delhi – 110 002

Tel.: 011-4356 0919

First Published: **July 2015**

ISBN: **978-81-7708-408-5**

Published by New Century Publications and printed at Salasar Imaging Systems, New Delhi

Designs: Patch Creative Unit, New Delhi

PRINTED IN INDIA

About the Book

It is well-known that in India, while one segment of the population has access to assortment of banking services encompassing regular banking facilities and portfolio counselling, the other segment of underprivileged and lower income group is totally deprived of even basic financial services. Exclusion of large segments of the society from financial services adversely affects the overall economic growth of a country. Apart from the rural areas, there is a significant degree of financial exclusion in urban areas as well. The cost of financial exclusion is recognised to be enormous for the society as well as for individuals, particularly in terms of inability to realise full potential due to financial constraints.

The recent developments in banking technology have transformed banking from the traditional brick-and-mortar infrastructure like staffed branches to a system supplemented by other channels like automated teller machines (ATMs), credit/debit cards, internet banking, online money transfers etc. However, access to such technology is restricted only to privileged segments of the society.

In order to ensure financial inclusion of the poor, particularly in rural areas, various initiatives have been taken by the Government of India and the Reserve Bank of India (RBI) from time to time. These have included nationalization of commercial banks in 1969 and 1980, establishment and expansion of rural credit co-operatives, regional rural banks (RRBs), urban co-operative banks (UCBs), micro finance and self-help groups (SHGs), mutual funds, pension funds and Pradhan Mantri Jan-Dhan Yojana (PMJDY), 2014.

There are several challenges that require concerted efforts from banks, the RBI and the Government to ensure convenient and cost-effective delivery of financial services to the public at large. In particular, the challenge is to introduce innovations in risk assessment, reduce transaction costs, devise new credit delivery channels, and use information technology to make financial inclusion a viable model. Looking to the immense potential lying ahead, rapid progress of financial inclusion efforts in India is the need of the hour. The stakeholders have come to realize the need for viable and sustainable business models which can sharply focus on accessible and affordable financial services, products and processes, synergistic partnerships with non-bank entities including the technology service providers.

Author's Profile

Dr. N. Mani is presently Head, Post-graduate and Research Department of Economics, Erode Arts and Science College, Erode, Tamil Nadu. He holds M.A., M.Phil. and Ph.D. degrees from Bharathiar University, Coimbatore. Specializing in development economics, he has 23 years of teaching experience to post-graduate and undergraduate classes. He successfully completed a major research project sponsored by University Grants Commission (UGC), New Delhi. He is currently engaged in a research project sponsored by Indian Council of Social Science Research (ICSSR), New Delhi.

Dr. Mani has published five books and several papers in reputed journals on varied subjects. He is also the President of Tamil Nadu Science Forum and was organizing secretary of the National Children Science Congress, 2006. He has successfully guided and supervised the works of 6 Ph.D. and 14 M.Phil. scholars. He is a member of various academic bodies including *Indian Society of Labour Economics* and *Indian Society of Agricultural Economics*.

Contents

Preface

It is a known fact that in India, while one segment of the population has access to assortment of banking services encompassing regular banking facilities and portfolio counselling, the other segment of underprivileged and lower income group is totally deprived of even basic financial services. Exclusion of large segments of the society from financial services affects the overall economic growth of a country. It is for this reason that financial inclusion is a global concern. In Sweden and France, banks are legally bound to open an account for anybody who approaches them. In Canada, law requires banks to provide accounts without minimum balance to all Canadians regardless of employment or credit history. In the United States, the Community Reinvestment Act (1977) is intended to encourage depository institutions to help meet the credit needs of the communities in which they operate, including low and moderate income neighbourhoods, consistent with safe and sound operations.

The present concern for financial inclusion can be traced to the United Nations Capital Development Fund (UNCDF) initiatives, which broadly underlined the main goals as also the broad frameworks and parameters of inclusive finance, as access to a range of financial services, including savings, credit, insurance, remittance and other banking/payment services to all 'bankable' households and enterprises at a reasonable cost.

According to UNCDF the main goals of inclusive finance are as under:

1. Access at a reasonable cost of all households and enterprises to the range of financial services for which they are 'bankable', including savings, short and long-term credit, leasing and factoring, mortgages, insurance, pensions, payments, local money transfers and international remittances.
2. Sound institutions, guided by appropriate internal management systems, industry performance standards, and performance monitoring by the market, as well as by sound prudential regulation where required.
3. Financial and institutional sustainability as a means of providing access to financial services over time.
4. Multiple providers of financial services, wherever feasible, so as to bring cost-effective and a wide variety of alternatives to customers (which could include any number of combinations of sound private, non-profit and public providers).

The problem of financial exclusion is not exclusive to the developing world. The developed countries too have been affected by it and many poor and disadvantaged people in the world still lack access to financial services. However, the type, degree and magnitude differ between the two worlds. Therefore, emphasis has been on empowerment of the disadvantaged groups for access to public goods and services including banking services in the developed countries. The UN General Assembly had designated the year 2005 as the International Year of Micro Credit stating that the year will be an important opportunity to give impetus to micro finance programmes throughout the world. Thus, the International Year of Micro Credit 2005 aimed at "Building Inclusive Financial Sectors to Achieve the Millennium Development Goals".

The nexus between economic growth, financial deepening and financial inclusion has been well-recognized in India's development strategy, particularly when the financial and economic reforms process was initiated in early 1990s. A more focused and structured approach towards financial inclusion has been, in effect, followed since the year 2005, when the Reserve Bank of India decided to implement policies to promote financial inclusion and urged the banking system to focus on this goal. Recent policy initiatives to drive financial inclusion, including formulation of a board approved financial inclusion policy (FIP) by the banks, also attempt to strike a balance between the requirements of financial inclusion and that of soundness of financial institutions and stability of the financial system.

The concept of financial inclusion has a special significance for a fast-emerging economy such as India, as it encompasses a large segment of the productive sectors of the economy under formal financial network to unleash their creative capacities. Over a period of time, several financial and economic policy measures are being taken by the banks in India to improve access to affordable financial services through financial education, awareness generation, business communication networking and leveraging technology.

In most developing countries, a large segment of society, particularly low-income people, has very little access to financial services, both formal and semi-formal. As a consequence, many of them have to necessarily depend either on their own or high cost informal sources of finance such as moneylenders. This is particularly true for the sporadic financing requirements of low income households for non-productive consumption purposes and other emergency requirements such as medical expenditure. Benefits of growth, therefore, tend to concentrate in the hands of those already served by the formal financial system.

According to the Committee on Financial Inclusion (Chairman: C. Rangarajan), 2008, "Financial inclusion may be defined as the process of ensuring access to financial services and timely and adequate credit where needed by vulnerable groups such as weaker sections and low income groups at an affordable cost".

The essence of financial inclusion is in trying to ensure that a range of appropriate financial services is available to every individual and enabling them to understand and access those services. Apart from the regular form of financial intermediation, it may include a basic no-frills banking account for making and receiving payments, a savings product suited to the pattern of cash flows of a poor household, money transfer facilities, small loans and overdrafts for productive, personal and other purposes, insurance (life and non-life) etc. While financial inclusion, in the narrow sense, may be achieved to some extent by offering any one of these services, the objective of *comprehensive financial inclusion* would be to provide a holistic set of services encompassing all of the above.

Census 2011 estimated that out of 24.67 crore households in the country, 4.48 crore (58.7 percent) households had access to banking services. Of the 16.78 crore rural households, 9.14 crore (54.46 percent) were availing banking services. Of the 7.89 crore urban households, 5.34 crore (67.68 percent) households were availing of the banking services. The banking network of the country (as on March 31, 2014) comprised of a bank branch network of 1,15,082 and a network of 1,60,055 ATMs. Of these, 43,962 branches (38.2 percent) and 23,334 ATMs (14.58 percent) were in rural areas.

Despite various measures for financial inclusion, poverty and exclusion continue to dominate socio-economic and political discourse in India even after 68 years of Independence. Though economy has shown impressive growth during post-liberalization era (1991 onwards), impact is yet to percolate to all sections of the society and therefore India is still home to 1/3rd of world's poor.

Indian economy in general and banking services in particular have made rapid strides in the recent past. However, a sizeable section of the population, particularly the vulnerable groups, such as weaker sections and low income groups, continue to remain excluded from even the most basic opportunities and services provided by the financial sector. Access to a well-functioning financial system, by creating equal opportunities, enables economically and socially excluded people to integrate better into the economy, so as to actively contribute to development and protect themselves against economic shocks.

Financial inclusion is new paradigm of economic growth which plays a major role in driving away the poverty. Lack of access to financial services in most of rural areas due to high informative barriers and low awareness, creates the need and scope of financial inclusion. Fruits of development have hardly reached to nearly half of Indian population because of lack of access to loans and insurance services. Financial inclusion is integral to the inclusive growth process and sustainable development of the country. It should, therefore, ideally be a policy of involving a much wider section of population deposit mobilization and credit intermediation.

Access to formal banking system is affected by several implementation and policy barriers such as culture, financial literacy, gender, income and assets, proof of identity, remoteness of residence etc. Over a period of time, several measures have been taken by the banks in India to improve access to affordable financial services through financial education, awareness generation, business communication networking and leveraging technology. The lack of awareness, low incomes and assets, social exclusion, illiteracy are the barriers from demand side. The distance from bank branch, branch timings, cumbersome banking procedure and requirements of documents for opening bank accounts, unsuitable banking products or schemes, language, high transaction costs and attitudes of bank officials are the barriers from supply side. Hence, there is a need for financial inclusion to build uniform economic development through greater accessibility and transparency in fund-flow regime for ushering in greater economic and social equity.

The foundation for promoting greater financial access in India can be traced to the findings of the All-India Rural Credit Survey in the early 1950s. In order to ensure financial inclusion various initiatives have been taken by the Government of India and the Reserve Bank of India (RBI) from time to time. These have included nationalization of commercial banks in 1969 and 1980, establishment and expansion of rural credit co-operatives, regional rural banks (RRBs), urban co-operative banks (UCBs), micro finance and self-help groups (SHGs), mutual funds, pension funds and Pradhan Mantri Jan-Dhan Yojana (PMJDY), 2014.

There is substantial progress towards opening of accounts, providing basic banking services during the recent years. However, it is essential that all the sections be financially included in order to have financial stability and sustainability of the economic and social order. There is urgent need to push forward the financial inclusion agenda to ensure that people at the bottom of the pyramid join the mainstream of the formal financial system.

There are several challenges that require concerted efforts from banks, the RBI and the Government to ensure convenient and cost-effective delivery of financial services to the public at large. In particular, the challenge is to introduce innovations in risk assessment, reduce transaction costs, devise new credit delivery channels, and use information technology to make financial inclusion a viable model. Looking to the immense potential lying ahead, rapid progress of financial inclusion efforts in India is the need of the hour. The stakeholders have come to realize the need for viable and sustainable business models which can sharply focus on accessible and affordable financial services, products and processes, synergistic partnerships with non-bank entities including the technology service providers.

May 2015 **N. Mani**
Erode

Abbreviations/Acronyms

ACLF	Additional Collateralised Lending Facility
ACTI	Advisory Council on Trade and Industry
ACU	Asian Clearing Union
ADB	Asian Development Bank
ADR	Assets Development Reserve
ADRs	American Depository Receipts
ADs	Authorised Dealers
AIDBs	All India Development Banks
AIFIs	All India Financial Institutions
ALM	Asset Liability Management
AMC	Asset Management Company
AML	Anti-Money Laundering
AMS	Aggregate Measure of Support
APEC	Asia Pacific Economic Cooperation
APMC	Agriculture Produce Market Committee
ARC	Agricultural Refinance Corporation
ARC	Asset Reconstruction Company
ARDC	Agricultural Refinance and Development Corporation
ASEAN	Association of South East Asian Nations
ATMs	Automated Teller Machines
BCBS	Basel Committee for Banking Supervision
BCSBI	Banking Codes and Standards Board of India
BFRS	Board for Financial Regulation and Supervision
BFS	Board for Financial Supervision
BIFR	Board for Industrial and Financial Reconstruction
BIS	Bank for International Settlements
BPSS	Board for Payment and Settlement Systems
BSE	Bombay Stock Exchange
CAAP	Capital Adequacy Assessment Process
CAC	Capital Account Convertibility
CAMELS	Capital Adequacy, Asset Quality, Management, Earnings, Liquidity and Systems Control
CAR	Capital to Assets Ratio
CBLO	Collateralised Borrowing and Lending Obligations
CCFF	Compensatory and Contingency Financing Facility
CCIL	Clearing Corporation of India Ltd.

CDBMS	Centralised Database Management System
CDOs	Collateralised Debt Obligations
CDR	Corporate Debt Restructuring
CDR	Credit-Deposit Ratio
CDs	Certificates of Deposit
CFMS	Centralised Funds Management System
CFSs	Consolidated Financial Statements
CIBIL	Credit Information Bureau of India Ltd.
COC	Controller of Currency
CPC	Credit Planning Cell
CPR	Consolidated Prudential Reporting
CP	Commercial Paper
CPSS	Committee on Payment and Settlement Systems
CPSUs	Central Public Sector Undertakings
CR	Contingency Reserve
CRAR	Capital to Risk-Weighted Assets Ratio
CRISIL	Credit Rating Information Services of India Ltd.
CRR	Cash Reserve Ratio
CSF	Consolidated Sinking Funds
CVPS	Currency Verification and Processing Systems
DBD	Department of Banking Development
DBO	Department of Banking Operations
DBOD	Department of Banking Operations and Development
DBS	Department of Banking Supervision
DCA	Department of Company Affairs
DCCBs	District Central Cooperative Banks
DCM	Department of Currency Management
DEIO	Department of External Investment and Operations
DFIs	Development Finance Institutions
DIC	Deposit Insurance Corporation
DICGC	Deposit Insurance and Credit Guarantee Corporation
DM	Deutsche Mark
DPs	Depository Participants
DPSS	Department of Payment and Settlement Systems
DRI	Differential Rate of Interest
DRT	Debt Recovery Tribunals
DSB	Dispute Settlement Body
DSR	Debt Service Ratio
DSS	Debt Swap Scheme

ECBs	External Commercial Borrowings
E-Commerce	Electronic Commerce
ECR	Export Credit Refinance
ECS	Electronic Clearing Service
EDMU	External Debt Management Unit
EFF	Extended Fund Facility
EFT	Electronic Funds Transfer
EMEs	Emerging Market Economies
E-Money	Electronic Money
EMU	European Monetary Union
EXIM Bank	Export Import Bank of India
FCA	Foreign Currency Assets
FCCBs	Foreign Currency Convertible Bonds
FCNR(A)	Foreign Currency Non-Resident (Accounts)
FCNR(B)	Foreign Currency Non-Resident Accounts (Banks)
FDI	Foreign Direct Investment
FEMA	Foreign Exchange Management Act
FERA	Foreign Exchange Regulation Act
FIIs	Foreign Institutional Investors
FRBM	Fiscal Responsibility and Budget Management
FSQ	Free Sale Quota
GDRs	Global Depository Receipts
GIC	General Insurance Corporation of India
HDFC	Housing Development Finance Corporation Ltd.
HFCs	Housing Finance Companies
IBA	Indian Banks' Association
IBRD	International Bank for Reconstruction and Development
ICAI	Institute of Chartered Accountants of India
ICDs	Inter-Corporate Deposits
ICICI	Industrial Credit and Investment Corporation of India
ICRA	Information and Credit Rating Agency
IDBI	Industrial Development Bank of India
IDBs	India Development Bonds
IDFC	Infrastructure Development Finance Company Ltd.
IFC	International Finance Corporation
IFCI	Industrial Finance Corporation of India Ltd.
IMF	International Monetary Fund
IRDA	Insurance Regulatory and Development Authority
IRDP	Integrated Rural Development Programme

IRS	Interest Rate Swaps
ISDA	International Swap and Derivatives Association
ISQ	Internal Sale Quota
IT	Information Technology
ITEs	Intra-group Transaction and Exposures
KYC	Know Your Customer
LAF	Liquidity Adjustment Facility
LAN	Local Area Network
LERMS	Liberalised Exchange Rate Management System
LIBOR	London Inter-Bank Offered Rate
MFs	Mutual Funds
MNCs	Multinational Companies
MoU	Memorandum of Understanding
NABARD	National Bank for Agriculture and Rural Development
NAIS	National Agricultural Insurance Scheme
NBFCs	Non-Banking Financial Companies
NBFIs	Non Banking Financial Institutions
NFA	Net Foreign Assets
NFEA	Net Foreign Exchange Assets
NHB	National Housing Bank
NLR	Net Liquidity Ratio
NPAs	Non-Performing Assets
NREGS	National Rural Employment Guarantee Scheme
NRI	Non-Resident Indian
NSE	National Stock Exchange
NSSF	National Small Savings Fund
NSSO	National Sample Survey Organisation
ODs	Overdrafts
OGL	Open General License
OMO	Open-Market Operations
OMS	Open-Market Sales
ORFS	On-Line Return Filing System
OSS	Off-Site Surveillance System
OTC	Over the Counter
PACS	Primary Agricultural Credit Societies
PDS	Public Distribution System
PLR	Prime Lending Rate
PPP	Purchasing Power Parity
PSBs	Public Sector Banks

PSU	Public Sector Undertaking
RBI	Reserve Bank of India
RBS	Risk-Based Supervision
REER	Real Effective Exchange Rate
REPO	Repurchase Agreement
RRBs	Regional Rural Banks
RTGS	Real Time Gross Settlement
SBI	State Bank of India
SBS	Shredding and Briquetting System
SCBs	Scheduled Commercial Banks
SCBs	State Cooperative Banks
SDRs	Special Drawing Rights
SEBI	Securities and Exchange Board of India
SENSEX	Sensitive Index
SFC	State Finance Corporation
SHG	Self-help Group
SIDBI	Small Industries Development Bank of India
SLR	Statutory Liquidity Ratio
SPV	Special Purpose Vehicle
SARFAESI	Securitisation and Reconstruction of Financial Assets and Enforcement of Security Interest Act
SRP	Supervisory Review Process
SSIs	Small-scale Industries
STCI	Securities and Trading Corporation of India
TBs	Treasury Bills
TRAI	Telecom Regulatory Authority of India
UCBs	Urban Co-operative Banks
UNCTAD	United Nations Conference on Trade and Development
UNDP	United Nations Development Programme
USAID	United States Agency for International Development
UTI	Unit Trust of India
VaR	Value at Risk
VAT	Value-added Tax
WMA	Ways and Means Advances
WTO	World Trade Organization
YTM	Yield-to-maturity

Unit and Currency Conversion Table

Unit Conversion

1 lakh = 0.1 million
10 lakh = 1.0 million
1 crore = 10.0 million
100 crore = 1.0 billion

Currency Conversion

The unit of currency in India is Indian Rupee, symbolized as ₹. As per reference rate of Reserve Bank of India (RBI) for May 8, 2015,

US$ 1 = 64.04
UK£ 1 = 99.03
Euro (€) 1 = 71.76
Japanese Yen (¥) 100 = 53.41

Fiscal Year

Fiscal year in India runs from April 1 to March 31 of the following year

Pre- and Post-metric Systems of Currency and Measures in India

Metric system of currency in India was introduced from April 1, 1957
In the Pre-metric system, one Rupee was = 16 annas and one anna was = 4 paise
In the Post-metric system,
One Rupee = 100 paise
One mile = 1.6 kilometres
One yard = 0.9144 metre
One acre = 0.4046 hectare

Part I:
Indian Economy, Poverty and Financial System

1

Indian Economy: An Overview

Prior to Independence in 1947, India was a dependency of the United Kingdom and consisted of British India, and the Princely States. It encompassed the entire area which now forms the four countries of India, Pakistan, Myanmar, and Bangladesh.

The British came to India as merchants in the middle of the 17th century. After gaining foothold on the coastline, they spread to every corner of the Indian peninsula. They gained political supremacy around the middle of the 18th century. After winning the Battle of Plassey in 1757 and the Battle of Buxer in 1764, they established themselves firmly as the rulers of India and ruled it till 1947 to subserve their economic interests. At the time of the arrival of the British, Indian economy was, by and large, self-sufficient, possessing a fine balance between agriculture and industry.

The British rule in India can be divided into two periods: (a) the rule of the East India Company from 1757 to 1858, and (b) the rule of the British Government from 1858 to 1947. The British interests in India were governed by the requirements of the Industrial Revolution which started in Britain in the middle of the 18th century and then spread to other regions of Europe. These were two-fold: (a) to secure raw materials from India for factories in Britain, and (b) to ensure permanent market in India for the British manufactures. To fulfil these objectives, they adopted the measures which proved disastrous for the Indian economy.

Thus, on the eve of Independence, India was a typically backward economy. It exhibited the following features: (a) traditional and stagnant agriculture, (b) poor technological and scientific capabilities, (c) limited and lop-sided industrialization, (d) underdeveloped means of transport and communications (e) grossly inadequate health and educational facilities, and (f) virtually non-existent social security arrangements. In short, the country suffered from the twin problems of rampant poverty and widespread unemployment, both making for low general standard of living.

After 65 years of planned economic development, India is presently one of world's fastest growing economies. Lately, it has emerged as a global economic power, a leading outsourcing destination and a favourite of international investors. Indian economy has matured in several important respects. It is now much more integrated with the world economy and has benefited from this integration in many ways. The outstanding success of information technology (IT) and IT-enabled services (ITES) has demonstrated what Indian skills and enterprise can do, given the right environment. Similar strength is now evident in sectors such as pharmaceuticals, auto components and, more recently in textiles.

Many predict that India will emerge as third largest economy in the world (after US and China) in a couple of decades. Members of the global economy, including businesses and foreign governments, have started taking note of India's rise and recognizing opportunities for investments and enterprise. India's massive workforce and democratic functioning suggest that the future of labour-intensive industry lies here. No doubt, India is poised to claim its rightful place as world economic power in the 21st century, being referred to as the Asian Century.

1.1 Human and Natural Resources

1.1.1 Human Resources: After China, India is the most populated country in the world with a headcount of 121 crore in 2011. Mainland China's population is 135 crore. India's population has increased rapidly since Independence in 1947. The population increased from 36.1 crore in 1951 to 43.9 crore in 1961, to 54.8 crore in 1971, and to 68.5 crore in 1981. The Census of 1991 enumerated the population at 84.4 crore which rose to 102.9 crore in 2001 and was estimated at 121 crore in 2011. Thus, after China it is India that has crossed the 1 billion (100 crore) population mark. According to United Nations *World Population Prospects* (2010), India's population is projected to peak at 1.718 billion (171 crore) in 2060. At its peak, India will be the most populous country in the world. China at its peak in 2025 will have 1.395 billion (139.5 crore) people. In fact, when China peaks, India will have already surpassed it in population.

The unabated growth of population is attributable to a sharp decline in death-rate coupled with relatively high birth-rate. The death-rate has fallen due to improved health conditions, control of epidemics, better handling of famine conditions, and general improvement in the standard of living. There has been a significant decline in the infant mortality rate since Independence. However, birth-rate in India is still very high, hovering in the vicinity of 26 per thousand. Many social and economic factors are responsible for high birth-rate. These include universality of marriage, preference for male children, illiteracy, and poverty. The rapid growth of population has seriously hampered developmental efforts.

1.1.2 Natural Resources: Natural resources give India a large potential for agricultural and industrial production, and their rapid development is an essential condition for the achievement of a self-reliant and self-sustained economy which can provide to the mass of the people continually rising living standards and opportunities for gainful employment.

The most important natural resource of India is land which is the base for agricultural production. While population grows, the land surface is fixed and only a certain proportion of it is available for cultivation. The non-expandable land resources have to accommodate the competing demands for production of food, fodder, fibre and fuel, minerals, urbanisation, non-agricultural land use etc. for the increasing human and animal population.

India is endowed with substantial water resources. The country's average annual rainfall is about 1,194 mm. The outstanding feature of the rainfall in India is its unequal distribution during the year and its variation from year to year in respect of quantity, incidence and duration.

Substantial water supplies for irrigation, industrial and municipal uses are available from under-ground waters. Wells have been constructed in all parts of India for domestic water supply and for irrigation of land and they are in use from times immemorial. However, large-scale irrigation from this source is possible only with the help of tube wells operated by power pumps.

Forests play a vital role in social, cultural, historical, economic and industrial development of India and in maintaining its ecological balance. They are the resource base for sustenance of its population and a storehouse of biodiversity. Other vocations of land use, such as agriculture and animal husbandry, are dependent on forests and forestlands. Forests not only maintain and improve the moisture regime and provide clean air but also produce humus and maintain soil fertility.

Amongst natural resources, minerals form a special category as they are wasting assets. Once they are taken out of the ground and utilised, they are lost for ever. They should, therefore, be treated on a different footing from replenishable natural resources. Minerals figure in the export trade of India and contribute to the earning of foreign exchange. They are exported, however, largely in the raw state.

Coal, iron ore, manganese ore, mica, limonite and kyanite are produced in quantities of real importance to industry and other sectors of economy. Of these, mica, manganese ore, kyanite and limonite are wholly or largely exported. Private sector participation in coal mines has been allowed in recent years to fill the gap between coal demand and production.

1.2 Poverty, Five Year Plans and Economic Reforms

1.2.1 Poverty: The root cause of social insecurity in India is poverty and that is largely due to lack of adequate or productive employment opportunities. It is described as chronic or structural social insecurity, arising from insufficient degree of overall economic development. It is associated with other insecurities emanating from conventional contingencies such as the loss of employment, disability, old age, death etc. which are called the *second-order* type of insecurities or conventional social insecurity.

Poverty is a widespread social evil in underdeveloped countries of the world, particularly in Asia and Africa. There is no standard definition of poverty for all the countries of the world. Being a relative concept, the meaning of poverty differs from country to country. In India, poverty is defined in terms of a minimum (subsistence) level of living rather than a reasonable level of living. Thus, minimum physical quantities of cereals, pulses, clothing etc. are determined for a subsistence level. These physical quantities are multiplied by their prices and converted into monetary terms, determining the per capita consumption/income for subsistence level. Persons whose income/consumption is below this determined figure are considered to be below the poverty line.

1.2.2 Five Year Plans: India began the process of planned economic development with the start of the First Five Year Plan on April 1, 1951. The main objective of planning was identified as that of initiating a process of development which will raise living standards and open out to the people new opportunities for a richer and more varied life. The manner in which this objective has been translated into specific objectives has varied from Plan to Plan.

However, in a broad sense, the basic objectives of planning in India can be grouped under four heads: (a) growth, (b) modernisation, (c) self-reliance, and (d) social justice. In one form or another, these objectives, albeit with varying emphasis, reflect the views of all sections of the population and represent a national consensus on the aims of planning.

Since 1951, India has completed eleven Five Year Plans and the implementation of the Twelfth Five Year Plan (2012-13 to 2016-17) is underway. Each Plan takes into account the experience of the previous Plan and attempts to make the necessary directional changes and emphasis. In fact, the beginning and the end of a Plan are important dates in the economic history of India. Each Plan is both an assessment of the past and a call for the future.

1.2.3 Economic Reforms: The last decade of the 20th century was momentous in the economic history of India as it witnessed a successful transition of India from a controlled, inward-looking, and slow-growing economy to a liberalised and open economy that has now found a place amongst the fastest growing economies in the world.

Responding to the macroeconomic crisis of late 1980s, a programme of liberalisation, privatisation, and globalisation was initiated in July 1991. This programme encompassed wide-ranging reform measures in the areas of industry, public finances, banking and insurance, foreign trade and exchange rate management. The purpose of these economic reforms was two-fold: (a) to restore macroeconomic stability on both domestic and external fronts, and (b) to place the economy on a higher growth path through enhanced levels of investment, and improvements in productivity, efficiency and competitiveness.

When the Indian economy was opened to external competition in the early 1990s, many feared a set back for domestic companies which had enjoyed protection through high tariff and non-tariff walls for about half a century since Independence. These fears were true but short-lived. After facing global competition for about a decade and half, Indian industry is emerging much stronger to find its rightful place not only in the domestic market but also in foreign lands.

Economic reforms have well addressed the external payments and debt crises but the problem of budgetary deficits continues to persist, both at the level of the Centre and the States.

1.3 Agriculture and Allied Activities

At the time of Independence in 1947, Indian agriculture was traditional and stagnant in every respect. It was characterised by feudal land relations, primitive technology, and the resultant low productivity per hectare. The first task of Indian Government in the immediate post-Independence period was, therefore, to initiate growth process in agriculture on modern lines. Modernisation of agriculture was required both in terms of technological and institutional changes. Abolition of intermediaries in agriculture, like *zamindars* and *jagirdars*, was accomplished soon after Independence.

The process of planned economic development in India began with the launching of First Five Year Plan in April 1951. At that time, the country was faced with severe food shortage and mounting inflation. The Plan accorded pride of place to programmes for agriculture and community development. This was a natural priority for the Plan which sought to raise the standard of living in rural areas and cope with food shortages.

In the mid-1960s, a new technology in the form of high-yielding varieties (HYVs) was introduced for cereals. Apart from the new technology, public investment in agriculture, particularly in irrigation, was stepped up significantly. The public sector played an important role in promoting agricultural research and education. Large investments were made for the development of research system under the aegis of the Indian Council of Agricultural Research (ICAR) and the State Agricultural Universities. Simultaneously, a well-designed extension network was created for disseminating new technologies to the farmers.

Successive Five Year Plans have aimed at improving irrigation facilities, encouraging the use of fertilisers, improved varieties of seeds, implements and machinery and institutional credit. As a result, there has been a significant increase in the use of modern inputs leading to higher productivity and production. Satisfactory progress has been made not only in the production of major foodgrains but also in horticultural crops.

Another change of consequence was the introduction of a system of support prices, procurement and public distribution of major items of agricultural produce. Several changes have taken place in agricultural credit and marketing. The system of cooperative credit has spread, lessening the dependence of the cultivators on the exploitative practices of the village moneylenders. In agricultural marketing, the dominant role of the Food Corporation of India and the growth of marketing and processing cooperatives has helped both farmers and consumers. These and other changes in the field of credit and marketing have altered the very unequal relationship between the farmer and the trader.

Although agriculture is still the backbone of the Indian economy, at least in terms of employment, the impulses of reforms have been relatively less in scope and depth in this sector. It is noteworthy that reforms in agricultural sector were introduced only towards the end of the 1990s. Nevertheless, a series of policy initiatives have been undertaken in this sector as well. These include: (a) partial decontrol of fertiliser prices, (b) removal of bottlenecks in agricultural marketing, (c) relaxation of restrictions under the Essential Commodities Act, 1955, (d) introduction of forward trading in important commercial crops, (e) replacement of the Revamped Public Distribution System with Targeted Public Distribution System, (f) establishment of Rural Infrastructural Development Fund, and (g) replacement of quantitative controls by tariff.

Still further, micro credit, routed through self-help groups (SHGs), has emerged as a visible credit channel to the poor as their access to conventional credit channels is constrained by the requirement of collateral and high transaction cost. The National Horticulture Mission was launched on April 1, 2005. The Mission will ensure end-to-end approach having backward and forward linkages covering research, production, post-harvest management, processing and marketing.

The current deceleration in agriculture is the root cause of the problem of rural distress that has surfaced in many parts of the country and reached crisis levels in some. Government's strategy to raise agricultural output comprises the following elements: (a) improve water management, rain water harvesting and watershed development, (b) reclaim degraded land and focus on soil quality, (c) bridge the knowledge gap through effective extension, (d) diversify into high value outputs, fruits, vegetables, flowers, herbs and spices, medicinal plants, bamboo, bio-diesel etc., but with adequate measures to ensure food security, (e) promote animal husbandry and fishery, (f) provide easy access to credit at affordable rates, (g) improve the incentive structure and functioning of markets, and (h) refocus on land reforms issues.

1.4 Rural Development

Rural development implies both the economic betterment of people as well as greater social transformation. Increased participation of people in the rural development process, decentralisation of planning, better enforcement of land reforms and greater access to credit and inputs go a long way in providing the rural people with better prospects for improved quality of life. Improvements in health, education, drinking water, energy supply, sanitation and housing coupled with attitudinal changes also facilitate their social development.

According to 2011 Census, rural population was 68.8 percent of total population. With prospect of industrialisation and the consequent migration of rural population to urban areas, the percentage share of rural population in total population is expected to decline to 60 percent by 2030. Nevertheless, in the present scenario the bulk of India's population lives in rural areas.

Mahatma Gandhi National Rural Employment Guarantee Act (MGNREGA), 2005 was notified on September 7, 2005. The Act came into force on February 2, 2006 when 200 selected districts of the country were brought under its purview (Phase I, 2006-07). MGNREGA was extended to additional 130 districts in Phase II during 2007-08. The remaining rural areas were notified with effect from April 1, 2008. Total no. of job cards issued at the end of financial year 2014-2015 stood at 12.09 crore.

The objective of the MGNREGA is to enhance the livelihood security of unorganised workers in rural areas by guaranteeing 100 days of wage employment in a financial year to a rural household whose members volunteer to do unskilled manual work. The Act further aims at creating durable assets and strengthening the livelihood resource base of the rural poor. The choice of works suggested in the Act address causes of chronic poverty like drought, deforestation, soil erosion, etc.

The significance of MGNREGA lies in the fact that it creates a right-based framework for wage employment programmes and makes the Government legally bound to provide employment to those who seek it. In this way the legislation goes beyond providing a social safety net, and towards guaranteeing the right to employment. By prioritizing natural resource management and emphasizing the creation of durable assets it holds the potential of becoming a growth engine for sustainable development of an agriculture-based economy.

Shelter is an essential component of human survival. Shortage of shelter is a universal phenomenon faced by majority of countries and particularly the developing nations. More often than not, however, it is perceived more as an urban problem. However, the magnitude of the housing shortage in rural areas is enormous. Indira Awaas Yojana (IAY) is the flagship scheme of the Ministry of Rural Development (MoRD), Government of India to provide houses to the below-poverty-line (BPL) families in the rural areas. It has been in operation since 1985-86.

IAY is one of the very popular schemes of MoRD and has caught the imagination of the rural people. Funds are released in instalments directly to the beneficiaries and there is no credit portion as part of the assistance which enables timely release of funds. The beneficiaries construct the houses as per their own choice of design, technology and requirement.

Pradhan Mantri Gram Sadak Yojana (PMGSY) was launched on December 25, 2000 as a fully-funded Centrally-sponsored scheme to provide all weather road connectivity in rural areas of the country. The programme envisages connecting all habitations with a population of 500 persons and above in the plain areas and 250 persons and above in the hill States.

Rajiv Gandhi Grameen Vidyutikaran Yojana (RGGVY) was launched on April 4, 2005 for rural electricity infrastructure and household electrification. Rural Electrification Corporation (REC) is the nodal agency for the programme.

National Rural Health Mission (NRHM) was launched on April 12, 2005, to provide accessible, affordable and accountable quality health services to the poorest households in the remotest rural regions.

1.5 Industry and Minerals

1.5.1 Industry: India's industrial policy soon after Independence in 1947 was shaped broadly in terms of the Industrial Policy Resolution of 1948. That Resolution emphasised clearly the responsibility of the Government in promoting, assisting and regulating the development of industry in the national interest. It envisaged for the public sector an increasingly active role. This role was to be particularly significant in the establishment and development of heavy and basic industries. Certain crucial sectors for industrial development were reserved for Government initiative.

The 1948 Resolution was reviewed in the light of experience gained, and the new Industrial Policy Resolution was placed before Parliament by the Prime Minister on April 30, 1956.

Industrial sector of the Indian economy developed fairly rapidly during the first fifteen years (1951-66) of planned economic development. After that the pace of industrialisation slowed down, particularly in the capital goods sector. This so-called industrial retrogression was explained in terms of a host of factors, the chief among them being:

1. Exogenous causes like Chinese aggression (1962), Indo-Pak conflict (1965), and Bangladesh crisis (1971).
2. Successive droughts of 1965-66 and 1966-67 and again in 1971-72 which disrupted the supply of raw materials and the demand for industrial goods emanating from the rural sector.
3. Oil crisis of 1973 resulting in cost-push inflation.

Some economists believe that the rigid industrial licensing policies and other controls coupled with bureaucratic hurdles also hampered the growth of the industrial sector after the mid-1960s.

Responding to the macroeconomic crisis of late 1980s, a programme of liberalisation, privatisation, and globalisation was initiated in July 1991 when the Government announced its new industrial policy in the Parliament. It removed industrial licensing, reduced the number of industries reserved for the public sector, abolished restrictions on investment and expansion under the Monopolies and Restrictive Trade Practices (MRTP) Act, 1969, allowed automatic approval of foreign investment, eliminated quantitative import restrictions on intermediate and capital goods. No doubt, the reform measures have created a favourable environment for industry to upgrade its technology and build-up capacity in order to cater to growing domestic and external demand.

Following the reform measures, there was an initial spurt in industrial activities. However, it was short-lived and deceleration set in from 1996-97. The industrial deceleration was due to a number of structural and cyclical factors such as normal business and investment cycles, a lack of both domestic and external demand, continuing high real interest rates, infrastructure bottlenecks in power and transport, and lack of reforms in land and labour markets.

The process of industrial liberalisation started in 1991 is continuing. Private sector has been invited to invest in oil exploration and refining. Similarly, power sector is now open to both domestic and foreign private investment. Government has also allowed private sector activities in the mining industry. Industrial liberalisation after 1991 has proved a boon for the Indian economy, though there are some grey areas.

In another significant move, the Government enacted the Micro, Small and Medium Enterprises Development (MSMED) Act, 2006. This legislation for facilitating promotion and development and enhancing the competitiveness of micro, small and medium enterprises became operational from October 2, 2006.

By and large, Indian industry has upgraded technology and product quality to a significant degree and met the challenge of openness after being protected for so long. The Competition Act, 2002 passed by the Parliament seeks to establish a pro-competitive legal framework, contain anti-competitive practices and abuses of dominance and yield better regulation of markets.

Industrial progress of India over the last 67 years since Independence has been quite satisfactory. The country has achieved near self-sufficiency in the production of manufactured goods as reflected in the composition of imports which mainly consist of petroleum products, chemicals, and capital goods. Industrial progress has also led to the growth of technological and managerial skills, and industrial and scientific research.

1.5.2 Minerals: The metallurgical and mineral industries constitute the bedrock of industrial sector as they provide the basic raw materials for most of the industries. Amongst natural resources, minerals form a special category as they are wasting assets. Once they are taken out of the ground and utilised, they are lost for ever. They should, therefore, be treated on a different footing from replenishable natural resources.

India's per capita mineral consumption is one of the lowest in the world. The growth in cement and energy sector has been faster than growth in the metallic sector. Realising the need for a faster pace of industrialisation, the country has pursued an integrated approach to mineral development, attempting to augment the mineral base by establishing giant exploration and exploiting agencies. Presently the country is comfortably placed in the field of bauxite, iron ore, limestone, dimensional and decorative stones and coking coal and a major breakthrough is required for augmenting the reserves of diamond, platinum, base metals, fertiliser and industrial minerals.

The mineral wealth of India, though by no means inexhaustible, comprises an adequate range of useful products that are necessary for the industrial development of the country. An appraisal of the reserves shows that while in respect of minerals essential for basic industries—coal and iron—the reserves are ample, the country is deficient in a fairly long list of vital minerals like ores of copper, tin, lead, zinc, nickel, cobalt and in sulphur and most important of all, petroleum. The position with regard to aluminium ore, refractories, abrasives, limestone etc. may be considered as fairly adequate while in respect of titanium and thorium ores and of mica, the country has considerable reserves. The power resources in India comprise coal, oil and hydro electricity. India's coal mining is centred mainly in Jharkhand and West Bengal.

1.6 Infrastructure Development

Adequate, efficient and affordable infrastructural facilities constitute the core of development strategy and efforts. In the absence of infrastructure services, enterprises are forced to seek higher-cost alternatives which impact profits and production levels adversely. The demand for infrastructural services has increased rapidly after industrial liberalisation of the Indian economy. Unfortunately, infrastructural bottlenecks remain the biggest stumbling block of industrial progress in the country. By their very nature, infrastructure projects involve huge initial investments, long gestation periods and high risk.

Rapid economic growth cannot be realised if energy is not available at reasonable costs. Electricity is a crucial energy input in this context. Power sector reforms were initiated in 1991 to encourage competition in each sub-element of the sector, namely generation, transmission and distribution under an independent and transparent regulatory regime. With this objective in mind a Central Electricity Regulatory Commission (CERC) was set up at the national level and State Electricity Regulatory Commissions (SERCs) were set up at the level of States. Private sector participation was also set in motion with the enactment of the Electricity Laws (Amendment) Act in 1998. The Government of India has taken a number of measures, in consultation with State Governments and other stakeholders, to improve power situation in the country.

The transport sector, comprising the railways, roads, ports and civil aviation, has been one of the principal areas of government intervention in India. Given the transport sector's fundamental contribution to economic growth and social welfare, government intervention was perceived to be necessary, as in the case of many other infrastructure sectors, because of: (a) high risk perception emanating from long gestation periods, (b) irregular revenue flows, and (c) economies of scale leading to monopolistic tendencies. Public sector ownership, management and financing of the transport sector in India, however, suffers from several forms of inefficiencies and has been found to be unresponsive to user demand. Further, services are usually priced below costs which impedes the generation of adequate internal surpluses, in turn, leading to excessive dependence on budgetary support.

In India, transport system comprises a number of distinct modes and services, viz. railways, roads, road transport, ports, inland water transport, coastal shipping, airports and airlines. Railways and roads are the dominant means of transport. In a vast country like India, it is necessary to develop various transport modes in an integrated manner to build up an efficient, sustainable, safe and regionally balanced transportation system. Each mode of transport should operate in its field of economy and usefulness, with competitive and non-discriminatory prices that are adequate to support progressive development of transport infrastructure and services. This would also enable the comparative advantages and economic efficiencies to be properly reflected in the user costs.

Recent liberalization of the Indian economy has brought home the urgency of developing an efficient transportation system for increasing productivity and enabling the country to compete effectively in the world market. Adequacy and reliability of transport infrastructure and services are important factors, which contribute towards the ability of the country to compete in the field of international trade and attract foreign direct investment. The Government has a major role to play in this sphere. Even in a market economy, the framework that national governments provide for the transport sector largely determines the level of cost and transport operations. It is, therefore, necessary to create a policy environment that encourages competitive pricing and coordination between alternative modes in order to provide an integrated transport system that assures the mobility of goods and people at maximum efficiency and minimum cost.

Improved communication is vital for productivity in all spheres of activity: agriculture, industry, trade and commerce. In addition, with the increasing movement of people within and outside the country, easy communication is essential for enhancing human welfare so that families, friends and acquaintances can overcome the barriers of distance. For a developing economy like India, it is thus important that policies and programmes be initiated, and resources committed to bring about rapid growth in the sector.

Telecommunication has emerged as a key driver of economic and social development and in an increasingly knowledge intensive global scenario India needs to play a leadership role. The National Telecom Policy 2012 (NTP, 2012) was conceived with a vision to transform the country into an empowered and inclusive knowledge-based society, using telecommunications as a platform. NTP 2012 seeks to make a major effort in achieving a high degree of self reliance in telecom equipment manufacturing besides promoting innovation and IPR creation.

India has emerged over the last decade as the most preferred destination for outsourcing of IT services. The vibrant IT industry is contributing immensely by providing information about latest technology and international business practices. Various sectors of the Indian economy such as industry, finance, insurance, communications and transport have adopted information technology in a big way. However, agricultural sector of the economy is lagging behind in utilizing IT services. Some efforts have been made in this regard but they are by no means adequate.

Trade in information technology and information technology enabled services (IT and BPO services) has been the main driver of growth in India's trade in services in recent years. India's exports of IT and BPO services fall in three broad categories, IT services, BPO and Software products and Engineering Services.

The Special Economic Zones Act, 2005, was passed by Parliament in May 2005 which received the Presidential assent on June 23, 2005.

After extensive consultations, the SEZ Act, 2005, supported by SEZ Rules, came into effect on February 10, 2006, providing for drastic simplification of procedures and for single window clearance on matters relating to Central as well as State Governments. The main objectives of the SEZ Act are the following:

1. Generation of additional economic activity.
2. Promotion of exports of goods and services.
3. Promotion of investment from domestic and foreign sources.
4. Creation of employment opportunities.
5. Development of infrastructure facilities.

The SEZ Act, 2005 envisages key role for the State Governments in export promotion and creation of related infrastructure. A single window SEZ approval mechanism has been provided through a 19 member inter-ministerial SEZ Board of Approval (BoA).

The applications duly recommended by the respective State Governments/UT Administrations are considered by BoA periodically. All decisions of the BoA are with consensus.

SEZs in India seek to promote value addition component in exports, generate employment and mobilize foreign exchange. SEZs when operational are expected to offer high quality infrastructure facilities and support services, besides allowing for the duty free import of capital goods and raw materials.

Additionally, attractive fiscal incentives and simpler customs, banking and other procedures are offered in such zones. Setting up of SEZs is also treated as an infrastructure development activity and offered same incentives. SEZs in India closely follow the Chinese model.

1.7 Fiscal Policy

Fiscal policy is an important instrument of the general economic policy of a government. It is concerned with the use of a government's taxation and expenditure powers to influence economic activities in an economy at the aggregate level. It also deals with financial relations between different tiers of government in a federal polity. Through the medium of budget, it determines government expenditure, borrowing requirements and issue of new currency. It also determines private spending through taxation measures.

It may be recalled that the external payments crisis of 1991, which led to the initiation of economic reforms in India, was the result of deteriorating fiscal situation during the latter half of 1980s. This period was marked by high and persistent fiscal deficits, accompanied by large revenue deficits. This had led to a significant enlargement of Government borrowings from financial intermediaries and increased financing of Government deficit through automatic monetisation which aggravated price rise. When the Indian economy faced an unprecedented macroeconomic crisis in 1991, fiscal consolidation constituted a major objective of the policy response. This consolidation was to be achieved through reduction in the size of budget deficit and public debt in relation to GDP. For this purpose, it became necessary to: (a) enhance tax and non-tax revenue, (b) curtail current expenditure growth, (c) restructure public sector undertaking, including disinvestment, (d) improve fiscal-monetary co-ordination, and (e) deregulate financial system.

Apart from these reforms aimed at fiscal consolidation, a number of institutional measures were also taken during the 1990s. Public sector restructuring and disinvestments were undertaken with a view to increase the efficiency of the public sector undertakings and also to provide additional resources to the Government. The need for improvements in budgetary practices led to the enactment of the Fiscal Responsibility and Budget Management (FRBM) Act, 2003 which ushered the Indian economy in an era of fiscal consolidation based on fiscal policy rules.

The financing of fiscal deficit is another area, which underwent significant changes in the post-reforms period. With the discontinuation of *ad hoc* 91-day Treasury Bills in April 1997, automatic monetisation of deficits was eliminated. Greater reliance on borrowing at market-related interest rates has led to a substantial lowering of statutory pre-emption of institutional resources for the Government. This has also facilitated development of the market for Government securities which has witnessed remarkable changes in the last few years.

Tax reforms since June 1991 have helped in correcting structural imbalances in the tax system. They are *soft* on industry with a view to create new investment climate and make India internationally competitive. By lowering the tax rates, the Government expects speedy industrial development and hence buoyancy in tax revenues.

1.8 Monetary Policy, Prices and Credit Management

Monetary policy refers to the expansion or contraction of money and credit supply in an economy. Since monetary policy includes the regulation of both the volume and allocation of credit therefore credit policy is a part of the overall monetary policy. Monetary policy operates through changes in the stock of money and changes in the cost and availability of credit. The operation of monetary policy rests on the interrelationship between the stock of money, output and prices. Through money creation, credit is made available to productive enterprises. The availability of credit has favourable impact on output.

Simultaneously, increase in money supply raises demand, exerting pressure on prices. The output effect and the price effect must be considered together to assess the overall effect of a monetary measure on the economy.

In tune with the national economic objectives, RBI has followed a monetary policy usually called the policy of *controlled expansion.* The money supply has expanded sufficiently to meet the growing needs of industry and trade. However, it has been ensured that the expansion is not reckless. Broadly speaking, the expansion of money supply has been somewhat more than the increase in output thereby allowing a reasonable increase in the price level.

Budgetary deficits of the Central Government are an important cause for monetary expansion in India. In fact, monetary policy has played a subservient role to fiscal policy in India. Therefore, the main emphasis of the RBI has been on controlling secondary expansion of money, i.e. credit given by commercial banks to other sectors of the economy. While restraining the banking system in this regard, the RBI has ensured that the credit needs of priority sectors (agriculture, small-scale industries) are adequately met.

Price stability is of prime concern for a developing country like India. The term price stability is not used here in a rigid sense to mean price fixity. A modest increase of 2-3 percent in price level per annum is compatible, sometimes even desirable, with the general connotation of price stability. Since price rise is closely linked with the supply of money therefore monetary policy holds the key to price stability. This is why the economists stress growth with stability as the ideal objective of economic policy of a country.

Price stability is desired in the Indian context because majority of the population belongs to unorganised sector without protection against the onslaughts of inflation. Price stability is a pre-requisite for a successful development strategy, particularly in the context of the implementation of Five Year Plans. Domestic price stability is required also to boost exports.

Judicious demand and supply management policies are required to counteract inflationary tendencies. In spite of strong inflationary pressures in the world economy, India has successfully prevented inflation from getting out of hand. Government has focused attention on the price stability of certain essential commodities. This has been ensured by maintaining demand and supply balance at commodity level.

Following are the important elements of the price policy of the Government of India: (a) Some basic commodities like foodgrains and sugar are made available to consumers at fixed prices through a vast network of fair price shops, (b) Buffer stock operations are undertaken to maintain open market prices of certain essential goods with reasonable range, and (c) Imports of essential goods (e.g. vegetable oils and sugar) are allowed when necessary and exports held back to ensure adequate supplies of essential commodities (e.g. tea).

The RBI has pursued its monetary policy through a variety of instruments at its command. These include: bank rate policy, open market operations, variable reserve ratio and selective credit controls (now abolished). The twin objectives of monetary policy, viz. maintaining price stability and ensuring availability of adequate credit to productive sectors of the economy to support growth have remained unchanged, though their relative emphasis has varied depending on the circumstances. In line with this, in recent years, a preference emerged for a soft and flexible interest rate environment within the framework of macroeconomic stability. At the same time, the large inflows of external capital have contributed to the liquidity conditions remaining very comfortable. Consequently, the emphasis of monetary policy within the broad objectives of price stability and growth has been on liquidity management so as to ensure orderly conditions in financial markets without impeding the legitimate credit needs of industry.

The Reserve Bank of India (RBI) has largely been successful in bringing the organised sector of the money market well under its control. RBI is also playing a more active role in the provision of rural finance and is devoting special attention to the problem of promoting banking development in parts of the country in which it has hitherto been lacking. These developments have strengthened the credit system materially. RBI has wide powers for regulation and supervision of the credit policy of banks. More than these legal powers, it is the moral prestige of the RBI and the close understanding between its management and the management of public sector and private sector banks that is of special importance in the alignment of the banking system to the needs of a planned economy.

1.9 Financial Institutions, Financial Markets and Financial Instruments

Soon after Independence in 1947, Government of India followed a policy of social control of important financial institutions. This was reflected in the nationalisation of the Reserve Bank of India (RBI) in 1948, takeover of the then Imperial Bank of India (rechristened as State Bank of India) in 1956, nationalisation of life insurance business and the creation of Life Insurance Corporation of India (LIC) also in 1956, nationalisation of 14 major commercial banks in 1969, nationalisation of general insurance companies and the setting up of General Insurance Corporation (GIC) in 1972, and nationalisation of 6 more commercial banks in 1980.

As a result of state domination, India's financial system was characterised by barriers to entry, control over pricing of financial assets, high transaction costs and restrictions on movement of funds from one market segment to another. It was in this backdrop that wide-ranging financial sector reforms were introduced as an integral part of the economic reforms programme started in early 1990s. These reforms have paved the way for integration among various segments of the financial system. It is widely accepted that reduction/removal of financial repression has enhanced the efficiency and potential growth of the Indian economy.

1.9.1 Financial Institutions: Financial institutions (intermediaries) in India consist of commercial banks, regional rural banks (RRBs), urban co-operative banks (UCBs), rural co-operative credit institutions, development finance institutions (DFIs), non-banking financial companies (NBFCs), mutual funds, pension funds, and insurance organisations. These institutions, which provide a meeting ground for the savers and the investors, form the core of India's financial sector. Through mobilisation of resources and their better allocation, financial intermediaries play an important role in the development process of underdeveloped countries.

Financial institutions in India have transited since the mid-1990s from an environment of an administered regime to a system dominated by market-determined interest and exchange rates, and migration of the central bank from direct and quantitative to price-based instruments of monetary policy and operations. However, increased globalisation has resulted in further expansion and sophistication of the financial sector, which has posed new challenges to regulation and supervision, particularly of the banking system. In this context, the capabilities of the existing regulatory and supervisory structures also need to be assessed by benchmarking them against the best international practices.

1.9.2 Financial Markets: Developed and well-integrated financial markets are critical for sustaining high growth, for the effective conduct of monetary policy, for developing a diversified financial system, financial integration and ensuring financial stability. The question therefore is not whether developed financial markets are needed, but how to go about in developing them fully. Financial markets presently deal with complex and sophisticated products. Introduction of such products would require clear regulatory frameworks, appropriate institutions and development of human resource skills. The speed for further changes in the financial markets would thus depend on how quickly are we able to meet these requirements.

Money market is the most important segment of the financial system as it provides the fulcrum for equilibrating short-term demand for and supply of funds, thereby facilitating the conduct of monetary policy. It is a market for short-term funds with a maturity of up to one year and includes financial instruments that are close substitutes for money. The main instruments comprising the money market are: (a) call money/notice money, (b) certificates of deposit (CDs), (c) treasury bills (abolished with effect from April 1997), (d) repurchase agreements (repos), (e) commercial bills, (f) commercial paper (CPs), and (g) inter-corporate funds.

In India, the government securities market has witnessed significant transformation in its various dimensions, viz. market-based price discovery, widening of the investor base, introduction of new instruments, establishment of primary dealers and electronic trading and settlement infrastructure. This is the outcome of persistent and high-quality reforms in developing the government securities market. There are still areas where further development needs to be undertaken. Increased transparency and disclosures, gradual scaling down of mandated instruments and development of newer instruments are some major areas which could be considered. Regulatory incentives to increase the size of the trading book could be considered as a measure to further develop the government securities market.

Capital market is a market for long-term funds. The distinction between capital market and money market is not watertight. Broadly speaking, capital market focuses on financing of fixed investment (machinery and equipment) while money market provides working capital finance (raw material etc.)

The Securities and Exchange Board of India (SEBI) was constituted on April 12, 1988 as a non-statutory body through an Administrative Resolution of the Government for dealing with all matters relating to development and regulation of the securities market and investor protection and to advise the government on all these matters. SEBI was given statutory status and powers through an Ordinance promulgated on January 30, 1992. SEBI was established as a statutory body on February 21, 1992. The Ordinance was replaced by Securities and Exchange Board of India Act, 1992 on April 4, 1992.

With this ended all controls related to raising of funds from the market. The move was aimed at enhancing the efficiency, safety, integrity and transparency of the market. Presently, issuers of capital are required to meet the guidelines of SEBI on disclosures and protection of investors.

SEBI has emerged as an autonomous and independent statutory body. Its legally mandated objectives are the following:

1. Protection of the interests of investors in securities.
2. Development of the securities market.
3. Regulation of the securities market.
4. Matters connected therewith and incidental thereto.

The SEBI prohibits fraudulent and unfair trade practices, including insider trading. It also regulates substantial acquisition of shares and takeovers. In order to ensure protection of investors and to safeguard the integrity of the markets, there is a comprehensive surveillance system. Stock exchanges are the primary targets for detection of market manipulation, price rigging and other regulatory breaches regarding capital market functioning.

The SEBI regulates and supervises the securities market through its various regulations, guidelines and schemes issued from time to time.

In India, the foreign exchange market is a three-level structure consisting of: (a) Reserve Bank of India (RBI) at the top, (b) authorised dealers licensed by the RBI, and (c) customers (exporters, importers, companies, and other foreign exchange earners). In addition to these main market players, there are foreign exchange money changers who bring buyers and sellers together, but are not permitted to deal in foreign exchange on their own account.

Dealings in the foreign exchange market include transactions between authorised dealers and the exporters/importers and other customers, transactions among authorised dealers themselves, transactions with overseas banks and transactions between authorised dealers and the RBI.

The Indian foreign exchange market is a decentralised multiple dealership market comprising two segments—the spot and the derivatives market. In the spot market, currencies are traded at the prevailing rates and the settlement or value date is two business days ahead. The two-day period gives adequate time for the parties to send instructions to debit and credit the appropriate bank accounts at home and abroad.

The RBI intervenes in the market essentially to ensure orderly market conditions. The RBI undertakes sale/purchase of foreign currency in periods of excess demand/supply in the market.

1.9.3 Financial Instruments: The maturity and sophistication of financial system depends upon the prevalence of a variety of financial instruments to suit the varied investment requirements of heterogeneous investors so as to enable it to mobilize savings from as wide section of the investing public as possible. Since early 1990s, the Indian financial system has witnessed tremendous growth in financial product innovation by corporates as well as financial institutions.

Capital market instruments fall into two broad groups: (i) direct instruments, and (ii) derivates instruments. Direct instruments include the following:

1. Ordinary (or equity) shares.
2. Preference shares.
3. Debentures.

While the ordinary and preference shares represent ownership instruments, debentures and innovating debt instruments are creditorship securities.

In recent years, complex financial products such as asset-backed securities, derivatives, credit-default swaps (CDSs) and collateralised debt obligations

(CDOs) have proliferated in developed countries. These products have become highly popular with banks and financial institutions as they allow them to hedge their risks and manage their regulatory and economic capital more efficiently.

India has introduced different equity derivatives in a phased manner. This phased approach was adopted in India with index futures being introduced in June 2000, index options in June 2001 and individual stock options in July 2001.

1.10 Labour and Employment

Economic security is one of the main components of human security. It constitutes the crux of social security in the conventional sense. Economic security requires employment and an assured source of income adequate for meeting one's basic needs. As in other developing countries, unemployment is a serious problem of the Indian economy. The poverty of the masses in India is closely related to the problem of unemployment. Hence, expansion of employment opportunities has been an important objective of development planning in India. There has been a significant growth in employment during successive Five Year Plans. However, a relatively higher growth of population and labour force has led to an increase in the volume of unemployment from one plan period to another.

1.10.1 Unorganized Workers: According to the final report of the National Commission for Enterprises in the Unorganized Sector (NCEUS) [Chairman: Arjun Sengupta] released in April 2009, workers in the unorganized (or informal) sector constitute more than 93 percent of the total workforce of India. Unorganized sector workers are those who do not have any job security, income security or social security and are therefore extremely vulnerable to exogenous shocks.

The workers in the informal economy are clearly the overwhelming proportion of the workforce and most of these suffer from various forms of insecurities and vulnerabilities. It follows that policies have to focus on improving their conditions. However, the extent to which policy should focus upon increasing the share of the workforce in the organized sector has been a matter of some debate.

1.10.2 Agricultural Workers: Agricultural workers constitute by far the largest segment in the unorganized sector. They are extremely vulnerable to exploitation on account of low level of literacy, lack of awareness, persistent social backwardness and absence of unionisation and other forms of viable organisation. Further, the high rates of migration, because of the seasonality of operations and lack of stability of employment, subject them to all sorts of hazards and exploitation.

1.10.3 Women Workers: In a semi-industrialised country like India, the working class in destined to be one of the weaker sections of society. Moreover, society being male-dominated, female labour receives very poor recognition or value. Not that there are no statutory provisions. In fact, the Constitution of India provides equal rights and opportunities to both the genders. In addition there are specific provisions for protection and welfare of working women in many of the labour laws. However, most of these statutes do not cover the units in small and informal sectors which are the predominant workplaces of women.

The problems of women workers in general, and in the unorganized sector in particular, deserve special emphasis and focus in view of their marginalised position. Even when a large segment of women are not employed in the sense of contributing to the national output, a considerable share of their time is consumed by socially productive and reproductive labour. This is what is called the *double burden of work* that distinguishes women from men.

1.10.4 Child Workers: The problems of child labourers are more complex and intertwined with the twin issues of poverty and lack of access to quality school education. It is also not rare to find situations when a child worker is a migrant and bonded to the employer. The susceptibility of such child workers to exploitation is the greatest. Therefore, urgent national level action programmes are required to cater to child workers and potential child workers—such as street children, children of pavement dwellers, migrants and sex workers—and provide opportunities to them to facilitate their entry into main stream education through non-formal education, bridge education, and vocational training.

Consistent with the approach for an employment-centred development strategy, public employment programmes are an integral part of planning and policy. Apart from the advantages that accrue to the unemployed, under-employed and the poorly-employed, such programmes have a positive macroeconomic impact via increase in effective demand from the hitherto poor and vulnerable segments of the population.

The Government has, with the new economic policy, tried to transform the economy into a vibrant, outward looking, liberalised market economy driven by the forces of competition, productivity and efficiency, and for this, it expects the employers and the workers to appreciate the inevitability of change and to maximise the benefits to be derived from the new work ethos.

The workers have opposed economic liberalisation policy for fear of unemployment while entrepreneurs have welcomed it in the hope of new opportunities to improve Indian industries. The new economic policy has directly affected industrial relations in the country, because the Government has to play a dual role, one of protecting the interest of the workers, and second to allow a free interplay of the market forces. The two roles can be conflicting, and the Government needs to make relevant changes in the labour legislations to balance the position. As a result of the new economic policy, there is increased competition in the market which Indian industries are finding difficult to face due to old technology, and legislations which do not allow for closures, retrenchments, layoffs etc. The management is, therefore, demanding major changes in labour legislations.

Due to the various structural changes taking place, the role of the trade unions is also undergoing a change. Till now the unions had basically been bargaining for security of job, wages, working conditions etc. In the changed scenario, they have to redefine their role and objectives, and come up with new ways of facing the management. They have now to give more importance to education, training, retraining and counselling of the workers.

Economic reforms, by removing barriers to entry, have created competitive markets. Fiscal stabilisation has resulted in drastic reduction in budgetary support to the public sector commercial enterprises while exposing these enterprises to increased competition from private sector. A shift from long protected non-competitive to increasingly competitive markets since 1991 has reduced wasteful utilisation of both capital and labour. Side by side, increasing competitive pressures have also involved a shift from high-margin-low-volume environment of the earlier period to the high-volume-low-margin situation. This is expected to induct greater labour force in the production process.

1.11 Health and Education

1.11.1 Health: Improvement in the health status of the population has been one of the major thrust areas in social development programmes of India since Independence. Over the past six decades, India has built up a vast health infrastructure and manpower at primary, secondary and tertiary care levels in the government, voluntary and private sectors manned by professionals and para-medicals. India has invested massive amounts under the successive Five Year Plans in medical education, training and research which has ensured large manpower from the super-specialists to the auxiliary midwives.

National Urban Health Mission (NUHM) which along with National Rural Health Mission (NRHM) forms the Sarva Swasthya Abhiyan (SSA). NUHM is designed to meet health needs of the urban poor, particularly the slum dwellers by making available to them essential primary health care services. This is done by investing in high calibre health professionals, appropriate technology through public-private partnership and health insurance for urban poor. NRHM was launched for meeting health needs of all age groups and reduce disease burden across rural India.

To change the behaviour of the community towards institutional delivery, the Government of India, under NRHM in 2005, modified the National Maternity Benefit Scheme (NMBS), from that of a nutrition-improving initiative to the Janani Suraksha Yojana (JSY). The scheme has the dual objectives of reducing maternal and infant mortality by promoting institutional deliveries. Though the JSY is implemented in all States and UTs, its focus is on States having low institutional delivery rate. The scheme is 100 percent centrally sponsored and integrates cash assistance with maternal care. It is funded through the flexi-pool mechanism.

Health sector trends suggest that no single system of healthcare has the capacity to solve all of society's health needs. Of late, there is a resurgence of interest in holistic systems of health care, especially in the prevention and management of chronic lifestyle-related non-communicable diseases and systemic diseases. India can be a world leader in the era of integrative medicine because it has strong foundations in western biomedical sciences and an immensely rich and mature indigenous medical heritage of its own.

Ayurveda, Yoga and Naturopathy, Unani, Siddha and Homeopathy (AYUSH) sector across the country supports a network of 3,277 hospitals and 24,289 dispensaries. The health services provided by this network largely focused on primary health care. In the private and not-for-profit sector there are several thousand AYUSH clinics and around 250 hospitals and nursing homes for in-patient care and specialized therapies like Panchkarma. In clinics and nursing homes there are anecdotal reports of the role of AYUSH in the successful management of several communicable and non-communicable diseases.

1.11.2 Education: Education has been a thrust sector ever since India attained Independence in 1947. Right from the inception of planning, the crucial role of education in economic and social development has been recognised and emphasised. Efforts to increase people's participation in education and to diversify educational programmes in order to promote knowledge and skills required for nation-building have characterised successive Five Year Plans. Despite a series of problems that the country faced soon after independence, it has been possible to create a vast educational infrastructure in terms of large enrolments and teaching force and massive capabilities for management, research and development.

In a historic move, the Constitution (Eighty-sixth Amendment) Act, 2002, amended the Constitution by inserting Article 21A which reads as follows: "The State shall provide free and compulsory education to all children of the age of six to fourteen years in such manner as the State may, by law, determine". This was a significant measure for achieving the goal of Education for All (EFA) by making free and compulsory elementary education a fundamental right for all children in the age group of 6-14 years.

Again, the year 2010 was a landmark for education in India as the Right of Children to Free and Compulsory Education (RTE), Act, 2009 was enforced with effect from April 1, 2010. RTE Act, 2009, representing the consequential legislation to the Constitution (Eighty-sixth Amendment) Act, 2002, secures the right of children to free and compulsory education till completion of elementary education in a neighbourhood school. RTE Act, 2009 lays down norms and standards relating to pupil teacher ratios, buildings and infrastructure, school working days and working hours of teachers.

In order to fulfil the constitutional obligation, *Sarva Shiksha Abhiyan* was launched in partnership with the States. The programme is an effort towards recognition of the need for improving the performance of the school system through a community-owned approach and ensuring quality elementary education in a mission mode to all children in the age group of 6-14 years by 2010. It also seeks to bridge gender and social gaps. This programme subsumed all existing programmes (except *Mahila Samakhya* and Mid-day Meal Schemes) including externally-aided programmes with its overall framework with district as the unit of programmes implementation.

1.12 Social Security of Vulnerable Groups

The final objective of all economic efforts is human development. Human development encompasses quality of life, the level of well-being and access to basic social services. In India, the emphasis on the achievement of higher economic growth along with social justice is manifest in the renewed focus on development initiatives in the social sectors.

The root cause of social insecurity in India is poverty and that is largely due to lack of adequate or productive employment opportunities. The pattern of economic development in India since Independence in 1947 has left in its trail a variety of inequalities which have caused socio-politico tensions. While the economy has performed well in terms of growth rate of gross domestic product (GDP), its performance in terms of human development indicators has been unsatisfactory.

Development and empowerment of scheduled castes (SCs), scheduled tribes (STs), other backward classes (OBCs), minorities, disabled and other social groups in order to bring them at par with the rest of society is a commitment enshrined in the Constitution. Policies of the Central and State Governments have tried to ensure equal rights, and access to benefits and resources to disadvantaged groups in society to enable them to develop their potential and capacities as agents of social change, through the process of planned development.

India's recent economic growth performance has, indeed, been creditable. However, such growth must make a demonstrable difference to the lives of the poorest and most vulnerable citizens. India has the potential and the means to secure a reasonable standard of living for all of its citizens. The socio-economically disadvantaged—particularly women in rural areas—are yet to benefit from development efforts.

The constitutional commitments made in favour of socially disadvantaged groups prompted the policy makers and the planners to accord high priority for the welfare and development of these groups right from the country's First Five Year Plan launched on April 1, 1951. During the 1950s, the general developmental programmes were so designed as to cater adequately to the backward classes. Efforts were also made to ensure that the benefits of economic development accrued more and more to the relatively less privileged classes of the society in order to reduce inequalities.

In spite of Constitutional Directives and a number of legislative and executive measures by the Government, the conditions of socially disadvantaged groups have not improved appreciably mainly due to the lack of economic support. Although special programmes have been formulated in the Five Year Plans for their socio-economic development, the basic problem of their poor economic base has remained almost untouched so far.

Continuing to pursue traditional occupations, they are unable to avail of the fruits of economic growth and participate fully in the process of modernisation. Even the few educated groups amongst them are unable to compete for job opportunities created while scheduled tribes still remain largely outside the main stream of development mainly because of their relative isolation and their exploitation by outside agencies. A large proportion of bonded labourers are also scheduled castes. In both these cases, social and economic impoverishment merges to form a single basic factor for backwardness.

1.13 Environment, Disaster Management and Climate Change

India has an elaborate legal framework of national laws for control of environmental pollution. The overarching legislation in this context is the Environment Protection Act of 1986, which was a response to the Bhopal Gas Tragedy of 1984, the worst such industrial disaster in the world. This Act provides for the protection and improvement of environment and for matters connected therewith. India participated at the United Nations Conference on Human Environment held in Stockholm in June 1972 and decided to take appropriate steps for the protection and improvement of environment and the prevention of hazards to human life and health, other living creatures, plants and property.

The Act empowers the Central Government to establish authorities [under Section 3(3)] charged with the mandate of preventing environmental pollution in all its forms and to tackle specific environmental problems that are peculiar to different parts of the country.

National Green Tribunal (NGT) was officially notified on October 19, 2010 with Justice Lokeshwar Singh Panta as chairman. The tribunal is exclusively dedicated to environmental issues. Established by an Act of Parliament (National Green Tribunal Act, 2010), it will have circuit benches across the country to try all matters related to and arising out of environmental issues.

The tribunal also consists of other members who are experts in the field of environmental and related sciences. It is empowered to issue directions for the compensation and restitution of damage caused from actions of environmental negligence.

This is the first body of its kind that is required by its parent statute to apply the *polluter pays* principle and the principle of sustainable development.

The erstwhile National Environment Appellate Authority ceased to exist with the launch of the NGT. All the functions of the authority were transferred to the NGT.

NGT would follow various decisions of the Supreme Court and 186 Reports of the Law Commission.

National Environmental Protection Authority (NEPA) is slated to be constituted soon and the two bodies would constitute the pillars of the reformed system of environmental governance in the country.

Disaster Management Act, 2005 was enacted for establishing requisite institutional mechanisms for drawing up and monitoring the implementation of disaster management plans, ensuring measures by various wings of Government for prevention and mitigating effects of disasters, and for undertaking a holistic, co-ordinated and prompt response to any disaster situation.

National Disaster Management Authority (NDMA) under the Chairmanship of the Prime Minister was set up in terms of the Disaster Management Act, 2005. NDMA is an apex body responsible for laying down of policies, plans and guidelines on disaster management so as to ensure timely and effective response to disaster. NDMA has prepared a Draft National Policy on Disaster Management and has taken up preparation of guidelines on prevention, mitigation, response and recovery in regard to various types of disasters such as earthquake, flood, landslides, industrial disaster etc. The guidelines on management of earthquake, chemical disasters and chemical (industrial) disasters have also been circulated.

NDMA, in consultation with National Informatics Centre (NIC), National Spatial Data Infrastructure (NSDI), National Remote Sensing Agency (NRSA) and Department of Space is actively promoting the use of GIS in all institutions concerned with disaster management. Priority will have to be given to highly vulnerable areas for generating database for mapping as well as hazard vulnerability and risk assessment related to disasters like cyclone, flood earthquake, chemical, industrial etc.

As a part of voluntary actions to address climate change related concerns, India launched National Action Plan on Climate Change (NAPCC) on June 30, 2008. It stresses that maintaining a high growth rate is essential for increasing living standards of the vast majority of people of India and reducing their vulnerability of the impacts of climate change. Accordingly, it identifies measures that promote the objectives of sustainable development of India while also yielding to benefits for addressing climate change.

The NAPCC is co-ordinated by the Ministry of Environment and Forests and implemented through the nodal Ministries and is aimed at advancing relevant actions in specific sectors/areas.

NAPCC advocates a strategy that promotes, firstly, the adaptation to climate change and secondly, further enhancement of the ecological sustainability of India's development path.

Government of India has set up an elaborate institutional mechanism to consider and address issues relating to climate change. A Council chaired by Prime Minister called Prime Minister's Council on Climate Change was constituted in June 2007 to coordinate national action for assessment, adaptation and mitigation of climate change. The Council provides the overall guidance to climate change related actions taken by various Ministries of the Government and other agencies.

1.14 Foreign Trade, Debt, Aid and Investment

1.14.1 Foreign Trade: Over the last 67 years, India's foreign trade has undergone a complete change in terms of composition and direction. Exports now cover a wide range of traditional and non-traditional items while imports mainly consist of capital goods, petroleum products, raw materials, and chemicals to meet the ever-increasing needs of a developing and diversifying economy.

For about 40 years (1950-90), foreign trade of India suffered from strict bureaucratic and discretionary controls. Similarly, foreign exchange transactions were tightly controlled by the Government and the Reserve Bank of India (RBI). From Independence in 1947 till mid-1990s, India, with some exceptions, always faced deficit in its balance of payments, i.e. value of imports always exceeded the value of exports. This was characteristic of a developing country struggling for reconstruction and modernisation of its economy. Imports galloped because of increasing requirements of capital goods, defence equipment, petroleum products, and raw materials. Exports remained relatively sluggish owing to lack of exportable surplus, competition in the international market, inflation at home, and increasing protectionist policies of the developed countries.

Beginning 1991, the Government of India introduced a series of reforms to liberalise and globalise the Indian economy. Reforms in the external sector of India were intended to integrate the Indian economy with the world economy. Reform of trade and exchange rate policy was a critical element in structural reform and a great deal was done in this area. The exchange rate adjustments in July 1991, and the trade policy announced subsequently, considerably reduced the reliance upon licensing control of imports and created a more favourable exchange rate for exports.

The major trade policy changes in the post-1991 period included simplification of procedures, removal of quantitative restrictions, and substantial reduction in the tariff rates. A significant development in the current account of balance of payments in the 1990s was the remarkable growth in the export of invisibles to the rest of the world. This was made possible by growth in information and communication related services like computer software, hardware, internet, e-commerce and telecommunication sector.

India's approach to openness has been cautious, contingent on achieving certain preconditions to ensure an orderly process of liberalisation and ensuring macroeconomic stability. This approach has been vindicated in recent years with the growing incidence of financial crises elsewhere in the world. All the same, the policy regime in India in regard to liberalisation of the foreign sector has witnessed very significant change.

Exports have acquired added significance in the wake of liberalisation wave sweeping across the world. The trend towards market economy in almost all the countries of the world has increased the role of exports in developmental efforts. Exports have become an important indicator of a country's economic performance.

In recent years, manufactured goods have constituted the bulk of exports—over 63 percent, followed by crude and petroleum products (including coal) with a 20 percent share and agriculture and allied products with a share of 13.7 percent share.

As per *Economic Survey, 2014-2015*, the top seven product groups accounting for nearly 80.9 percent of India's total exports in 2014-15 (April-December) were: petroleum products (19.4 percent); gems and jewellery (13.0 percent); agriculture and allied products (12.0 percent); textiles and allied products (11.6 percent); chemicals and related products (10.1 percent); transport equipment (8.5 percent) and machinery (6.3 per cent share).

The surge in exports relative to imports has provided a strong stimulus to domestic industrial growth. While software exports are a well-known success story, India is now an important venue for many tasks in services such as financial accounting, call centres, processing insurance claims, and medical transcription. The future potential for growth in these areas appears to be considerable.

The structure of India's imports has undergone changes since the opening up of the Indian economy. With the move away from import substitution and towards promotion of trade, based on dynamic advantage, the policy distinction between essential imports and otherwise has gradually subsided. Commodity-wise analysis reveals that petroleum still continues to have a dominant presence in India's imports and accounted for 36.6 percent of India's total imports in 2013-14. Capital goods and other intermediary products which emerged as key items of imports, have however witnessed a continuous decline from 2011-12 onwards.

There have been a number of subtle compositional shifts within the broad level of aggregation in recent years. For instance, within the petroleum imports, there has been a shift from import of petroleum products towards crude imports following a large scale increase of refinery capacity over time. Furthermore, India has transformed itself from a net importer of finished petroleum products to net exporter of the same.

1.14.2 External Debt and External Aid: A noteworthy development in external sector management has been the containment of the country's external debt. The improvement in India's external debt position is attributable to a conscious debt management policy that focussed on high growth rate of current receipts, encouraging non-debt creating flows, keeping the maturity structure as well as the total amount of commercial debt under manageable limits and encouraging stable non-resident deposits through interest rates close to international levels. In the recent period, external debt has been further consolidated through recourse to pre-payment by the Government as well as the corporates. The strategy that was actively put in place in the early 1990s has paid dividends with sustained improvement in external indebtedness position of the country, with India being classified presently as a less indebted country.

External assistance with high element of concessionality played a significant role in the development process in India till the early 1980s. For most of this period, external assistance formed almost 100 percent of the capital account flows. During the 1980s, however, the share of external assistance in the capital account declined as the widening current account deficit necessitated recourse to additional sources of foreign savings such as commercial borrowings and non-resident deposits. The lower recourse to official aid was also attributed to other factors such as structural changes in global capital flows, lack of matching resources, delays involved in project appraisals and tender finalisation due to administrative bottlenecks, lack of cost related tariff structure for power and delays in land acquisition.

1.14.3 Foreign Direct Investment (FDI): In the wake of economic liberalisation policy initiated in 1991, the Government of India has taken several measures to encourage foreign investment, both direct and portfolio, in almost all sectors of the economy. However, the emphasis has been on foreign direct investment (FDI) inflows in the: (a) development of infrastructure, (b) technological upgradation of Indian industry (c) projects having the potential for creating employment opportunities on a large scale, and (d) setting up Special Economic Zones and establishing manufacturing units therein. With a vast reservoir of skilled and cost-effective manpower, India is now recognized as one of the most attractive investment destinations by reputed international rating organisations.

Promotion of foreign direct investment forms an integral part of India's economic policies. The role of foreign direct investment in accelerating economic growth is by way of infusion of capital, technology and modern management practices. Government has put in place a liberal and transparent foreign investment regime where most activities are opened to foreign investment on automatic route without any limit on the extent of foreign ownership.

While the magnitudes of inflows have recorded impressive growth, they are still at a small level compared to India's potential. The policy reforms undertaken have undoubtedly enabled the country to widen the sectoral and source composition of FDI inflows. Within a generation, the countries of East Asia transformed themselves. China, Indonesia, Korea, Thailand and Malaysia today have living standards much higher than in India.

1.14.4 Foreign Portfolio Investment: One of the major forces changing the face and structure of international capital markets since 1990s has been the flow of cross border portfolio investments—especially by foreign institutional investors (FIIs), from developed countries to the developing countries. Portfolio investors provide institutional character to the capital markets, flavoured by highly intensive research and diversified investments. FII investments inject global liquidity into the markets, raise the price-earning ratio and thus reduce the cost of capital.

Policies relating to portfolio investment in India have been substantially liberalised since the early 1990s. The state of the domestic capital market is far more crucial to attracting foreign institutional investors than any special regime or dispensation. The focus, therefore, should be on improving the regulatory and supervisory framework governing the domestic capital markets and on technological modernisation of their operations. There has already been considerable progress in this regard, but it is still some distance away before the full range of financial instruments are introduced in India and innovations are expeditiously permitted. Finally, there is no reason to expect that external investor confidence can be at variance with that of the domestic investor. Therefore, the precondition to attracting greater foreigner portfolio investment is the return of the domestic investors to the Indian capital markets.

To sum up, for almost three decades after Independence in 1947, development pattern of India was characterised by strong centralised planning, government ownership of basic and key industries, excessive regulation and control of private enterprise, trade protectionism through tariff and non-tariff barriers and a cautious and selective approach towards foreign capital. It was quota, permit and license regime guided and controlled by a bureaucracy trained in colonial style. Indian economy grew at an average rate of 3.5 percent per annum during the first 30 years (1950-80) of planned economic development.

This so-called inward-looking, import substitution strategy of economic development began to be widely questioned with the beginning of 1980s. Policy makers started realising the drawbacks of this strategy which inhibited competitiveness and efficiency and produced a much lower rate of growth than expected.

Consequently, economic reforms were set in motion, though on a modest scale, when controls on industries were reduced by the 1985 industrial policy. The economic reforms programme got a big boost when the Government announced a new industrial policy in the Indian Parliament on July 24, 1991. Since then, it is liberalisation, privatisation and globalisation all the way and the process is underway. In the new liberalised industrial and trade environment, the Government is progressively assuming the role of a promoter, facilitator and catalytic agent instead of a regulator and controller of economic activities.

As at end-January 2015, India had the world's eighth largest foreign exchange reserves totalling US$ 328.7 billion. Technology, competition, and benchmarking to the best international practices are the driving forces of India's development efforts. The country is making rapid strides in all these areas. Technology is getting upgraded rapidly and competition in the market place has become fierce. The vibrant information technology (IT) industry is contributing immensely by providing information about latest technology and international business practices. It can safely be said that India is no longer a country of scarcities and shortages. India's gradual and cautious approach to economic reforms has proved well-founded and the country is placed on a firm footing for future forays into domestic and global economic activities.

The economy braced the global financial crisis (sub-prime crisis) of 2008-09 successfully and came out of it almost unscathed by registering a robust growth rate of 8.4 percent and 8.6 percent in 2009-10 and 2010-11 respectively. This was made possible due to fiscal stimulus given by the Central Government and liberal monetary policy of the Reserve Bank of India (RBI). However, fiscal stimulus and liberal monetary policy led to boost in consumption (without a matching increase in supply), resulting in worrisome current inflation. More worrying is the food inflation which continues to be higher than overall inflation. Hence, the RBI was forced to tighten the monetary policy as a result of which and other external factors, the investment climate in the country was adversely impacted. The economy slowed down, registering growth rates of 6.2 percent and 5.0 percent during 2011-12 and 2012-13 respectively.

Although India's recent slowdown is rooted mainly in domestic causes, external factors have also played a role. The unfolding of euro zone crisis, the austerity measures in advanced economies, recession in many euro zone countries, risk on/risk off behaviour of investors and the uncertainty surrounding the future of euro zone have adversely affected the global economy and so also the Indian economy. Though India's growth rate has moderated to 6 to 6.5 percent, it is still satisfactory when seen in the global context. Many euro zone countries are facing austerity measures and budgetary cuts (reduced public expenditure), leading to unemployment. China has also slowed down due to environmental problems.

The fallout for the Indian economy has been a sharp deceleration in exports. Import demand, however, has remained resilient because of the continued high international oil prices that did not decline, unlike what happened after the Lehman meltdown of September 2008. The high value of gold imports contributed to the high import bill and widening of the trade deficit. The main fallout of euro zone crisis is global uncertainty. This has led to investors' alternating between risk-on/risk-off behaviour, with consequent implications for surge and reversal of capital to emerging economies.

As the things stand, Central and State Governments are trying frantically for private investments—both domestic and foreign. Recently, Government has allowed FDI in retail which is expected to boost investment in new technology and marketing of agricultural produce in the country.

According to *Economic Survey,* 2012-13, the economy is expected to grow in the range of 6.1 to 6.7 percent in 2013-14 [1]. Commenting on the recent slowdown of the Indian economy, it observed, "Why has the economy slowed down so rapidly despite recovering strongly from the global financial crisis? A number of factors are responsible. *First*, the boost to demand given by monetary and fiscal stimulus following the crisis was large. Final consumption grew at an average of over 8 percent annually between 2009-10 and 2011-12. The result was strong inflation and a powerful monetary response that also slowed consumption demand. *Second*, starting in 2011-12, corporate and infrastructure investment started slowing both as a result of investment bottlenecks as well as the tighter monetary policy. *Thirdly*, even as the economy slowed, it was hit by two additional shocks: a slowing global economy, weighed down by the crisis in the Euro area and uncertainties about fiscal policy in the United States, and a weak monsoon, at least in its initial phase". [2]

Endnotes

1. Government of India, Ministry of Finance, *Economic Survey*, 2012-13, p. 14.
2. Ibid., p. 3.

2

Poverty in India: Concept, Causes and Incidence

The final objective of all economic efforts is human development which encompasses quality of life, the level of well being and access to basic social services. The Fundamental Rights that India's Constitution guarantees to every citizen include the right to life and the right to livelihood is inherent in the right to life.

2.1 Problem of Poverty

The root cause of social insecurity in India is poverty and that is largely due to lack of adequate or productive employment opportunities. It is described as chronic or structural social insecurity, arising from insufficient degree of overall economic development. It is associated with other insecurities emanating from conventional contingencies such as the loss of employment, disability, old age, death etc. which are called the *second-order* type of insecurities or conventional social insecurity.

The provision of adequate and stable incomes will enable the poor to satisfy their basic needs. Till then, the State has to assume the basic responsibility of providing social security, especially in respect of those contingencies which would be difficult for individuals to cover without assistance from the State. The State also has the responsibility to provide the means of livelihood to those who cannot work and earn their living due to childhood, old age or other infirmities.

Poverty is a widespread social evil in underdeveloped countries of the world, particularly in Asia and Africa. There is no standard definition of poverty for all the countries of the world. Being a relative concept, the meaning of poverty differs from country to country. The concept, causes and incidence of poverty in India are discussed below.

2.2 Meaning of Poverty Line

In India, poverty is defined in terms of a minimum (subsistence) level of living rather than a reasonable level of living. Thus, minimum physical quantities of cereals, pulses, clothing etc. are determined for a subsistence level. These physical quantities are multiplied by their prices and converted into monetary terms, determining the per capita consumption/income for subsistence level.

Persons whose income/consumption is below this determined figure are considered to be below the poverty line.

Thus, poverty line is based on the definition of a norm which takes nutritional requirements into account and all persons below the norm are classified as poor. More specifically, the level of consumption below which people are living in poverty is set by determining the overall expenditure level at which consumers could purchase a food intake of 2,400 calories in rural areas or 2,100 calories in urban areas, which was estimated as the minimum necessary food intake. This overall expenditure sum was evaluated for a base period in 1979 and has then been updated using price indices. In 2004-05, the poverty level was ₹ 356 and ₹ 538 per person per month in rural and urban areas respectively.

For Planning Commission Estimates of Poverty Released in March 2012, see Section 2.8 of this chapter below.

2.3 Causes of Poverty

Widespread poverty in India is attributable to a host of factors, viz. population explosion, lack of industrialisation, failure of land reforms and failure of fiscal policy to narrow the gap between the rich and the poor.

Industrial development of the country has neither been on desirable lines nor at expected rate. Undue emphasis on capital-intensive industries has failed to generate sufficient jobs for the labour force.

Land reforms programme was started with great fanfare soon after Independence. However, it has failed to achieve the desired results. The incidence of poverty in rural areas is mainly due to the failure of land reforms.

Similarly, taxation and expenditure policies of the government have not been used effectively to bridge the gap between the rich and the poor.

Poverty in India is a chronic and multi-dimensional phenomenon. There is geography of poverty, with poverty being concentrated in the rural areas of certain states. There is sociology of poverty, with certain social groups suffering the most. There are identifiable occupational features of the poor: they are concentrated in agricultural labour and artisanal households in rural areas, and among casual labourers in urban areas. Casual labourers in urban areas are essentially distress migrants from rural areas in States where agricultural land-man ratio is very adverse, and where agricultural incomes have not been growing.

2.4 Poverty and Millennium Development Goals

In 2000, the 191 members of the United Nations, including India, committed to achieving 8 Millennium Development Goals by 2015. The Goals, with poverty reduction assuming top priority, are as under:

1. **Eradicate Extreme Poverty and Hunger:**
- Reduce by half the proportion of people living on less than a dollar a day.
- Reduce by half the proportion of people who suffer from hunger.
2. **Achieve Universal Primary Education:**
- Ensure that all boys and girls complete a full course of primary schooling.
3. **Promote Gender Equality and Empower Women:**
- Eliminate gender disparity in primary and secondary education preferably by 2005, and at all levels by 2015.
4. **Reduce Child Mortality:**
- Reduce by two thirds the mortality rate among children under five.
5. **Improve Maternal Health:**
- Reduce by three quarters the maternal mortality ratio.
6. **Combat HIV/AIDS, Malaria and Other Diseases:**
- Halt and begin to reverse the spread of HIV/AIDS. Halt and begin to reverse the incidence of malaria and other major diseases.
7. **Ensure Environmental Sustainability:**
- Integrate the principles of sustainable development into country policies and programmes; reverse loss of environmental resources.
- Reduce by half the proportion of people without sustainable access to safe drinking water.
- Achieve significant improvement in lives of at least 100 million slum dwellers, by 2020.
8. **Develop a global partnership for development:**
- Develop further an open trading and financial system that is rule-based, predictable and non-discriminatory, and includes a commitment to good governance, development and poverty reduction—nationally and internationally.
- Address the least developed countries' special needs. This includes tariff- and quota-free access for their exports, enhanced debt relief for heavily indebted poor countries, cancellation of official bilateral debt, and more generous official development assistance for countries committed to poverty reduction.
- Address the special needs of landlocked and small-island developing States.
- Deal comprehensively with debt problems of developing countries through national and international measures to make debt sustainable in the long-term.
- In cooperation with the developing countries, develop decent and productive work for youth.
- In cooperation with pharmaceutical companies, provide access to affordable essential drugs in developing countries.

- In cooperation with the private sector, make available the benefits of new technologies, especially information and communications technologies.

2.5 Incidence of Poverty

Widespread poverty in India has attracted the attention of a number of economists and organisations. Leading studies on poverty have been conducted by Dandekar and Rath, B.S. Minhas, P.K. Bardhan, World Bank and the Planning Commission of India. In their book *Poverty in India* (1971), Dandekar and Rath made a path-breaking study of the poverty phenomenon in India. Using the NSS data on consumption, they concluded that in 1960-61, about 40 percent of the rural population and about 50 percent of the urban population lived below the poverty line. The Planning Commission has been estimating the incidence of poverty at the national and state level using the methodology contained in the report of the Expert Group on Estimation of Proportion and Number of Poor (Lakdawala Committee) and applying it to consumption expenditure data from the large sample surveys on consumer expenditure conducted by the National Sample Survey Organization (NSSO) at an interval of approximately 5 years.

2.5.1 Eleventh Plan on Poverty:

A. Percentage Share of Poor in the Population: Over the years, the headcount ratio of the poor has steadily declined. In this connection, Eleventh Five Year Plan (2007-12) observed, "India has successfully reduced the share of the poor in the population by 27.3 percentage points from 54.8 in 1973 to 27.5 in 2004. Between 1973 and 1983, the headcount ratio of the poor had declined from 54.8 percent to 44 percent, and it fell further to 36 percent in 1993-94 and to 27 percent by 2004-05 (Table 2.1). Thus, sixty years after Independence, over a quarter of our population still remains poor. There is growing consensus that the poverty line (₹ 356 monthly per capita consumption expenditure for rural areas and ₹ 458 for urban areas in 2004-05) in India is much too low, and continues to be based on a consumption basket. If the poverty line was higher, the share of the population below the poverty line would be accordingly higher". [1]

B. Absolute Number of the Poor: Though the percentage of poor in the population has fallen appreciably over the last three-four decades, the absolute number of poor has registered only a marginal fall. This is clear from Table 2.2. In this context the Eleventh Five Year Plan (2007-12) remarked, "India is a nation of over 300 million poor people, a number that has barely declined over the last three decades of development. It is therefore essential that the Eleventh Five Year Plan addresses the task of reducing the numbers of the poor frontally. All growth benefits the poor, but the appropriate definition of pro-poor growth should be that it benefits them disproportionately. It is clear that rapid growth will be essential to reduce the number of the poor and sustainable poverty reduction, but for growth to benefit the poor disproportionately, it will have to be accompanied by more rapid employment expansion than hitherto, greater investment in health, education, water/sanitation and child nutrition than so far, and directly targeted poverty-reduction programmes". [2]

Table 2.1: Percentage of Population below Poverty Line in India (1973-2004)

Year	Rural	Urban	Combined
1973	56.4	49.0	54.9
1983	45.7	40.8	44.5
1993	37.3	32.3	36.0
2004	28.3	25.7	27.5

Source: Government of India, Planning Commission, *Eleventh Five Year Plan* (2007-12), Volume, III, p. 79.

Table 2.2: Number of Persons below Poverty Line in India (1973-2004)

(in Lakh)

Year	Rural	Urban	Combined
1973	2612.90	600.46	3213.36
1983	2519.57	709.40	3228.97
1993	2440.31	763.37	3203.68
2004	2209.24	807.96	3017.20

Source: Government of India, Planning Commission, *Eleventh Five Year Plan* (2007-12), Volume, III, p. 80.

It is discernible from Table 2.2 that the number of poor in rural areas in the country has declined from 2612 lakh in 1973 to 2209 lakh in 2004. However, in urban areas the number of poor has gone on increasing from 600 lakh in 1973 to 709 lakh in 1983, to 763 lakh in 1993 and to 807 lakh in 2004. Giving explanation for these trends, the Eleventh Five Year Plan (2007-12) observed, "The fact that the numbers of the poor have slightly declined in rural areas, and increased in urban areas over the last three decades suggests that to escape rural poverty, the poor migrate to urban areas. In fact, the total number of *migrant workers* in India in 1999-2000 was 10.27 crore, a staggering number. The number of seasonal or cyclical migrants in India may be 2 crore or so. But migration, both rural-rural (from relatively poor to relatively richer states and districts) and rural-urban, has the effect of disenfranchising the poor, leaving them without a safety net. Nevertheless, rural-urban migration will, and should continue; the policy imperative is that migrants are provided the basic social services that all citizens are entitled to according to the Constitution of India". [3]

2.6 Expert Group on Poverty (Chairman: Suresh Tendulkar), 2009

In view of the controversy around the measurement of poverty and other unresolved issues, the Planning Commission of India constituted this Expert Group in December 2005 to review the methodology for estimation of poverty. The Expert Group submitted its report in December 2009.

The Expert Group estimated India's aggregate poverty to be 37.2 percent—the poverty percentages for rural population and urban population being 41.8 and 25.7 respectively. The percentages of the population in poverty in rural and urban areas using official estimates and the Expert Group's estimates are indicated in the Table 2.3.

Table 2.3: Estimates of Population in Poverty (Percentage below the poverty line)

	Official Estimates			Estimates of Expert Group		
	Urban	Rural	Total	Urban	Rural	Total
1993-94	32.4	37.3	36.0	31.8	50.1	45.3
2004-05	25.7	28.3	27.5	25.7	41.8	37.2

Source: Government of India, Planning Commission, *Mid-term Appraisal of the Eleventh Five Year Plan*, p. 6.

The revised poverty lines for 2004-05 as recommended by the Expert Group were accepted by the Planning Commission. It is, however, worth clarifying that the higher estimates of the Expert Group for rural poverty in 2004-05—compared to existing estimates of the Planning Commission based on NSS data—did not reflect an increase in poverty, but merely a changed definition of what constitutes poverty. They indicate no change in the urban poverty estimates, but the rural poverty line is revised upwards significantly and as a consequence the percentage of the population below the poverty line in rural areas is higher than in the earlier estimates.

The Expert Group recommended that the urban poverty line need not be changed, but the rural poverty line should be raised to reflect the basket of commodities that can be purchased at the urban poverty line after allowing for the difference in urban and rural prices.

The findings of the Expert Group endorsed the earlier Planning Commission assessment that the growth process witnessed in India has led to a reduction in poverty between 1993-94 and 2004-05, though the reduction is less than what might have been expected. More importantly, this change tells us nothing about what has happened to poverty after 2004-05.

However, there is reason to expect that there will be a significant reduction in poverty over the Eleventh Plan period owing to: (a) accelerated GDP growth after 2004-05, (b) better distribution of GDP across States, (c) improvement in agriculture, (d) implementation of Mahatma Gandhi National Rural Employment Guarantee Act (MGNREGA), and (e) completion of Bharat Nirman programme.

An important programme contributing to poverty reduction in rural areas is the MGNREGA which began in the first year of the Eleventh Plan and was quickly expanded to cover the entire country. This programme is expected in 2009-10 to generate about three times the volume of employment generated by the rural wage employment programmes that were in place before it was introduced. There is evidence that implementation of MGNREGA has reduced distress migration and improved the bargaining power of agriculture labour leading to higher wages.

It must be emphasised however that while the MGNREGA provides much needed minimal employment security, it is not a substitute for the long-term solution to rural poverty. That requires shifting significant numbers of labour force out of low productivity employment in the agricultural sector to higher productivity employment in the non agricultural sector such as in labour intensive manufacturing and organised sector in general.

2.7 Twelfth Five Year Plan (2012-17) on Poverty

Striking an optimistic note on poverty reduction, the Approach Paper to Twelfth Plan observed, "The Eleventh Plan had set a more ambitious target of achieving a decline in poverty ratio of 2 percentage points per year. While the actual performance in this regard was below this target, it was better than it was in the earlier decade. Preliminary estimates using the latest NSS survey for 2009-10 suggest that the percentage of the population in poverty declined, at a faster pace than before, by approximately one percentage point per annum, during the five-year period 2004-05 to 2009-10. Since 2009-10 was a drought year, and poverty in that year could have increased temporarily, the underlying rate of decline is probably more than one percentage point per year. It is also possible that the pace of poverty reduction accelerated in the last two years of the Eleventh Plan period, since by then several Eleventh Plan programmes aimed at increasing inclusiveness would have begun to have a fuller impact. A summary assessment is that the pace of poverty reduction has accelerated, though it may still be short of the target. Nevertheless, it is heartening to note that looking ahead; India is well poised to meet the Millennium Development Goal target of 50 percent reduction of poverty between 1990 and 2015". [4]

2.8 Planning Commission Estimates of Poverty Released in March 2012

Data on poverty released by the Planning Commission on March 19, 2012 showed that poverty had significantly declined between 2004-05 and 2009-10. The estimates were based on a poverty line that averaged ₹ 672.8 per month (₹ 22.43 per day) in rural areas and ₹ 859.6 per month (₹ 28.65 per day) in urban areas for 2009-10. As per these bench-marks, poverty across the country declined by 7.3 percentage points from 37.2 percent in 2004-05 to 29.8 percent in 2009-10. Rural poverty declined faster, down 8 percentage points to 33.8 percent from 41.8 percent. Urban poverty declined by 4.8 percentage points to 20.9 percent. In absolute terms, there were 35.5 crore poor people in 2009-10 against 40.7 crore in 2004-05.

The decline was attributed to various rural welfare schemes including Mahatma Gandhi National Rural Employment Guarantee Scheme (MGNREGS). It is noteworthy that a host of Centrally-sponsored social security schemes for the poor are meant for below poverty line (BPL) people, and those above poverty line (APL) are excluded thereof.

However, Government soon rejected these definitions/estimates of poverty by the Planning Commission in the face of stiff opposition from various quarters.

The latest estimates of poverty are available for the year 2011-12. These estimates have been made following Tendulkar Committee methodology using household consumption expenditure survey data collected by the NSSO in its sixty-eighth round (2011-12). Over a span of seven years the incidence of poverty declined from 37.2 percent to 21.9 percent in 2011-12 for the country as a whole, with a sharper decline in the number of rural poor (Table 2.4).

Table 2.4: Poverty Estimates for the Year 2011-12

Year	Poverty line (₹)		Number of poor (million)			Poverty ratio (percent)		
	Rural	Urban	Rural	Urban	Total	Rural	Urban	Total
2004-05	446.68	578.80	326.3	80.8	407.1	41.8	25.7	37.2
2011-12	816.00	1000.00	216.5	52.8	269.3	25.7	13.7	21.9

Source: Government of India, *Economic Survey, 2014-15*, Volume II, Chapter 9, Table 9.3.

2.9 Direct Benefit Transfer (DBT) Scheme

Government introduced DBT scheme on January 1, 2013. To begin with, benefits under 26 schemes will directly be transferred into the bank accounts of beneficiaries in 43 identified districts across respective states and union territories

(UTs). Thus, benefits such as scholarships, pensions, and MGNREGA (Mahatma Gandhi National Rural Employment Guarantee Act) wages will be directly credited to the bank or post office accounts of identified beneficiaries.

The DBT scheme will not substitute entirely for delivery of public services for now. It will replace neither food and kerosene subsidies under the TPDS (Targeted Public Distribution System) nor fertilizer subsidies. The DBT is designed to improve targeting, reduce corruption, eliminate waste, control expenditure, and facilitate reforms.

Transfers that are already taking place through paper and cash mode will now be done through electronic transfers.

This has been enabled by rapid roll out of Aadhar (Unique Identity) covering 833 million people as on May 5, 2015 (nearly 2/3 rd of the population). The DBT in tandem with such unique identification will ensure that the benefits reach the target groups faster and minimize inclusion and exclusion errors as well as corruption that are associated with manual processes.

Banks will ensure that all beneficiaries in these districts have a bank account. All public sector banks (PSBs) and regional rural banks (RRBs) have made provision so that the data collected by the Departments/Ministries/Implementing agency concerned can be used for seeding the bank account details in the core banking system (CBS) of banks with Aadhaar.

All PSBs have also joined the Aadhaar Payment Bridge of the National Payment Corporation of India for smooth transfer of benefits.

To sum up, from the statistical and other information available on the subject, the following facts emerge regarding the geo-social aspects of poverty in India.

1. Incidence of poverty is more in rural areas than in urban areas.
2. Incidence of poverty is the greatest among small farmers and landless workers in rural areas.
3. Poverty in urban areas is largely the overflow of rural poor into the urban areas.
4. Urban poverty is concentrated in the casual labour households.
5. Wide inter-state disparities are visible in the poverty ratios. Uttar Pradesh, Bihar, Madhya Pradesh, Odisha and Rajasthan account for most of the poor in India.
6. Among the social groups, scheduled castes, scheduled tribes and backward castes account for more percentage of the poor than their share in the population

Poverty eradication may either be left to the automatic mechanism of growth process and/or to programmes aimed at direct assault on poverty. The initial thinking of the Government relied on the automatic benefits of growth coupled with a progressive taxation policy. However, this strategy did not work on desired lines. As the Eighth Five Year Plan (1992-97) observed, "The equity objective was sought to be pursued through redistribution of assets. But, land reforms could not be implemented effectively. The problem of poverty could not be tackled through growth, which itself was slow over a long period of time. Hence, direct intervention through poverty alleviation programmes became necessary". [5] Lately, the Government has increasingly resorted to direct attack on poverty through rural development and rural employment schemes.

The socio-economically disadvantaged are yet to benefit from economic reforms. The challenge to overcome the scourge of poverty remains a daunting task. The support of the poor for reforms and their involvement in the development process can be achieved only if they start benefiting from the policies. It is necessary to ensure that the poor and the deprived have greater stake in economic reforms than at present for mobilising their enthusiastic participation in the development process. Economic reforms must be guided by compassion and distributive justice. Improvement of living conditions of the poorest and the weakest sections of society should be high priority areas.

Endnotes

1. Government of India, Planning Commission, *Eleventh Five Year Plan* (2007-12), Volume, III, p. 79.
2. Ibid., p. 79.
3. Ibid., p. 80.
4. Government of India, Planning Commission, *An Approach to the Twelfth Five Year Plan (2012-17)*, October 2011, p. 3.
5. Government of India, Planning Commission, *Eighth Five Year Plan* (1992-97), Volume I, p. 7.

3

Financial System and Regulators in India

Finance is the life blood of a modern economy. A financial system helps to mobilise the financial surpluses of an economy and transfer them to areas of financial deficit. It is the linchpin of any development strategy. The financial system promotes savings by providing a wide variety of financial assets to the general public. Savings collected from the household sector are pooled together and allocated to various sectors of the economy for raising production levels. If the allocation of credit is judicious and socially equitable, it can help achieve the twin objectives of growth and social justice.

3.1 Financial System: Theoretical Settings

3.1.1 Meaning, Importance and Functions of Financial System: Financial sector of an economy is a multi-faceted term. It refers to the whole gamut of legal and institutional arrangements, financial intermediaries, markets and instruments with both domestic and external dimensions.

A well-functioning financial system is a pre-requisite for the pursuit of economic growth with stability. The core function of a financial system is to facilitate smooth and efficient allocation of resources from savers to the ultimate users. The financial infrastructure contributes to the effective functioning of institutions and markets and thereby to stability. Hence, it serves as the foundation for adequate access to financial services and sustained financial development.

In the context of relatively under-developed capital market and with little internal resources, firms or economic entities depend largely on financial intermediaries for their fund requirements. In terms of sources of credit, they could be broadly categorised as institutional and non-institutional. For example, the major institutional sources of credit in India are commercial banks, development finance institutions (DFIs) and non-banking financial companies (NBFCs) including housing finance companies (HFCs). The non-institutional or unorganised sources of credit include moneylenders, indigenous bankers and sellers for trade credit. However, information about unorganised sector is limited and not readily available.

The relationship between finance and development has been a crucial subject of public policy for long. As early as in the 19th century, a number of economists stressed the importance of financial development for the growth of an economy.

The banking system was recognised to have important ramifications for the level and growth rate of national income via the identification and funding of productive investments. This, in turn, was expected to induce a more efficient allocation of capital and foster growth. A contrary view also prevailed at the same time suggesting that economic growth would create demand for financial services. This meant that financial development would follow growth more or less automatically. In other words, financial development could be considered as a by-product of economic development.

Following are some of the functions performed by a financial system:

1. It facilitates trading and hedging of risks. Risk mitigation reduces uncertainty and enables resources to flow towards most profitable projects. Such a situation raises the efficiency of investments and the rate of growth.
2. By acting as an efficient conduit for allocating resources, the financial system enables improvement in technical progress. Technological innovations take place when entrepreneurs exploit the best chances of successfully imitating technologies in their production processes and introducing new products.
3. To the extent that financial development leads to the creation of financial infrastructure and enables better and more efficient provision of goods and services, costs of transactions would be lower, with positive spill over on economic growth.

The role and importance of the financial sector in the process of economic growth has evolved over time along with the changing paradigms. Till the late 1960s, the role of financial intermediaries in general, and banks in particular, in the process of economic growth of a country was largely ignored.

3.1.2 From Financial Neutrality to Financial Activism: The views on neutrality of financial intermediaries to economic growth, however, came under attack during the late 1960s. It was pointed out that there exists a strong positive correlation between financial development and economic growth of a country. Financial experts started emphasising the negative impact of *financial repression*, under which the government determined the quantum, allocation and price of credit, on the growth process. They argued that credit is not just another input and instead, credit is the engine of growth.

The world of finance has changed markedly over the last 30 years or so. The change has been brought about by a number of events and circumstances. The growing dissatisfaction with the working of the fixed exchange rate system during the 1960s led many countries, especially of the industrialised world, to adopt a floating exchange rate system by the early 1970s. There was also a growing realisation that for achieving sustained growth with stability, it would be necessary to have freer trade, liberalised external capital movements, and a relatively flexible use of domestic monetary policy. With trade being subject to multilateral negotiations, industrialised countries and some of the emerging market economies took steps to liberalise capital movements across countries since about the middle of the 1970s. Simultaneously, efforts were made to remove distortions in the domestic financial sector through elimination or containment of reserve requirements and interest rate regulations. These initiatives coincided with the rapid technological improvements in electronic payments and communication systems. The interaction among these factors helped the process of internationalisation of financial markets.

Under the impact of economic liberalisation, the industrialised countries, as a group, improved their relative economic position in the world economy, and posted high growth rates in the 1980s and thereafter. This experience has confirmed the release of growth impulses following financial liberalisation.

Developing countries, on their part, have been adopting, since the early 1980s, market-oriented strategies of financial development, partly supported by international financial institutions, and partly to avail of the large pool of resources available in international financial markets. They either dismantled or sharply contained *financial repression* and undertook financial reforms with a view to enhancing allocative efficiency and competitiveness. Financial development required the deepening and widening of the existing financial markets as well as the introduction of new products and instruments to cater to the needs of savers and investors.

Financial development depends on market-based regulatory framework and incentives (disincentives) that promote market discipline. If market discipline is not well-understood or not complied with, there would arise possibilities of inefficiencies and/or volatilities in asset prices and capital movements. Financial stability, therefore, is a pre-requisite for sustained financial development which in turn would impact growth rate positively.

3.1.3 From Financial Volatility to Financial Stability: The process of deregulation and globalisation of financial markets gained momentum in the 1990s, and expanded the choices for investors, and helped to improve the prospects of reducing the costs of financial transactions and improving operational and allocative efficiency of the financial system. A number of developing countries, especially in Asia, that moved early on to the path of economic liberalisation had experienced large capital inflows through the 1980s and the first half of the 1990s. Large capital inflows, however, carry the risk of financial sector vulnerability, where the use of such flows is not administered by application of appropriate mix of macroeconomic measures. The currency and financial crises in Mexico and Thailand, followed by Korea and Indonesia, provide many insights about the problems that would arise when exchange rates are inflexible, and banking and financial systems are weak.

The experience of the crisis-affected countries highlights the need for setting in place regulatory and supervisory frameworks to ensure the safety and stability of financial systems. Their experience also underscores the premise that financial development is only a necessary condition for sustainable growth, and by no means a sufficient condition. In view of the costs of financial crises falling on the sovereign governments, financial stability has come to occupy a centre-stage in formulating public policy for economic development.

3.1.4 Role of the Government in Financial Development: An important aspect of the process of financial development has been the role of the government. In many developing economies the governments traditionally played a significant role in fostering financial development. In the context of developing countries, this role is all the more important because financial systems in these countries are characterised by nascent accounting frameworks and inadequate legal mechanisms.

Several developing countries, therefore, undertook programmes for reforming their financial systems. In the initial stages of the development process, the financial sector in developing countries was characterised by directed credit allocation, interest rate restrictions and lending criteria based on social needs etc. These policies retarded the nature of financial intermediation in developing countries and the recognition of the same paved the way for financial sector reforms. Since the late 1970s and the 1980s, financial sector reforms encompassing deregulation of interest rates, revamping of directed credit and measures to promote competition in the financial services became an integral part of the overall structural adjustment programmes in many developing economies.

The interface between financial system and economic development revolves around on a wide range of issues, the following being more prominent.

1. Extant of state ownership of financial entities vis-à-vis private sector ownership.
2. Corporate governance in banks and other segments of the financial system.
3. Transparency of policies and practices of monetary and financial agencies.
4. Prudential requirements of market participants.
5. Maintenance of best practices in accounting and auditing.
6. Comprehensive and efficient regulation and supervision of the financial system.
7. Collection, processing and dissemination of information in order to meet the market needs.

The commonality among these concerns has given rise to a wide recognition and acceptance of having a set of international standards and best practices that every country should strive to foster and implement.

3.1.5 Determinants of Access to Financial Services: In the literature on finance, a number of factors have been mentioned which affect the access to financial services. Some important factors among these are as under:

1. **Level of Income:** Financial status of people is always important in gaining

access to financial services. Extremely poor people find it difficult to access financial services even when the services are tailored for them.

2. **Type of Occupation:** Many banks have not developed the capacity to evaluate loan applications of small borrowers and unorganised enterprises and hence tend to deny loan requests by them.
3. **Legal Identity:** Lack of legal identities like identity cards, birth certificates or written records often exclude ethnic minorities, economic and political refugees and migrant workers from accessing financial services.
4. **Attractiveness of the Product:** Benefits of financial products offered and how their availability is marketed are crucial in accessing financial services.
5. **Terms and Conditions:** Terms and conditions attached to products such as minimum balance requirements and conditions relating to the use of accounts often dissuade people from using such products/services. Generally, transaction is free as long as the account has sufficient funds to cover the cost of transactions made. However, there is a range of other charges that have a disproportionate effect on people with low income.
6. **Socio-cultural Barriers:** Lack of financial literacy (basic accounting skills) and cultural and religious barriers to banking often constrain demand for financial services. Access to credit is often limited for women who do not have, or cannot hold title to assets such as land and property or must seek male guarantees to borrow.
7. **Living Conditions:** Factors like density of population, rural and remote areas, mobility of the population (i.e. highly mobile people with no fixed or formal address), insurgency in a location etc. also affect access to financial services.
8. **Age Factor:** Financial service providers usually target the middle of the economically active population, often overlooking older or younger customers.

3.1.6 Regulation and Supervision of Financial System: An efficient and robust regulatory structure is an essential pre-requisite for the stability of the financial system. The implications of increased cross-sectoral and cross-border conglomeration of financial companies highlight the need for increased focus on co-ordination and information sharing among regulators. The emergence of the holding company structure and its legal implications has given rise to concerns about their regulation and supervision. The recent international financial turbulence has shown that there is no single fail-proof method of financial regulation and that an ideal system would have elements of both principles-based and rules-based regulation.

The recent global financial crisis has highlighted the importance of liquidity management for institutions. In this context, it is imperative to have an adequate liquidity infrastructure in place. In the Indian context, active liquidity management has been an integral part of the Reserve Bank of India's monetary operations and it is being achieved through various instruments. However, the use of monetary policy requires to be further honed in order to deal with the impact of external capital flows.

3.1.7 Financial Globalisation: No major economy in the world today can be viewed in isolation from the rest of the world. Given the size and the growing magnitude of interaction—in terms of trade, services, and capital flows—and the greater openness to globalisation, India is in a different economic milieu today than it was two decades ago. India is virtually part of the world of globalised finance and is learning to walk, negotiating the strong currents, both positive and negative, generated by the forces of financial globalisation.

The 1990s witnessed a paradigm shift towards market-oriented economic policies and a careful dismantling of obstacles in its wake. This has helped the smaller, emerging economies gain access to world markets, emergent technologies and collaborations. This has also given them a window to the developed world and helped them understand the significant role of globalisation as an instrument, which could be utilised not just to achieve economic efficiency, but also eradicate poverty.

Globalisation has also resulted in the creation of a new business framework. More changes can be expected in the business scenario specifically in terms of openness, adaptiveness and responsiveness. The most important dimensions of economic globalisation are: (a) breaking down of national barriers; (b) international spread of trade, financial and production activities, and (c) growing power of transnational corporations and international financial institutions in these processes. While economic globalisation is a very uneven process, with increased trade and investment being focused in a few countries, almost all countries are greatly affected by this process.

A major feature of globalisation is the growing concentration and monopolisation of economic resources and power by transnational corporations and by global financial firms and funds. This process has been termed transnationalisation, in which fewer and fewer transnational corporations are gaining a large and rapidly increasing proportion of world economic resources, production and market shares. Where a multinational company used to dominate the market of a single product, a big transnational company (TNC) now typically produces or trades in an increasing multitude of products, services and sectors. Through mergers and acquisitions, fewer and fewer of these TNCs now control a larger and larger share of the global market, whether in commodities, manufactures or services.

3.2 State Domination of India's Financial Sector (1947-1990)

At the time of Independence in 1947, India had a fairly well-developed banking system. The process of financial development in independent India has hinged effectively on the development of commercial banking, with impetus given to industrialisation based on the initiatives provided in the five year plans.

Soon after Independence in 1947, Government of India followed a policy of social control of important financial institutions. The nationalisation of the Reserve Bank of India (RBI) in 1948 marked the beginning of this policy. This was followed by the takeover of the then Imperial Bank of India in 1955 which was rechristened as State Bank of India. In 1956, 245 life insurance companies were nationalised and merged into the newly created Life Insurance Corporation of India (LIC). In another significant development, Government nationalised 14 major commercial banks in 1969. The year 1972 saw the nationalisation of general insurance companies and the setting up of General Insurance Corporation (GIC). In 1980, 6 more commercial banks were nationalized and brought under public ownership.

Trade and industrial activities during the 1950s, and the 1960s reflected the dominance of banking as the critical source. The number of banks and branches had gone up, notwithstanding the consolidation of small banks, and the support given to the community-operative credit movement. Functionally, banks catered to the needs of the organised industrial and trading sectors. The primary sector consisting of agriculture, forestry, and fishing had to depend largely on their own financing and on sources outside the commercial banks.

The course of development of financial institutions and markets during the post-Independence period has been largely guided by the process of planned development pursued in India with emphasis on mobilisation of savings and channelising investment to meet Plan priorities. The adoption of bank-dominated financial development strategy was aimed at meeting the sectoral credit needs, particularly of agriculture and industry. Towards this end, the RBI (nationalised in 1948) concentrated on regulating and developing mechanisms for institution building. The commercial banking network was expanded to cater to the requirements of general banking and for meeting the short-term working capital requirements of industry and agriculture. Specialised development finance institutions (DFIs) with majority ownership of the RBI were set up to meet the long-term financing requirements of industry and agriculture. To facilitate the growth of these institutions, a mechanism to provide concessional finance to these institutions was also put in place by the RBI.

3.2.1 Nationalisation of Imperial Bank of India (1955): Soon after Independence, India launched its First Five Year Plan (1951-56). The Plan accorded high priority to the development of rural India, particularly agriculture. The All India Rural Credit Survey Committee recommended the creation of a State-partnered and State-sponsored bank by taking over the Imperial Bank of

India and integrating with it the former State-owned or State-associated banks. Accordingly, an Act was passed in the Parliament in May 1955 and the State Bank of India was constituted on July 1, 1955. Later, the State Bank of India (Subsidiary Banks) Act was passed in 1959 enabling the State Bank of India to take over eight former State-associated banks as its subsidiaries.

3.2.2 Nationalisation of Life Insurance Business (1956): By the Life Insurance (Emergency Provisions) Ordinance, 1956, promulgated by the President of India on January 19, 1956, the management and control of life insurance business in India, including the foreign business of Indian insurers, and the Indian business of foreign insurers, vested with immediate effect in the Central Government. With this, the life insurance business passed from the private sector to the public sector. This was a step never before attempted any where in the world on such a large scale.

Though the Ordinance was promulgated in January 1956, the Life Insurance Corporation Act was passed in the next session of Parliament. According to this Act the Life Insurance Corporation of India came into existence on September 1, 1956.

3.2.3 Nationalisation of Commercial Banks (1969 and 1980): The process of state domination of financial sector was given impetus with the adoption of the policy of social control over banks in 1967, reinforced in 1969 by the Nationalisation of 14 major scheduled commercial banks. In April 1980, government nationalised 6 more commercial banks. Driven largely by public sector initiative and policy activism, commercial banks have a dominant share in total financial assets and are the main source of financing for the private corporate sector. They also channel a sizeable share of household savings to the public sector. Besides, in recent years, they have been performing most of the payment system functions. With increased diversification in recent years, banks in both public and private sectors have been providing a wide range of financial services.

3.2.4 Nationalisation of General Insurance Business (1973): The general insurance business was nationalized with effect from January 1, 1973, through the General Insurance Business (Nationalization) Act, 1972. However, as a prelude to the above Act, the Government took over the management of all the operating companies in 1971 through General Insurance (Emergency Provision) Act, 1971. The emergency Act provided for the appointment of custodians who were empowered to exercise control over these companies subject to the directions of the Central Government. At the time of nationalization of these companies, there were a total of 107 companies underwriting general insurance business in India. All these companies were amalgamated and grouped into four, namely the National Insurance Company Limited, the New India Assurance Company Limited, the Oriental Insurance Company Limited, and the United India Insurance Company Limited with head offices at Kolkata, Mumbai, Delhi and Chennai respectively. The General Insurance Company (GIC) was formed as a holding company in November 1972. The GIC was constituted for the purpose of superintending, controlling and carrying out the business of general insurance. The entire capital of GIC was subscribed by the Government and that of four companies by the GIC on behalf of the Government of India.

Broadly speaking, financial development in India up to the early 1990s was, by and large, a state-induced activity.

3.2.5 Rethinking on State Domination of Financial Sector: Nationalisation of commercial banks in 1969 and 1980 was a mixed blessing. After nationalisation there was a shift of emphasis from industry to agriculture. The country witnessed rapid expansion in bank branches, even in rural areas. However, bank nationalisation created its own problems like excessive bureaucratisation, red-tapism and disruptive tactics of trade unions of bank employees.

Being a near-monopoly of the Government, the banking sector suffered from lack of competition, low capital base, low productivity and high intermediation cost. The role of technology was minimal and the quality of service was not given adequate importance. Banks also did not follow proper risk management systems and the prudential standards were weak. All these resulted in poor asset quality and low profitability.

Among non-banking financial intermediaries, development finance institutions (DFIs) operated in an over-protected environment with most of the funding coming from assured sources at concessional terms.

The mutual fund industry also suffered from lack of competition and was dominated for long by one institution, viz. the Unit Trust of India (UTI).

Non-banking financial companies (NBFCs) grew rapidly, but there was no regulation regarding their asset side. Financial markets were characterised by control over pricing of financial assets, barriers to entry, high transaction costs and restrictions in movement of funds between the market segments. This, apart from inhibiting the development of the markets, also affected their efficiency.

Similarly, capital market structure in India was subject to several controls and opaque procedures. The trading and settlement system was outdated and not in tune with international practices. Raising of capital from the market was regulated by the Capital Issues (Control) Act, 1947 which was administered by the Controller of Capital Issues (CCIs) in the Ministry of Finance, Government of India. The scheme of controls under the Act required all the companies to obtain prior consent for issues of capital to the public. Pricing as well as the features of the capital structure (such as debt-equity ratios), were controlled by the Government. The Securities Contracts (Regulation) Act was administered by the Directorate of Stock Exchanges also in the Ministry of Finance. It empowered the

Government to recognise/derecognise stock exchanges, stipulate rules and bye-laws for their functioning, compel listing of securities by public companies etc. Such a system of regulation and control was fragmented and inadequate in the context of liberalisation wave sweeping across the world. Urgent measures were needed to relax controls and modernise the functioning of capital market.

Furthermore, state monopoly of insurance business resulted in limited availability of insurance products, lack of information technology and poor quality of insurance services. In this connection, the Committee on Reforms in Insurance Sector (Chairman: R.N. Malhotra), which was set up in April 1993 and which submitted its report in January 1994, remarked,

- "Indian insurance industry lacks depth, diversity and reach, both geographically as well as in terms of insurable population, as there was immensely vast potential yet to be tapped;
- It provides poor customer service in terms of pricing, adequacy and appropriateness of covers and the much needed and timely claims settlement;
- It lacks the global dimensions having remained in isolation too long".

In fact, the environment in the financial sector till the initiation of reforms in 1991 was not particularly conducive for the development of deep and wide financial markets. In fact, it had resulted in segmented and underdeveloped markets characterised by paucity of instruments, and limited number of participants. Banks and financial institutions functioned in a highly regulated environment, characterised by an administered interest rate structure, quantitative restrictions on credit flows, fairly high reserve requirements and pre-emption of significant proportion of lendable resources for the priority and Government sectors. While the quantitative restrictions resulted in credit rationing for the private sector, interest rate controls led to suboptimal use of credit resulting in low levels of investment and growth. These, coupled with other factors such as the absence of proper accounting, transparency and prudential norms, resulted in a large build-up of non-performing assets in the banking system. All this led to erosion of profitability in the banking sector, besides decline in productivity and efficiency. The bank-based and highly controlled regime turned out to be inimical to financial market development.

Thus, until the early 1990s, the role of the financial system in India was primarily restricted to the function of channelling resources from surplus to deficit sectors. Whereas the financial system performed this role reasonably well, its operations came to be marked by some serious deficiencies over the years. The Indian Government determined the quantum, allocation and the price of credit, a situation referred to as *financial repression* [1] by some experts.

It was in this backdrop, that wide-ranging financial sector reforms in India were introduced as an integral part of the economic reforms initiated in the early 1990s. [2]

3.3 Financial Sector Reforms since 1991

Considering the strategic importance of the financial sector, the Government of India set up a Committee on Financial System (Chairman: M. Narasimham) in 1991. It was asked to examine all aspects relating to the structure, organisation, functions and procedures of the Indian financial system. The Committee submitted its report in November 1991. It was presented to Parliament in December 1991. The report focussed mainly on enabling and strengthening measures for the financial sector. The Committee on Banking Sector Reforms (Chairman: M. Narasimham), 1998 placed greater emphasis on structural measures and improvement in standards of disclosure and levels of transparency in order to align the Indian standards with international best practices. Pursuant to the recommendations of the two Committees, financial reforms introduced in India have brought about considerable improvements as reflected in various parameters relating to capital adequacy, asset quality, profitability and operational efficiency.

3.3.1 From Financial Repression to Financial Liberalisation: Financial sector reforms since 1991 have focused on the following:

1. Elimination of segmentation across various markets in order to facilitate transmission of impulses across markets.
2. Easing the liquidity management process.
3. Making resource allocation more efficient across the economy.

For above purposes, restrictions on pricing of assets have been removed and new instruments introduced. Technological infrastructure has been strengthened. Liberalisation of the financial sector has included, among others, the following measures.

1. Deregulation of interest rates.
2. Introduction of new products.
3. Relaxation in investment norms for financial intermediaries, especially banks.
4. Lowering of restrictions on specialisation/diversification of banks.
5. Emergence of new institutions such as primary dealers and mutual funds.
6. Withdrawal of reserve requirements on inter-bank borrowings.
7. Withdrawal of credit controls and excessively high reserve requirements.
8. Deregulation and development of markets.
9. Moves toward privatisation of financial services.
10. Easing of restrictions in respect of banks' foreign currency investments.
11. Easing of restrictions on current and capital account convertibility.
12. Lowering of entry barriers/limits on participation of foreign banks.

These reforms have paved the way for integration among various segments of the financial system. It is widely accepted that reduction/removal of financial repression has enhanced the efficiency and potential growth of the Indian economy.

A. Banking Sector Reforms: The key objective of reforms in the banking sector has been to enhance the stability and efficiency of banks. To achieve this objective, various reform measures were initiated that could be categorised broadly into three main groups: (a) enabling measures, (b) strengthening measures, and (c) institutional measures.

Enabling measures were designed to create an environment where banks could respond optimally to market signals on the basis of commercial considerations. Salient among these included reduction in statutory pre-emptions so as to release greater funds for commercial lending, interest rate deregulation to enable price discovery, granting of operational autonomy to banks and liberalisation of the entry norms for financial intermediaries.

The strengthening measures aimed at reducing the vulnerability of banks in the face of fluctuations in the economic environment. These included, *inter alia*, capital adequacy, income recognition, asset classification and provisioning norms, exposure norms, improved levels of transparency, and disclosure standards.

Institutional measures focused on reforms in the legal framework pertaining to banks and creation of new institutions.

3.3.2 India's Approach to Financial Sector Reforms: Financial sector reforms in India have formed an important component of the overall economic reforms process initiated in the early 1990s. These reforms have followed a well calibrated approach.

The general approach to financial sector reforms has been a transparent, collaborative and consultative process aimed at resolving many possible dilemmas. The reform process itself was characterised by caution with a tilt towards preserving stability, careful sequencing of measures, mutually reinforcing monetary measures and ensuring consistency and complementarity with other policies.

Further, reforms in the financial markets have been undertaken within the overall monetary policy framework and in co-ordination with reforms in the money and foreign exchange markets. Many of the major reforms have been implemented in phases, allowing for transition so as not to destabilise market conditions or any group of participants or the financial system in general.

In the context of maximising benefits of financial integration and minimising the risks, the link with the real sector cannot be ignored. In India, reforms in the financial sector started early in the reform cycle which imparted efficiency and stability to the real sector. The financial sector can add competitive strength and growth if reforms in the financial and real sectors keep apace. A major agenda for reform at this juncture for India, given the impressive all-round confidence in the economy, relates to the structure and functioning of institutions and in particular lowering the high transaction costs prevalent in the system. There are several dimensions to the transaction costs—ranging from legal provisions, the judicial system and procedures to attitudes.

The policy of gradualism that has been followed by India focuses on evolution of appropriate institutional framework and the sequencing of reforms based on the experience gained so far. The sequencing and pace of reforms are also vital to safeguard monetary and financial stability and avoid reversals. The issues in this context include: (a) whether bank-based or market-based system of development should be adopted, (b) order of sequencing of reforms of various segments of the financial market to be followed, and (c) whether or not capital account liberalisation should precede domestic financial market reform.

A. Lessons from East Asian Crisis: By following a gradualist approach, India has successfully avoided financial disasters as were experienced by some East Asian countries. A number of developing countries especially in Asia that moved early on to the path of economic liberalization had experienced large capital inflows through the 1980s and the first half of the 1990s. Large capital inflows, however, carried the risk of financial sector vulnerability, where the use of such flows is not regulated by application of appropriate mix of macroeconomic and structural policy measures. The recent currency and financial crises in Mexico and Thailand, followed by Korea and Indonesia, provide many insights about the problems that would arise when exchange rates are inflexible, and banking and financial systems are weak.

The experience of the crisis-affected countries highlights the need for setting in place regulatory and supervisory frameworks to ensure the safety and stability of financial systems. Their experience also underscored the premise that financial development is only a necessary condition for sustainable growth, and by no means sufficient. In fact, with the incidence of the costs of financial crisis falling on the sovereign governments, financial stability has come to occupy a centre-stage in public policy making along with the requirement of ensuring that the efficiency of the financial sector is high.

Implementation of the reforms process has had several unique features. Financial sector reforms were undertaken early in the reform cycle. Notably, the reforms process was not driven by any banking crisis, nor was it the outcome of any external support package. Besides, the design of the reforms was crafted through domestic expertise, taking on board the international experiences in this respect. The reforms were carefully sequenced with respect to the instruments to be used and the objectives to be achieved. Thus, prudential norms and supervisory strengthening were introduced early in the reform cycle, followed by interest-rate deregulation and a gradual lowering of statutory pre-emptions. The more complex aspects of legal and accounting measures were ushered in subsequently when the basic tenets of the reforms were already in place.

3.3.3 Strategy of Financial Sector Reforms: Reforms in the financial sector are wide-ranging, encompassing institutional, legal and technological aspects of the functioning of financial intermediaries and financial markets.

A. Developing and Strengthening Financial Infrastructure: Measures to improve market infrastructure must be implemented at an early stage of reform alongside appropriate legal framework. These conditions facilitate growth of financial transactions including inter-bank transactions and active liquidity management.

Presence of well-established institutions, soundness of bank balance sheets, existence of adequate safety nets and vigilant supervision are the pre-requisites for successful financial liberalisation. The reform process in India within the banking system has sought to strengthen the balance sheets of individual banks, empower banks to respond in the most optimal manner to market stimuli and to establish institutions to ensure a level playing field for all market participants and provide a back-up system for contingencies.

Competition has been infused into the financial system by licensing new private banks since 1993. Foreign banks have also been given more liberal entry.

Progress has also been generated through demonstration and spread effects of advanced technology and risk management practices accompanying new private banks and foreign banks. Given the fiscal constraint being faced by the Government and in keeping with the evolving principles of corporate governance, the Government permitted public sector banks to raise fresh equity from markets to meet their capital shortfalls or to expand their lending. Several public and private sector banks have accessed the domestic equity market. Public sector banks have also raised capital through GDR/ADRs while many banks have raised subordinated debt through the private placement route.

B. Financial Regulation and Supervision: The quality of financial regulation and supervision as well as of information and the legal system are important for reaping the benefits of globalisation. Hence, enactment of enabling legislation has been a priority area of the reforms. The Board for Financial Supervision (BFS) was constituted in 1994, with the mandate to exercise the powers of supervision and inspection in relation to the banking companies, financial institutions and non-banking financial companies.

With the switchover to international best practices on income recognition, asset classification and provisioning, the problem of non-performing assets (NPAs) assumed critical importance. It was widely perceived that the level of NPAs in India was high by international standards. The problem needed to be tackled urgently and from different fronts. A menu approach has been adopted to tackle this major constraint confronting the banking sector. These policy measures have resulted in reduction in gross NPAs in the banking system.

The need for monitoring and supervising becomes even more important systemically with the opening up of the economy. Thus, the prudential regulations were fortified by reorientation of *on-site inspections* and introduction of *off-site surveillance*. The focus of inspection has shifted from ensuring appropriate credit planning and credit allocation under a closed economy framework to assessment of the bank's safety and soundness and to identify areas where corrective action is needed to strengthen the institution and improve its performance.

In view of the growing liberalisation of the external sector and international banking by banks in India, monitoring of the cross-border flow of funds has assumed importance. RBI now compiles and disseminates international banking statistics (IBS) on the lines of the reporting system devised by the Bank for International Settlements (BIS). The locational banking statistics (LBS) provide the gross position of international assets and international liabilities of all banking offices located in India. They report exclusively banks' international transactions including the transactions with any of their own branches/subsidiaries/joint ventures located outside India.

C. Financial Openness: In India, opening up of the financial sector in terms of entry of foreign entities and easing of restrictions on international transactions took place within the broader process of reforms. The constant policy concern in this respect has been that of preparing the financial sector for global competition and taking preventive measures for the potential vulnerabilities that it might engender.

Despite their extensive branch network, the biggest banks in India are miniscule compared to most of the multinational banks, in terms of standard parameters like assets or deposits. Hence, the initial focus of reforms in the financial sector was to strengthen the domestic financial infrastructure, make it more competitive and to provide banks greater freedom in their foreign operations.

Since 1991, the presence of foreign entities within the Indian banking sector has increased and so also the international transactions of Indian banks.

International experience has shown that the cost of financial intermediation declines and quality of financial services improves with opening of the economy. However, openness should be preceded by deregulation and strengthening of institutional framework in order to limit contagious influences. The strategy adopted in India has been to maximise the beneficial effects of openness while minimising the adverse consequences. Financial crisis due to internal/external factors have been averted, while the financial system has been progressively deregulated and strengthened.

In short, India's financial sector has made rapid strides in reforming itself and aligning itself to the new competitive business environment. While the operational and supervisory practices in the sector have progressively approximated international best practices, the process of convergence is not yet complete. Greater conformity to prudential norms of international standards as also adoption of better systems of risk management will enhance the stability of the financial system even as banks expand the range and volume of their operations.

3.3.4 International Security Standards: There are at present a number of security standards available for different financial applications. Most of them are internationally accepted and part of the ISO standards. These international standards such as the BS7799 [3] have been accepted by the RBI. Banks, however, could also put in place measures which conform to their own policies and ensure regular and periodical audit.

The objectives of these standards are as listed below.

1. To provide management direction and support for information security which is a basic pre-requisite for BS7799.
2. To manage information security within the organisation, maintain the security of organisational information processing facilities and information assets accessed by third parties, and to maintain the security of information when the responsibility for information processing has been outsourced to another organisation.
3. To maintain appropriate protection of corporate assets and ensure that information assets receive an appropriate level of protection.
4. To reduce risks of human error, theft, fraud or misuse of facilities and minimise the damage from security incidents and malfunctions and learn from such incidents.
5. To ensure the correct and secure operation of information processing facilities, minimise the risk of systems failures, to protect the integrity of software and information and maintain the integrity and availability of information processing and communication.
6. To control access to information, prevent unauthorised access, detect unauthorised activities and ensure information security when using mobile computing and tele-networking facilities.
7. To ensure security is built into operational systems, to prevent loss, modification or misuse of user data in application systems.
8. To counteract interruptions to business activities and critical business processes from the effects of major failures or disasters.
9. To prevent breaches of any criminal or civil law, statutory, regulatory or contractual obligations and of any security requirements, ensure compliance of systems with organisational security policies and standards and minimise interference to/from the system audit process.

3.3.5 Basel II and Migration to Basel III Norms: With a view to ensuring smooth transition to the revised framework and providing opportunity to banks to streamline their systems and strategies, banks in India were required to commence a parallel run of the revised framework with effect from April 1, 2006. All scheduled commercial banks (except regional rural banks) were required to implement the revised capital adequacy framework with effect from March 31, 2007. Basel II framework in India became fully operational from end-March 2009.

Several measures were undertaken by the RBI to prepare the banking system to make a smooth migration to Basel II. Following the amendment to the Banking Companies (Acquisition and Transfer of Undertakings) Act in 1994, several public sector banks (PSBs) have raised capital both in India and abroad through global depository receipts (GDRs). Several PSBs have also raised subordinated debt through the private placement. Concurrently, a series of regulatory initiatives were taken by the RBI relevant for Basel II.

As per a circular issued by the Reserve Bank of India on March 27, 2014, it was stated that, in view of the implementation of Basel III Capital Regulations, banks need to improve and strengthen their capital planning processes.

In terms of Basel III Capital Regulations issued by the Reserve Bank of India, the Capital Conservation Buffer (CCB) was scheduled to be implemented from March 31, 2015 in phases and to be fully implemented by March 31, 2018. However, it has been decided that the implementation of CCB will begin as on March 31, 2016. Consequently, Basel III Capital Regulations will be fully implemented as on March 31, 2019. Implementation of Basel III framework will throw various challenges for Indian banks and its adoption by Indian banks would push down their return on equity (RoE) to an extent.

3.3.6 Accounting and Auditing Standards: Indian accounting standards are generally in alignment with international accounting standards, except for some modifications to suit local customs, usages and level of development in the country. There has been significant progress in accounting standards though some issues remain to be addressed. There are suggestions that Institute of Chartered Accountants of India (ICAI) needs to be made an autonomous body with its own staff and independent funding. Need has also been felt to develop country-specific/sector-specific standards where similar standards are not developed by International Accounting Standards Board (IASB). Similarly, ICAI should make attempts to attain convergence with International Financial Reporting Standards (IFRS).

India is one of the earliest countries to have adopted International Standards on Auditing by amending them to suit Indian requirements. There has been significant progress since ROSC-2004. However, there are some areas which need attention. Auditing and Assurance Standards Board (AASB) needs to take steps to attain convergence with International Standards on Auditing. It needs to take proactive steps by bringing out more technical guidance and other literature to help small and medium practitioners to understand standards. There is a need to give functional independence to AASB.

A. Marking-to-market: The Indian accounting standards are generally aligned to the International Financial Reporting Standards, though there are some differences. India is yet to fully adopt the marking-to-market requirements as available in the international standards. The Indian standards are relatively conservative and do not permit recognition of unrealised gains in the profit and loss account or equity, though unrealised losses are required to be accounted. Banks are required to mark-to-market the investments in the held for trading (HFT) and available for sale (AFS) categories at periodical intervals, on a portfolio basis, and provide for the net losses and ignore the net gains. This has proved to be a stabilising factor, inasmuch as it has not induced an imbalance in the incentive structures and has also proved to be less pro-cyclical.

3.3.7 Technological Solutions for Financial Services: Most of the initiatives regarding technology are aimed at providing better and more efficient customer service by offering multiple options to the customer. The death of distance, which is a by-product of technology, has become a reality in the banking sector. Technology is also playing a key role in banks' strategy for gaining a competitive edge.

Many banks have commenced the process of setting up core banking solutions, which are at various stages of implementation. While such systems are already in place in respect of new private sector banks, a few old private sector banks and public sector banks are also quickly moving to set up such processes. This would benefit the customer in the banking sector. Computerisation of the business of banks has been receiving high importance. The public sector banks have already crossed the 70 percent level of computerisation of their business. The directive from the Central Vigilance Commission (CVC) to achieve 100 percent computerisation has resulted in renewed vigour towards computerisation of branches.

Networking has been receiving focused attention by banks. This activity is also being monitored by the RBI. Most banks have their own corporate networks to facilitate inter-branch and branch-controlling office communication in an electronic mode. Inter-bank and inter-city communication takes place through the Indian Financial Network (INFINET). As part of the INFINET, the terrestrial lines have been augmented to provide for increased data transfer capabilities. All these have resulted in the dependence of banks on network-based computing which has benefited the customer.

INFINET also provides for safe and secure transmission of electronic messages with the use of public key infrastructure (PKI) which has the legal backing of Information Technology Act, 2000. It also provides for messages to flow in a structured environment, using the structured financial messaging solutions (SFMS), which provides for inter-operability of messages so that straight through processing (STP) is achieved.

Another major development witnessed in recent years is the growth in multiple delivery channels to customers such as internet-based banking, mobile banking and anywhere banking. This has benefited the customers and the banks alike. While customers have now a wide variety of options to choose from, banks have been able to reduce costs which have had a positive impact on their profitability.

These developments have, however, also posed certain challenges. In a world where geographical barriers are losing significance, it is essential that security is given prime importance in a transnational scenario where large sums of money are at stake. While the challenges relating to physical security could be confronted with relative ease, the position is much more complicated in respect of IT security. The RBI has, therefore, provided guidelines on information system (IS) security as also IS audit which banks can use for their benefit. These are generic in nature and do not have any prescriptive tones.

3.3.8 Legal Reforms for Strengthening Financial Sector: An efficient financial system requires a regulatory framework with well-defined objectives, adequate and clear legal framework and transparent supervisory procedure. This, in turn, requires comprehensive legislations to enable the regulatory authorities to discharge their responsibilities effectively. The RBI has, therefore, been making constant efforts to upgrade and strengthen the legal framework in tune with the changing environment.

Some recent Acts enacted by the Parliament are as under:

A. Prevention of Money Laundering Act (PMLA), 2002: PMLA, 2002 was enacted in January 2003. The Act along with the Rules framed thereunder came into force with effect from July 1, 2005. Section 3 of PMLA defines offence of money laundering as whosoever directly or indirectly attempts to indulge or knowingly assists or knowingly is a party or is actually involved in any process or activity connected with the proceeds of crime and projecting it as untainted property shall be guilty of offence of money-laundering. It prescribes obligation of banking companies, financial institutions and intermediaries for verification and maintenance of records of the identity of all its clients and also of all transactions and for furnishing information of such transactions in prescribed form to the Financial Intelligence Unit-India (FIU-IND). It empowers the Director of FIU-IND to impose fine on banking company, financial institution or intermediary if they or any of their officers fails to comply with the provisions of the Act.

PMLA empowers certain officers of the Directorate of Enforcement to carry out investigations in cases involving offence of money laundering and also to attach the property involved in money laundering. PMLA envisages setting up of an Adjudicating Authority to exercise jurisdiction, power and authority to confirm attachment or order confiscation of attached properties. It also envisages setting up of an Appellate Tribunal to hear appeals against the order of the Adjudicating Authority and the authorities like Director FIU-IND.

PMLA envisages designation of one or more courts of sessions as Special Court or Special Courts to try offences punishable under PMLA and offences with which the accused may, under the Code of Criminal Procedure, 1973, be charged at the same trial. PMLA allows Central Government to enter into an agreement with Government of any country outside India for enforcing the provisions of the PMLA, exchange of information for the prevention of any offence under PMLA or under the corresponding law in force in that country or investigation of cases relating to any offence under PMLA.

PMLA seeks to combat money laundering in India and has three main objectives:

1. To prevent and control money laundering.
2. To confiscate and seize the property obtained from the laundered money.
3. To deal with any other issue connected with money laundering in India.

Special Courts have been set-up in a number of States/UTs by the Central Government to conduct the trial of the offences of money laundering. The authorities under the Act, like the director, adjudicating authority and the appellate tribunal, have been constituted to carry out the proceedings related to attachment and confiscation of any property derived from money laundering.

In order to enlarge the scope of this Act and to achieve the desired objectives, the Act provides for bilateral agreements between countries to cooperate with each other and curb the menace of money laundering. These agreements shall be for the purpose of either enforcing the provisions of this Act or for the exchange of information which shall help in the prevention in the commission of an offence under this Act or the corresponding laws in that foreign State.

In certain cases the Central Government may seek/provide assistance from/to a contracting State for any investigation or forwarding of evidence collected during the course of such investigation. The Act provides for reciprocal arrangements for processes/assistance with regard to accused persons.

The Government constituted the Financial Intelligence Unit-India, in November, 2004. The organization has started receiving Cash Transaction Reports and Suspicious Transaction Reports from the banking companies etc. in terms of Section 12 of the PMLA.

B. Credit Information Companies (Regulation) Act, 2005: It is aimed at providing for regulation of credit information companies and to facilitate efficient distribution of credit. No company can commence or carry on the business of credit information without obtaining a certificate of registration from the RBI. The Act sets out procedures for obtaining certificate of registration, the requirements of minimum capital and management of credit information companies. The Act also empowers the RBI to determine policy in relation to functioning of credit information companies and to give directions to such companies, credit institutions and specified users.

The Act also lays down the functions of credit information companies, powers and duties of auditors, obtaining of membership by credit institutions in credit information companies, information privacy principles, alterations of credit information files and credit reports, regulation of unauthorised access to credit information, offences and penalties, obligations as to fidelity and secrecy.

Other salient features of the Act include settlement of disputes between credit institutions and credit information companies or between credit institutions and their borrowers. The Act also provides for amendment of certain enactments so as to permit disclosure of credit information.

C. Government Securities Act, 2006: This Act was enacted by the Parliament with a view to consolidating and amending the law relating to Government securities and its management by the Reserve Bank of India. The Act applies to Government securities created and issued, whether before or after the commencement of the Act, by the Central or a State Government. Accordingly, the Public Debt Act, 1944 ceased to apply to the Government securities. The Indian Securities Act, 1920 was repealed.

The new Act would facilitate widening and deepening of the Government securities market and its more effective regulation by the Reserve Bank in various ways, such as:

1. Stripping or reconstitution of Government securities.
2. Legal recognition of beneficial ownership of the investors in Government securities through the constituents' subsidiary general ledger (CSGL).
3. Statutory backing for the Reserve Bank's power to debar subsidiary general ledger (SGL) account holders from trading, either temporarily or permanently, for misuse of SGL account facility.
4. Facility of pledge or hypothecation or lien of Government securities for availing of loan.
5. Extension of nomination facility to hold the securities or receive the amount thereof in the event of death of the holder.
6. Recognition of title to Government security of the deceased holder on the

basis of documents other than succession certificate such as will executed by the deceased holder, registered deed of family settlement, gift deed, deed of partition, etc., as prescribed by the Reserve Bank of India.

7. Recognition of mother as the guardian of the minor for the purpose of holding Government Securities.
8. Statutory powers to the Reserve Bank to call for information, cause inspection and issue directions in relation to Government securities.

D. Payment and Settlement Systems Act, 2007: This Act, along with Payment and Settlement Systems Regulations, 2008, stipulates that no person other than the Reserve Bank of India (RBI), shall commence or operate a payment system except under and in accordance with an authorisation issued by the RBI under the provisions of the Act.

All persons currently operating a payment system or desirous of setting up a payment system, as defined in Section 2(1)(i) of the Act should apply for authorisation to the Reserve Bank, unless specifically exempted in terms of the Act. Existing payment systems will cease to have the right to carry on their operations, unless they obtain an authorisation within six months from the commencement of the Act (i.e. August 12, 2008). The Payment and Settlement Systems Regulations, 2008 detail the form and manner in which the application is to be made to the Reserve Bank for grant of authorisation.

3.3.9 High Level Committee on Financial Sector Reforms, 2008: With a view to outlining a comprehensive agenda for the evolution of the financial sector—indicating especially the priorities and sequencing decisions which the Government of India must keep in minds—a High Level Committee on Financial Sector Reforms was set up by the Planning Commission of India in August 2007. The Committee (Chairman: Raghuram G. Rajan) submitted its report in September 2008, and made the following main recommendations:

1. Allow more entry to private well-governed, deposit-taking small finance banks.
2. Liberalise the banking correspondent regulation so that a wide range of local agents can serve to extend financial services. Use technology both to reduce costs and to limit fraud and misrepresentation.
3. Offer priority sector loan certificates (PSLC) to all entities that lend to eligible categories in the priority sector. Allow banks that undershoot their priority sector obligations to buy the PSLC and submit it towards fulfilment of their target.
4. Sell small under-performing public sector banks, possibly to another bank or to a strategic investor, to gain experience with the process and gauge outcomes.
5. Create stronger boards for large public sector banks, with more power to

outside shareholders (including possibly a private sector strategic investor), devolving the power to appoint and compensate top executives to the board.

6. After starting the process of strengthening boards, delink the banks from additional government oversight, including by the Central Vigilance Commission and Parliament, with the justification that with government-controlled boards governing the banks, a second layer of oversight is not needed.
7. Be more liberal in allowing takeovers and mergers, including by domestically incorporated subsidiaries of foreign banks.
8. Free banks to set up branches and ATMs anywhere.

3.3.10 Committee on Financial Sector Assessment (CFSA), 2009: In March 2009, the Government and RBI jointly released the report of the Committee on Financial Sector Assessment (CFSA) that was co-chaired by Deputy Governor Rakesh Mohan and Finance Secretary Ashok Chawla. The report is the culmination of work started in September 2006 to undertake a comprehensive self-assessment of India's financial sector, particularly focusing on stability assessment and stress testing and compliance with all financial standards and codes.

CFSA owed its origins to the Financial Sector Assessment Programme (FSAP) that was initiated in 1999 and carried out jointly by the IMF and the World Bank after the Asian crisis. Several countries, including India, participated in this long-drawn and resource-intensive exercise. This programme so far has been conducted by the IMF and the World Bank using experts from around the world to carry out the assessment with participation from the host country.

The CFSA followed a forward-looking and holistic approach to self-assessment, based on three mutually reinforcing pillars:

1. Financial stability assessment and stress testing.
2. Legal, infrastructural and market development issues.
3. Assessment of the status of implementation of international financial standards and codes.

The first pillar is essentially concerned with stability assessment. Taking into account the legal, regulatory and supervisory architecture in India, the CFSA felt the need for involving, and associating closely, all the major regulatory institutions in the financial sector—RBI, SEBI and IRDA [4], besides the relevant government departments. Direct official involvement at different levels brought about enormous responsibility, ownership, and commitment to the process, ensuring constructive pragmatism when faced with contentious issues.

Since the assessment required comprehensive domain knowledge in the various technical areas examined, the CFSA initially constituted Technical Groups comprising officials with first-hand experience in handling the respective areas from the regulatory agencies concerned as well as the government to undertake the preliminary assessment and to prepare technical notes and background material in the concerned areas. This ensured that officials who are well-conversant with their own systems and are aware of the existing strengths and weaknesses could identify the best alternative solutions.

To ensure an impartial assessment, the CFSA constituted four external independent advisory panels, comprising non-official experts drawn from within the country. These Panels made their assessments after thorough debate and rigorous scrutiny of inputs provided by the technical groups. To further strengthen the credibility of this assessment, the advisory panels' assessments were reviewed by eminent international experts.

The CFSA then drew up its own overview report at the final stage, drawing upon the assessments, findings and recommendations of the advisory panels and the comments of the peer reviewers. The assessments and recommendations comprise six volumes.

Overall, the CFSA found that India's financial system is essentially sound and resilient, and that systemic stability is by and large robust. India is broadly compliant with most of the standards and codes though gaps were noted in the timely implementation of bankruptcy proceedings.

Of immediate interest, and related closely to the current macroeconomic conditions, the CFSA also carried out single-factor stress-tests for credit and market risks and liquidity ratio and scenario analyses. These tests show that there are no significant vulnerabilities in the banking system. This does not mean that NPAs will not rise in this economic slowdown. NPAs may indeed rise. However, given the strength of the banks' balance sheets, that rise is not likely to pose any systemic risks, as it might in many advanced countries.

Risk assessment, however, is a continuous process and the stress tests need to be conducted taking into account the macroeconomic linkages as also the second round and contagion risks.

3.3.11 Financial Sector Legislative Reforms Commission (FSLRC), 2013: The Indian financial system is increasingly out of touch with the requirements of the economy today and the even greater requirements of the economy in the future. Most changes in the framework of financial regulation in India have been made in response to the need of the hour. This has meant piecemeal changes to the various laws that give powers to regulators to regulate finance.

In recent years, a consensus has emerged about the direction of reforms through a series of expert committees, which have drawn on hundreds of independent experts and a body of research on the failings of Indian finance.

However, many of the changes proposed are incompatible with the basic structure of existing laws.

With a view to revamping financial sector laws to bring them in tune with current requirements, the Government set up the FSLRC (Chairman: B.N. Srikrishna) on March, 24, 2011. [5] FSLRC in its Report, submitted in March 2013, gave wide-ranging recommendations, both legislative and non-legislative, on the institutional, legal, and regulatory framework and operational changes in the Indian financial sector. The draft Indian Financial Code (IFC) was proposed by FSLRC has provisions that aim at replacing a large numbers of existing financial laws. FSLRC has designed a modified financial regulatory architecture which would increase accountability by achieving clarity of purpose for each organization and avoid conflicts of interest. The modified arrangements also facilitate achieving economies of scope and scale of related activities, for the private sector and for the government.

The FSLRC was set up to review and redraft the laws so that Indian finance can be reformed to prepare India for growing into a modern economy, without having to constantly amend existing laws to incorporate each new step for the financial system.

The task for FSLRC was to question the fundamental arrangements between regulators, the Government, the regulated, and the consumer for whose protection regulation is ultimately being done. FSLRC proposed a new draft law, viz. the Indian Financial Code. This law puts consumer protection at the heart of all financial regulations. In order to protect the consumer without putting a burden on the taxpayer, regulators do micro-prudential regulation and reduce the risk of failure of financial firms. They protect policy holders and prevent unsuitable products from being sold through regulations about consumer protection and through redressal forums. When financial firms fail, shareholders should bear the full brunt of the failure, but consequences for consumers and the economy should be blocked using a resolution corporation. Through systemic risk regulation, the regulators and the government prevent a large-scale disruption of financial services. This adds up to a rational approach to interventions by financial agencies in the financial system, as opposed to the existing approach of command and control.

A major theme of many of the recommendations of previous committee reports in India has been the impediments placed by financial agencies against progress. This issue has been addressed by FSLRC by giving regulators clear objectives and enumerated powers. The regulator in this scenario needs to demonstrate that the regulation is required to meet the objectives assigned to him, and it lies within his powers, and that a cost-benefit analysis of the regulation shows that the additional cost, monetary or otherwise, of complying with this regulation is going to bring clear benefits to the economy.

The Indian Financial Code is on the legislative agenda. This legislative and non-legislative work is now the centrepiece of financial reforms in India.

3.3.12 Financial Stability and Development Council (FSDC): Following the recent global financial crisis, several nations have been revisiting their regulatory architecture. India has also been prompt to act on this front. In pursuance of the announcement made in the Budget 2010-11, an apex-level Financial Stability and Development Council was set up under the Chairmanship of the Finance Minister for strengthening and institutionalizing the mechanism for maintaining financial stability and enhancing inter-regulatory coordination. The FSDC is a non-statutory apex council for coordination among various regulatory bodies, since in India's increasingly complex economy, issues arise that straddle multiple financial jurisdictions and so risk falling through the cracks or getting caught in the crossfire.

A sub-committee of the FSDC has also been set up under the chairmanship of the Governor of Reserve Bank of India (RBI). Under the aegis of the FSDC, two empowered technical groups (i.e. Technical Group on Financial Literacy and Financial Inclusion and Inter-Regulatory Technical Group) have been formed.

3.3.13 Financial Action Task Force (FATF): Financial Action Task Force (FATF) is an inter-governmental policy-making body established in 1989 by the Ministers of its Member jurisdictions. The objectives of the FATF are to set standards and promote effective implementation of legal, regulatory and operational measures for combating money laundering, terrorist financing and other related threats to the integrity of the international financial system. The FATF is therefore a *policy-making body* which works to generate the necessary political will to bring about national legislative and regulatory reforms in these areas.

The FATF has a ministerial mandate to establish international standards for combating money laundering and terrorist financing. India joined the FATF as its 34th member in June 2010. At present the FATF has 36 members comprising 34 countries and two organizations, namely the European Union and Gulf Cooperation Council. India participated in the FATF plenary and Working Group Meetings held in Mexico from June 20-24, 2011.

FATF has developed a series of Recommendations that are recognised as the international standard for combating of money laundering and the financing of terrorism and proliferation of weapons of mass destruction. They form the basis for a co-ordinated response to these threats to the integrity of the financial system and help ensure a level playing field. First issued in 1990, the FATF Recommendations were revised in 1996, 2001, 2003 and most recently in 2012 to ensure that they remain up to date and relevant, and they are intended to be of universal application.

FATF monitors the progress of its members in implementing necessary measures, reviews money laundering and terrorist financing techniques and counter-measures, and promotes the adoption and implementation of appropriate measures globally. In collaboration with other international stakeholders, the FATF works to identify national-level vulnerabilities with the aim of protecting the international financial system from misuse.

FATF's decision making body, the FATF Plenary, meets three times per year.

3.3.14 Achievements of Financial Sector Reforms and Areas of Concern: Financial sector in the Indian economy since the early 1990s has undergone a transformation towards a vibrant, competitive and diversified system, with a multiplicity of financial institutions having different risk profiles intermediating in various segments of the market spectrum. The evolution of the Indian financial system from somewhat of a constricted and an undersized one to a more open, deregulated and market oriented one and its interface with the growth process are the major areas of reforms still underway.

The financial system has exhibited considerable dynamism in recent years. The system today is varied, with a well-diversified structure of financial institutions, financial companies and mutual funds. The setting up of some specialised financial institutions and refinance institutions has provided depth to financial intermediation outside the banking sector. These developments, coupled with increased financial market liberalization, have enhanced competition. A number of existing financial institutions have diversified into several new activities, such as, investment banking and infrastructure financing, providing guarantees for domestic and offshore lending for infrastructure projects.

Rapid expansion of non-banking financial companies (NBFCs) has taken place, providing avenues for depositors to hold assets and for borrowers to enhance the scale of funding of their activities. Various types of NBFCs have provided varied services that include equipment leasing, hire purchase, loans, investments, mutual benefit and chit fund activities. More recently, NBFCs activity has picked up in the area of housing finance.

Financial development is also reflected in the growing importance of mutual funds. In the 1990s, they enabled sizable mobilisation of financial surpluses of the households for investment in capital markets. Capital markets themselves have become an important source of financing corporate investments, especially after firms were permitted to charge share premium in a flexible manner.

An understanding of the organisational structure of markets for financial assets is vital for knowing the limitations and prospects with regards to efficiency, integration and stability. Financial markets in India comprise, in the main: the credit market, the money market, the foreign exchange market, the debt market and the capital market. Of late, the derivatives market has also emerged. With banks having already been allowed to undertake insurance business, bancassurance market is also likely to emerge in a big way.

Most of the financial markets were characterised, till the early 1990s, by controls over the pricing of financial assets, restrictions on flows or transactions, barriers to entry, low liquidity and high transaction costs. These characteristics came in the way of development of the markets and allocative efficiency of resources channelled through them.

The initiation of financial sector reforms in the early 1990s was essentially to bring about a transformation in the structure, efficiency and stability of financial markets, as also an integration of the markets.

In spite of the significant improvements in the banking industry as a result of reforms, several challenges lie ahead, the most important being the need to bring down the NPAs. Commercial banks continue to face the problem of non-performing assets (NPAs), attributable, *inter alia*, to factors such as weak debt recovery mechanism, non-realisation of collateral and poor credit appraisal techniques. Policy measures have not yielded the desired results. The recent enactment of the Securitisation and Reconstruction of Financial Assets and Enforcement of Security Interest Act, 2002 has increased the momentum for the recovery of NPAs. However, banks need to intensify their efforts to recover their overdues and prevent generation of fresh NPAs.

Co-operative banks constitute an important segment of the Indian banking system. They have an extensive branch network and reach out to people in remote areas. They have traditionally played an important role in creating banking habits among the lower and middle-income groups and in strengthening the rural credit delivery system. Unfortunately, financial reforms have not impacted the functioning of co-operative banks. Since the introduction of reforms, there has been very little perceptible improvement in either stability or efficiency of co-operative banks. In particular, the asset quality and profitability of co-operative banks has shown some deterioration in the reform period. Positive impact of reforms, as has been witnessed in the case of commercial banking sector, may take longer to get manifested for co-operative banks given the late start of the reform process in this sector.

Financial institutions, which constitute an important source of funds for the commercial sector, have been losing ground fast. The situation has come about as a result of the distinction between development and commercial banking getting blurred, high cost of funds and asset-liability mismatches. With reforms in the financial sector, the facility of low cost funds under long-term operations funds,

funds from bilateral and multilateral agencies and bond issues under statutory liquidity ratio is no more available. Now the financial institutions are raising funds at market-related rates of interest. The Reserve Bank of India (RBI) has been advising financial institutions to chart a path for their evolution into universal banks. The merger of ICICI with the ICICI Bank was approved by the RBI in April 2002.

Competitive pressures as well as prudential regulatory requirements have made banks risk-averse, preferring their investment in relatively risk-free gilt instruments. The behaviour and strategies of bank business would need to change from the present so that they can factor in their own risk assessment even while performing their core activities. There is a need to ensure long term finance to support development and growth in the economy, even as restructuring takes place through mergers and universal banking.

True, there has been a significant progress towards globalisation in the recent past in India, the extent to which the country is globalised is considerably low as compared with other emerging economies. This indicates not only the existence of enormous opportunities but also challenges in terms of transition from a non-entity to a major player in the global financial system.

To recapitulate, in the context of the balance of payments crisis of 1991, a comprehensive structural and financial sector reform process was initiated in India as recommended by the Committee on the Financial System (Chairman: M. Narasimham, 1991) which became the starting point for gradual deregulation of the financial sector and development and integration of various segments of the financial market. Measures were initiated to streamline functioning of the financial system to create a sound, competitive and efficient banking system capable of meeting the increasing challenges of liberalisation and globalisation.

A safe and sound financial sector is a prerequisite for sustained growth of any economy. Globalisation, deregulation and advances in information technology in recent years have brought about significant changes in the operating environment for banks and other financial institutions. These institutions are faced with increased competitive pressures and changing customer demands. These, in turn, have engendered a rapid increase in product innovations and changes in business strategies. While these developments have enabled improvement in the efficiency of financial institutions, they have also posed some serious risks. The regulatory and supervisory policies are, accordingly, being reshaped and reoriented to meet the challenge of containing systemic risks. In this changing milieu, the main challenge for the supervisors has been to maintain the stability of the financial system and, at the same time, provide sufficient flexibility to financial institutions so that they can respond effectively to the growing competition while taking advantage of business opportunities and technological developments.

With the liberalisation of financial markets, policy authorities in India have also had to contend with episodes of financial volatility as were witnessed in some East Asian countries. Recognising the strong complementarity between financial stability and macroeconomic stability, the operational settings for policies are being geared to dampen excessive volatility and the possible impairment of the ability of financial institutions to handle fluctuations in financial asset prices. Current macroeconomic and financial developments in the Indian economy highlight the evolving role of the financial sector in the functioning of the economy and the growing integration across financial markets.

Although the financial sector in India has grown fairly rapidly in recent years, in terms of the conventional metrics of financial deepening—such as a ratio of total financial claims or bank loans to GDP—India appears to be considerably behind other emerging markets. One of the most important gaps in our existing financial structure is the lack of a sufficiently large venture capital and angel investor community, which play important role in financing start-ups, especially in areas where technology is the key to success and risk capital is needed.

The financial sector in the Indian economy is undergoing a transformation towards a vibrant, competitive and diversified system, with a multiplicity of financial institutions having different risk profiles intermediating in various segments of the market spectrum. The development of banking is a critical element in the agenda of financial sector reforms in India. Financial sector reforms in India are by no means complete. Plans are afoot to modernise the financial system to make it compatible with best international practices.

3.4 Financial Regulators in India

Financial regulators in India are multiple. There is a plethora of legislations, rules and regulations to regulate and supervise the financial sector. In this context, the Report of the Financial Sector Legislative Reforms Commission (Chairman: B.N. Srikrishna), 2013 remarked, "The institutional framework governing the financial sector has been built up over a century. There are over 60 Acts and multiple rules and regulations that govern the financial sector. Many of the financial sector laws date back several decades, when the financial landscape was very different from that seen today. For example, the Reserve Bank of India (RBI) Act and the Insurance Act are of 1934 and 1938 vintage respectively. Financial economic governance has been modified in a piecemeal fashion from time to time, without substantial changes to the underlying foundations. Over the years, as the economy and the financial system have grown in size and sophistication, an increasing gap has come about between the requirements of the country and the present legal and regulatory arrangements". [6]

The Commission further observed, "The existing regulatory environment in India is fragmented and complex. There are multiple regulators, each one tasked with a silo within the financial sector. Given the fluidity and the fungibility of financial markets, such a fragmented approach cannot possibly achieve the results desired in terms of providing an organicunity to the sector in addressing domestic and global co-ordination, addressing financial development and inclusion, and dealing with systemic stability and other concerns. In fact, the experience of regulatory co-operation in India has not been very encouraging and has witnessed escalation of conflicts in the recent past. The Commission, therefore, feels that the fragmented approach to financial sector regulation in India has failed on many grounds, which need to be corrected. But at the same time, learning from the global crisis and the consequential regulatory rethinking in multiple jurisdictions, and the need for aligning the regulatory requirements to our own milieu, the Commission deliberated the issue of appropriate regulatory structure in detail". [7] See also section 3.3.11 of this chapter.

The chief regulators and supervisors of the Indian financial system are described below.

3.4.1 Ministry of Finance, Government of India: The work of the Ministry is divided into 5 departments.

A. Department of Economic Affairs (DEA): DEA is the nodal agency of the Union Government to formulate and monitor country's economic policies and programmes having a bearing on domestic and international aspects of economic management. A principal responsibility of this Department is the preparation of the Union Budget annually (excluding the Railway Budget). Other main functions include the following:

1. Formulation and monitoring of macroeconomic policies, including issues relating to fiscal policy and public finance, inflation, public debt management and the functioning of capital market including stock exchanges. In this context, it looks at ways and means to raise internal resources through taxation, market borrowings and mobilization of small savings.
2. Monitoring and raising of external resources through multilateral and bilateral official development assistance (ODA), sovereign borrowings abroad, foreign investments and monitoring foreign exchange resources including balance of payments.
3. Production of bank notes and coins of various denominations, postal stationery, postal stamps; and cadre management, career planning and training of the Indian Economic Service (IES).

B. Department of Expenditure: It is the nodal Department for overseeing the public financial management system in the Central Government and matters connected with State finances. The principal activities of the Department include the following:

1. Pre-sanction appraisal of major schemes/projects (both Plan and non-Plan expenditure).
2. Handling the bulk of the Central budgetary resources transferred to States.
3. Implementation of the recommendations of the Finance Commission and Central Pay Commission.
4. Overseeing the expenditure management in the Central Ministries/Departments through the interface with the financial advisors and the administration of the financial rules, regulations and orders through monitoring of audit comments and observations.
5. Preparation of Central Government Accounts.
6. Managing the financial aspects of personnel management in the Central Government.
7. Assisting Central Ministries/Departments in controlling the costs and prices of public services.
8. Assisting organizational re-engineering through review of staffing patterns and reviewing systems and procedures to optimize outputs and outcomes of public expenditure.

The Department also coordinates matters concerning the Ministry of Finance including Parliament-related work of the Ministry. The Department has under its administrative control the National Institute of Financial Management (NIFM), Faridabad.

C. Department of Revenue: It exercises control in respect of matters relating to all the Direct and Indirect Union Taxes through two statutory Boards namely, the Central Board of Direct Taxes (CBDT) and the Central Board of Excise and Customs (CBEC). Each Board is headed by a Chairman who is also ex-officio Special Secretary to the Government of India. Matters relating to the levy and collection of all Direct taxes are looked after by the CBDT whereas those relating to levy and collection of Customs and Central Excise duties and other Indirect taxes fall within the purview of the CBEC. The two Boards were constituted under the Central Board of Revenue Act, 1963.

D. Department of Financial Services: It looks after the following matters:

1. Citizen's Charter.
2. Banking.
3. Industrial finance and micro small and medium enterprise sector.
4. Insurance.
5. Pension reforms.

6. Work allocation.
7. Advertisements.

E. Department of Disinvestment: It promotes people's ownership of Central Public Sector Enterprises to share in their prosperity through disinvestment. The Mission of the Department is as follows:

1. List all profitable Central Public Sector Enterprises (CPSEs) on stock exchanges.
2. Listing to result in: (a) improvement in corporate governance, (b) higher disclosure levels due to listing to bring about greater transparency and accountability in the functioning of the CPSEs, and (c) adding market discipline to the functioning of CPSEs.
3. Disinvestment process to facilitate unlocking the true value of the CPSEs for all stakeholders—investors, employees, company and the Government.

3.4.2 Reserve Bank of India (RBI): There is only one central bank in a country whose main function is to control the operations of the rest of the banking system. Reserve Bank of India (RBI), the central bank of India, is the apex institution responsible for managing and supervising the monetary and financial system of the economy.

A. Changing Role of RBI in the Financial Sector: Since the setting up of the Reserve Bank of India in 1935, its role in the financial sector and financial market development has undergone significant changes. Emerging primarily as a bank-based financial system, the development of financial structure in India has been to finance the planned development efforts. To this end, institutional development received considerable attention of the RBI. The broad-based development of the banking sector to meet short-term financing needs was supplemented by the setting up of specialised development finance institutions by the RBI to cater to long-term financing needs. Since the early 1990s, the introduction of financial sector reforms has provided a strong impetus to the development of financial markets. The introduction of market-based monetary policy instruments, the liberalisation of capital controls and integration of the Indian economy with global markets have exposed the country to potentially volatile capital inflows, posing new challenges and dilemmas for the RBI in monetary and exchange rate management.

The RBI has been suitably reorienting the regulatory and supervisory framework so as to meet the challenges of a new environment. It has been the endeavour of the RBI to develop a competitive, strong and dynamic banking system so that it plays an effective role in supporting the growth process of the economy. The emphasis has been on safeguarding the financial stability of the overall system through increased emphasis on prudential guidelines and effective monitoring, improving institutional soundness, strengthening the regulatory and supervisory processes by aligning with international best practices and by developing the necessary technological and legal infrastructure. While the approach towards the reforms has essentially been gradual and relevant to the context, consultative processes and appropriate timing and sequencing of measures have succeeded in aiding growth, enhancing efficiency, avoiding crises and imparting resilience to the financial system.

B. Global Financial Crisis and the RBI: Though adversely affected by global meltdown, Indian economy has shown considerable absorption capacity and resilience. Soon after the start of the crisis, net portfolio flows to India turned negative as foreign institutional investors (FIIs) rushed to sell equity stakes in a bid to replenish overseas cash balances. This had a knock-on effect on the stock market which nosedived to record levels. Supply and demand imbalance in the foreign exchange market led to depreciation of rupee vis-à-vis other currencies. The current account was affected mainly after September 2008 through slowdown in exports. Despite setbacks, however, the balance of payments situation of the country has remained comfortable.

India has remained relatively immune from the fallout of the crisis due to several reasons including prudential, supervisory and regulatory framework of the Reserve Bank of India (RBI). Moral suasions on the part of Government of India, RBI and Securities and Exchange Board of India (SEBI) have also worked. More importantly, the Indian banking system has shown remarkable market discipline, docility, and sincerity of purpose as against the financial gimmicks and dubious practices of the financial institutions in the US. It is heartening to note that in India, complex structures like synthetic securitisations have not been permitted so far.

RBI has the necessary framework for provision of liquidity to the banking system, in terms of Sections 17 and 18 of the Reserve Bank of India Act, 1934. RBI can undertake purchase/sale of securities of the Central or State Governments and can purchase, sell and rediscount bills of exchange and promissory notes drawn on and payable in India and arising out of bonafide commercial or trade transactions for provision/absorption of liquidity for normal day-to-day liquidity management operations as also for provision of emergency liquidity assistance to the banks under the lender-of-last-resort function.

RBI is empowered under the existing legal framework to deal with the resolution of weak and failing banks. The Banking Regulation Act provides the legal framework for voluntary amalgamation and compulsory merger of banks under Sections 44 (A) and 45, respectively. The Deposit Insurance and Credit Guarantee Corporation (DICGC) offers deposit insurance cover in India. The mergers of many weak private sector banks with healthy banks have improved overall stability of the system. Not a single scheduled commercial bank in the country has capital adequacy ratio which is less than the minimum regulatory requirement of 9 percent.

RBI took a number of monetary easing and liquidity enhancing measures including reduction in cash reserve ratio (CRR), statutory liquidity ratio (SLR) and key policy rates. The objective has been to facilitate flow of funds from the financial system to meet the needs of productive sectors. RBI's monetary policy stance has consistently been to balance growth, inflation and financial stability concerns. It has taken a slew of measures aimed at infusing rupee as well as foreign exchange liquidity into the system and to maintain credit flow to productive sectors of the economy.

In tune with the national economic objectives, RBI has followed a monetary policy usually called the policy of *controlled expansion.* The money supply has expanded sufficiently to meet the growing needs of industry and trade. However, it has been ensured that the expansion is not reckless. Broadly speaking, the expansion of money supply has been somewhat more than the increase in output thereby allowing a reasonable increase in the price level.

3.4.3 Ministry of Corporate Affairs: The Ministry is primarily concerned with administration of the Companies Act, 2013 for regulating the functioning of the corporate sector in accordance with law. The Ministry is also responsible for administering the Competition Act, 2002. Besides, it exercises supervision over the three professional bodies—Institute of Chartered Accountants of India (ICAI), Institute of Company Secretaries of India (ICSI) and the Institute of Cost and Works Accountants of India (ICWAI)—which are constituted under three separate Acts of the Parliament for proper and orderly growth of the professions concerned. The Ministry also has the responsibility of carrying out the functions of the Central Government relating to administration of Partnership Act, 1932, the Companies (Donations to National Funds) Act, 1951 and Societies Registration Act, 1980.

A. Companies Act, 2013:

(a) Background: The Companies Act, 1956 Act was in need of a substantial revamp for quite some time, to make it more contemporary and relevant to corporates, regulators and other stakeholders in India. While several unsuccessful attempts were made in the past to revise the 1956 Act, the most recent attempt was the Companies Bill, 2009 which was introduced in the Lok Sabha on August 3, 2009. This Companies Bill, 2009 was referred to the Parliamentary Standing Committee on Finance, which submitted its report on August 31, 2010 and was withdrawn after the introduction of the Companies Bill, 2011. The Companies Bill, 2011 was also considered by the Parliamentary Standing Committee on

Finance which submitted its report on June 26, 2012. Subsequently, the Bill was considered and approved by the Lok Sabha on December 18, 2012 as the Companies Bill, 2012. The Bill was then considered and approved by the Rajya Sabha too on August 8, 2013. After having obtained the assent of the President of India on August 29, 2013, it came into effect.

(b) Significance: The 2013 Act introduces significant changes in the provisions related to governance, e-management, compliance and enforcement, disclosure norms, auditors and mergers and acquisitions. Also, new concepts such as one-person company, small companies, dormant company, class action suits, registered valuers and corporate social responsibility have been included.

An attempt has been made to reduce the content of the substantive portion of the related law in the Companies Act, 2013 as compared to the Companies Act, 1956. In the process, much of the aforesaid content has been left, *to be prescribed*, in the Rules which are yet to be finalised and notified.

The changes in the 2013 Act have far-reaching implications that are set to significantly change the manner in which corporates operate in India. The 2013 Act has introduced several new concepts and has also tried to streamline many of the requirements by introducing new definitions.

(c) Main Provisions:

(i) Types of Companies:

1. **One-person Company:** The 2013 Act introduces a new type of entity to the existing list i.e. apart from forming a public or private limited company, the 2013 Act enables the formation of a new entity a 'one-person company' (OPC). An OPC means a company with only one person as its member [Section 3(1) of 2013 Act].
2. **Private Company:** The 2013 Act introduces a change in the definition for a private company, *inter alia*, the new requirement increases the limit of the number of members from 50 to 200 [Section 2 (68) of 2013 Act].
3. **Small Company:** A small company has been defined as a company, other than a public company.

- Paid-up share capital of which does not exceed ₹ 50 lakh or such higher amount as may be prescribed which shall not be more than ₹ 5 crore.
- Turnover of which as per its last profit-and-loss account does not exceed ₹ 2 crore or such higher amount as may be prescribed which shall not be more than ₹ 20 crore:

  As set out in the 2013 Act, this section will not be applicable to the following: (a) a holding company or a subsidiary company, (b) a company registered under Section 8, and (c) a company or body corporate governed by any special Act [Section 2(85) of 2013 Act].

4. **Dormant Company:** The 2013 Act states that a company can be classified as dormant when it is formed and registered under this 2013 Act for a future project or to hold an asset or intellectual property and has no significant accounting transaction. Such a company or an inactive one may apply to the ROC in such manner as may be prescribed for obtaining the status of a dormant company [Section 455 of 2013 Act].

(ii) Mergers and Acquisitions: The 2013 Act features some new provisions in the area of mergers and acquisitions, apart from making certain changes from the existing provisions. While the changes are aimed at simplifying and rationalising the procedures involved, the new provisions are also aimed at ensuring higher accountability for the company and majority shareholders and increasing flexibility for corporates. The 2013 Act has streamlined as well as introduced concepts such as reverse mergers (merger of foreign companies with Indian companies) and squeeze-out provisions, which are significant. The 2013 Act has also introduced the requirement for valuations in several cases, including mergers and acquisitions, by registered valuers.

(iii) Prohibition of Association or Partnership of Persons Exceeding Certain Number: The 2013 Act puts a restriction on the number of partners that can be admitted to a partnership at 100. To be specific, the 2013 Act states that no association or partnership consisting of more than the given number of persons as may be prescribed shall be formed for the purpose of carrying on any business that has for its object the acquisition of gain by the association or partnership or by the individual members thereof, unless it is registered as a company under this 1956 Act or is formed under any other law for the time being in force.

As an exception, the aforesaid restriction would not apply to the following: (a) A Hindu undivided family carrying on any business, and (b) an association or partnership, if it is formed by professionals who are governed by special acts like the Chartered Accountants Act etc. [Section 464 of 2013 Act].

(iv) Insider Trading and Prohibition on Forward Dealings: The 2013 Act for the first time defines insider trading and price-sensitive information and prohibits any person including the director or key managerial person from entering into insider trading [Section 195 of 2013 Act]. Further, the Act also prohibits directors and key managerial personnel from forward dealings in the company or its holding, subsidiary or associate company [Section 194 of 2013 Act].

(v) Corporate Governance: The 2013 Act intends to improve corporate governance by requiring disclosure of nature of concern or interest of every director, manager, any other key managerial personnel and relatives of such a director, manager or any other key managerial personnel and reduction in threshold of disclosure from 20 percent to 2 percent. The term 'key managerial personnel' has now been defined in the 2013 Act and means the chief executive officer, managing director, manager, company secretary, whole-time director, chief financial officer and any such other officer as may be prescribed.

(vi) Accounts and Audit: The 2013 Act has introduced certain significant amendments in this chapter. It has also introduced several additional requirements such as preparation of consolidated financial statements, additional reporting requirements for the directors in their report such as the development and implementation of the risk management policy, disclosures in respect of voting rights not exercised directly by the employees in respect of shares to which the scheme relates, etc., in comparison with the requirements of the 1956 Act.

The 2013 Act features extensive changes within the area of audit and auditors with a view to enhance audit effectiveness and accountability of the auditors. These changes undoubtedly, have a considerable impact on the audit profession. However, it needs to be noted that these changes will also have a considerable impact on the company in terms of time, efforts and expectations involved. Apart from introducing new concepts such as rotation of audit firms and class action suits, the 2013 Act also increases the auditor's liability substantially in comparison with the 1956 Act.

Unlike the appointment process at each annual general meeting under the 1956 Act, the auditor will now be appointed for a period of 5 years, with a requirement to ratify such an appointment at each annual general meeting [Section 139(1) of 2013 Act].

(vii) Dividend: The 2013 Act proposes to introduce significant changes to the existing provisions of the 1956 Act in respect of declaration of dividend. The changes are likely to affect the existing practices followed by companies with regard to the declaration of dividend.

The existing provisions of the 1956 Act in relation to the transfer of a specified percentage of profit to reserve is no longer applicable and thus, companies will be free to transfer any or no amount to its reserves.

(viii) Revival and Rehabilitation of Sick Companies: Chapter XIX of the 2013 Act lays down the provisions for the revival and rehabilitation of sick companies. The chapter describes the circumstances which determine the declaration of a company as a sick company, and also includes the rehabilitation process of the same. Although it aims to provide comprehensive provisions for the revival and rehabilitation of sick companies, the fact that several provisions such as particulars, documents as well as content of the draft scheme in respect of application for revival and rehabilitation, etc. have been left to substantive enactment, leaves scope for interpretation.

The coverage of this chapter is no longer restricted to industrial companies, and the determination of the net worth would not be relevant for assessing whether a company is a sick company.

(ix) Corporate Social Responsibility: The 2013 Act makes an effort to introduce the culture of corporate social responsibility (CSR) in Indian corporates by requiring companies to formulate a corporate social responsibility policy and at least incur a given minimum expenditure on social activities.

3.4.4 Securities and Exchange Board of India (SEBI): SEBI is an autonomous and independent statutory body. Its legally mandated objectives are the following: (a) protection of the interests of investors in securities, (b) development of the securities market, (c) regulation of the securities market, and (d) matters connected therewith and incidental thereto.

3.4.5 Pension Fund Regulatory and Development Authority (PFRDA): PFRDA was established by Government of India on August 23, 2003. The Government has, through an executive order dated October 10, 2003, mandated PFRDA to act as a regulator for the pension sector. The mandate of PFRDA is development and regulation of pension sector in India.

3.4.6 Insurance Regulatory and Development Authority (IRDA): Regulatory and supervisory control of insurance companies in India is exercised by IRDA and its powers flow from Insurance Act, 1938 as well as from IRDA Act, 1999. IRDA Act, 1999 states: "Subject to the provisions of this Act and any other law for the time being in force, the Authority shall have the duty to regulate, promote and ensure orderly growth of insurance business and reinsurance business".

3.4.7 Monitoring Framework for Financial Conglomerates (FCs): The quickening pace of technological innovations coupled with blurring of sectoral distinctions has enabled financial intermediaries to effectively compete in sectors beyond their domain by deconstructing and recombining risks. Financial liberalisation has led to the emergence of financial conglomerates, cutting across not only various financial sectors such as banking, insurance and securities but across geographical boundaries as well.

These developments have also ushered in the attendant risks like that of contagion whereby the problems of different sectors and different geographies could have an adverse impact upon the balance sheets of parent regulated entity viz. the bank, insurance company or the securities company. Supervisors have realised the inadequacy of the sectoral regulations to deal with the complexities interwoven into operations of financial conglomerates.

In order to address the limitations of the segmental approach to supervision, the Reserve Bank, in consultation with SEBI and IRDA, decided upon putting in place a special monitoring system for systemically important financial intermediaries (SIFIs) or financial conglomerates. Accordingly, a financial conglomerates (FCs) monitoring mechanism was put in place in June 2004.

For the purpose of monitoring of FCs, the above three regulators are designated as the principal regulators to whom the identified FCs submit the FC Returns through their designated entities. The mechanism involves a quarterly reporting of relevant data by the identified FCs to their respective principal regulators with a focus on the extent of intra-group transactions and exposures of the identified groups. Primarily, the review of the intra-group transactions is conducted with a view to track build-up of large exposures to entities within the Group, to outside counterparties and to various financial market segments (equity, debt, money market, and derivatives markets), identify cases of migration/transfer of 'losses' and detecting situations of regulatory/supervisory arbitrage. The monitoring mechanism, thus, seeks to capture the 'contagion risk' within the group as also its cumulative exposure to specific outside entities, sectors and market segments.

The identification of financial groups for specialized monitoring under the FC framework is incumbent upon the scale of their operations in respective financial market segments (banking, insurance, securities, and non-banking finance). The size of the off-balance sheet position of the entities is also being additionally included as a parameter for determining the size of operations of the entities in respective market segments. While a group having a significant presence in two or more of these financial market segments qualifies to be an *identified FC*, few other financial groups which are otherwise important from a *systemic* standpoint (mainly on account of their size, involvement in specialised transactions like derivatives and securitisation and on account of market feedback), also get identified as FCs and are subjected to focused monitoring.

Since the monitoring framework also covers the housing finance segment which falls under the jurisdiction of the National Housing Bank (NHB), it has been named as a specified regulator.

The High Level Co-ordination Committee on Financial Markets (HLCCFM) Technical Committee on RBI Regulated Entities has been designated as the inter-regulatory forum for having an overarching view of the FC monitoring mechanism and for providing guidance/directions on concerns arising out of analysis of FC data and for sharing of other significant information in the possession of the Principal Regulators, which might have a bearing on the Group as a whole.

Thus, the FC monitoring framework endeavours to identify contagion like situations at the incipient stage, which could snowball into a systemic concern unless addressed promptly. The framework also aims at addressing market disruptions issues by undertaking assessments of sources of liquidity for the group which is quite critical from a financial stability angle.

Endnotes

1. Financial repression includes: (a) high required reserve ratios, (b) subsidised or directed credit programmes, (c) credit rationing, (d) ceilings on deposit, and (e) fixing maximum interest rates on loans.
2. As a matter of fact, the reform process started from the mid-1980s with initiation of several measures following the recommendations of the Committee to Review the Working of the Monetary System in India, 1985 (Chairman: Sukhamoy Chakravarty) and the Working Group on the Money Market, 1987 (Chairman: N. Vaghul). The process, however, gathered momentum in the early 1990s with wide ranging reforms in all segments (money, forex and Government securities) of the financial market. A gradual approach to market reform has been followed in India so as to avoid destabilising effects.
3. BS7799 is comprehensive in its coverage of security issues, containing a significant number of control requirements. Hence, compliance with it is a major task for most organisations. By following this standard, financial institutions including banks can ensure compliance to most of the information security requirements.
4. The supervisory control of insurance companies is exercised by Insurance Regulatory and Development Authority (IRDA) and these powers flow from Insurance Act, 1938 as well as from IRDA Act, 1999. IRDA Act 1999 states: "Subject to the provisions of this Act and any other law for the time being in force, the Authority shall have the duty to regulate, promote and ensure orderly growth of insurance business and reinsurance business". Regulatory and supervisory powers of the IRDA are wide and pervasive.
5. Government of India, Ministry of Finance, *Report of the Financial Sector Legislative Reforms Commission* (Chairman: B.N. Srikrishna), March 2013.
6. Government of India, Ministry of Finance, *Report of the Financial Sector Legislative Reforms Commission* (Chairman: B.N. Srikrishna), Volume I, March 2013, p. xiii.
7. Ibid., p. 9.

Part II:
Financial Inclusion Institutions in India

4

Financial Inclusion: Conceptual Framework

4.1 Origins of the Current Approach to Financial Inclusion

The present concern for financial inclusion can be traced to the United Nations Capital Development Fund (UNCDF) initiatives [1], which broadly underlined the main goals as also the broad frameworks and parameters of inclusive finance, as access to a range of financial services, including savings, credit, insurance, remittance and other banking/payment services to all 'bankable' households and enterprises at a reasonable cost.

According to UNCDF the main goals of inclusive finance are as under:

1. Access at a reasonable cost of all households and enterprises to the range of financial services for which they are 'bankable', including savings, short and long-term credit, leasing and factoring, mortgages, insurance, pensions, payments, local money transfers and international remittances.
2. Sound institutions, guided by appropriate internal management systems, industry performance standards, and performance monitoring by the market, as well as by sound prudential regulation where required.
3. Financial and institutional sustainability as a means of providing access to financial services over time.
4. Multiple providers of financial services, wherever feasible, so as to bring cost-effective and a wide variety of alternatives to customers (which could include any number of combinations of sound private, non-profit and public providers).

The Report of the Centre for Global Development (CGD) Task-Force on Access to Financial Services further laid down the broad policy principles for expanding financial access, including the implicit institutional mechanisms, with particular emphasis on the need for ensuring data collection, monitoring and evaluation. [2]

G-20 Toronto Summit [3] had also outlined the "Principles for Innovative Financial Inclusion", which serves as a guide for policy and regulatory approaches aimed at fostering safe and sound adoption of innovative, adequate, low-cost financial delivery models, helping provide conditions for fair competition and a framework of incentives for the various bank, insurance, and non-bank actors involved in the delivery of a full-range of affordable and quality financial services. The G-20's highest priority, as declaration goes, is to safeguard and strengthen the recovery and lay the foundation for strong, sustainable and balanced growth, and strengthen our financial systems against risks.

The problem of financial exclusion is not exclusive to the developing world. The developed countries too have been affected by it and many poor and disadvantaged people in the world still lack access to financial services. However, the type, degree and magnitude differ between the two worlds. Therefore, emphasis has been on empowerment of the disadvantaged groups for access to public goods and services including banking services in the developed countries. The UN General Assembly had designated the year 2005 as the International Year of Micro Credit stating that the year will be an important opportunity to give impetus to micro finance programmes throughout the world. Thus, the International Year of Micro Credit 2005 aimed at “Building Inclusive Financial Sectors to Achieve the Millennium Development Goals”.

The nexus between economic growth, financial deepening and financial inclusion has been well-recognized in India’s development strategy, particularly when the financial and economic reforms process was initiated in early 1990s. A more focused and structured approach towards financial inclusion has been, in effect, followed since the year 2005, when the Reserve Bank of India decided to implement policies to promote financial inclusion and urged the banking system to focus on this goal. Recent policy initiatives to drive financial inclusion, including formulation of a board approved financial inclusion policy (FIP) by the banks, also attempt to strike a balance between the requirements of financial inclusion and that of soundness of financial institutions and stability of the financial system.

The concept of financial inclusion has a special significance for a fast-emerging economy such as India, as it encompasses a large segment of the productive sectors of the economy under formal financial network to unleash their creative capacities. Over a period of time, several financial and economic policy measures are being taken by the banks in India to improve access to affordable financial services through financial education, awareness generation, business communication networking and leveraging technology.

4.2 Financial Exclusion and Financial Inclusion Defined

In most developing countries, a large segment of society, particularly low-income people, has very little access to financial services, both formal and semi-formal. As a consequence, many of them have to necessarily depend either on their own or high cost informal sources of finance such as moneylenders. This is particularly true for the sporadic financing requirements of low income households for non-productive consumption purposes and other emergency requirements such as medical expenditure. Benefits of growth, therefore, tend to concentrate in the hands of those already served by the formal financial system.

Despite the rapid spread of banking over the years, a significant segment of the population, predominantly in the rural areas, is excluded from the formal financial system. It is well-known that poor people, potential entrepreneurs, small enterprises and others are excluded from the financial sector, which leads to their marginalisation and denial of opportunity for them to grow and prosper. Therefore, access to a greater proportion of the population to the organised financial system should be high on the agenda of the Government of India. The key issue, however, is how to mainstream the institutional sources so as to achieve wider coverage in terms of extending credit. There are also a large number of households with low income and small savings, which need to be mobilised.

Apart from the rural areas, there is significant degree of financial exclusion in urban areas as well. The cost of financial exclusion is recognised to be enormous for the society as well as for individuals, particularly in terms of inability to realise full potential due to financial constraints.

The recent developments in banking technology have transformed banking from the traditional brick-and-mortar infrastructure like staffed branches to a system supplemented by other channels like automated teller machines (ATMs), credit/debit cards, internet banking, online money transfers etc. However, the access to such technology is restricted only to certain segments of the society. Indeed, some trends, such as increasingly sophisticated customer segmentation technology—allowing, for example, more accurate targeting of sections of the market—have led to restricted access to financial services for some groups. There is a growing divide, with an increased range of personal finance options for a segment of high and upper middle income population and a significantly large section of the population who lack access to even the most basic banking services. This is termed *financial exclusion*. These people, particularly, those living on low incomes, cannot access mainstream financial products such as bank accounts, credit, remittances and payment services, financial advisory services, insurance facilities etc.

Merely having a bank account may not be a good indicator of financial inclusion. The ideal definition should look at people who want to access financial services but are denied the same. If genuine claimants for credit and financial services are denied the same, then that is a case of exclusion. As this aspect would raise the issue of credit worthiness or bankability, it is also necessary to dwell upon what could be done to make the claimants of institutional credit bankable or creditworthy. This would require re-engineering of existing financial products or delivery systems and making them more in tune with the expectations and absorptive capacity of the intended clientele.

According to the Committee on Financial Inclusion (Chairman: C. Rangarajan),

2008, "Financial inclusion may be defined as the process of ensuring access to financial services and timely and adequate credit where needed by vulnerable groups such as weaker sections and low income groups at an affordable cost".

The essence of financial inclusion is in trying to ensure that a range of appropriate financial services is available to every individual and enabling them to understand and access those services. Apart from the regular form of financial intermediation, it may include a basic no-frills banking account for making and receiving payments, a savings product suited to the pattern of cash flows of a poor household, money transfer facilities, small loans and overdrafts for productive, personal and other purposes, insurance (life and non-life) etc. While financial inclusion, in the narrow sense, may be achieved to some extent by offering any one of these services, the objective of *comprehensive financial inclusion* would be to provide a holistic set of services encompassing all of the above.

4.3 Advantages of Financial Inclusion

The objective of financial inclusion is to extend financial services to the large hitherto unserved population of the country to unlock its growth potential. In addition, it strives towards a more inclusive growth by making financing available to the poor in particular. Government of India has been actively pursuing the agenda of financial inclusion, with key interventions in four groups, viz. expanding banking infrastructure, offering appropriate financial products, making extensive and intensive use of technology and through advocacy and stakeholder participation.

Access to safe, easy and affordable credit and other financial services by the poor and vulnerable groups, disadvantaged areas and lagging sectors is recognised as a pre-condition for accelerating growth and reducing income disparities and poverty. A developing country can benefit from financial inclusion in the following ways:

1. Access to a well-functioning financial system—by creating equal opportunities—enables economically and socially excluded people to integrate effectively into the economy and contribute to development and protect themselves against economic shocks.
2. Availability of external finance to potential entrepreneurs and small firms enables new entrants, leading to increased competition to incumbents. This, in turn, encourages entrepreneurship and productivity.
3. Inclusive finance—including safe savings, appropriately designed loans for poor and low-income households and for micro, small and medium-sized enterprises, and appropriate insurance and payments services—can help people to enhance incomes, acquire capital, manage risk, and come out of poverty.
4. Access to financial services contributes to higher production and social protection, as the financial sector—through stored savings, credit and

insurance—serves as a measure of crisis mitigation.

5. Financial inclusion can improve the efficiency of the process of intermediation between savings and investments while facilitating change in the composition of the financial system with regard to the transactions that take place, the clients that use the various services, the new risks created, and possibly the institutions that operate in newly created or expanded markets. As the balance sheet of the financial sector grows more diversified and encompasses a broader spectrum of economic agents, its contribution to a more resilient economy is commensurately higher.
6. For financial institutions, especially banks, financial inclusion helps provide a more stable retail base of deposits. As the recent global crisis also demonstrated, stable retail sources of funding, as against reliance on borrowed funds, can greatly enhance the soundness and resilience of financial institutions and can reduce volatility in earnings. It has been well-recognised that access to financial services facilitates making and receiving financial payments and reduces transaction costs. Financial inclusion enables to finance activities or firms or individuals that are at the margin, thereby promoting their growth-inducing productive activities.
7. Financial inclusion facilitates greater participation by different segments of the economy in the formal financial system. The presence of a large informal sector can impair the transmission of monetary policy as a significant segment of financially excluded households and small businesses make financial decisions independent of and un-influenced by, the monetary policy actions of the central bank. As the share of the formal financial sector increases through greater financial inclusion, it yields an important positive externality by making monetary policy transmission more effective.
8. To the extent that financial inclusion helps people move from the cash economy to bank accounts which can be monitored, it helps facilitate implementation of anti-money laundering and combating the financing of terrorism.
9. Financial inclusion can contribute to enhanced financial stability through contributing to the improved health of the household sector, of small businesses and, to some extent, that of the corporate sector. The health of the household sector is improved through improved economic linkages, reducing reliance on the costly informal sector and through improved ability to make and receive payments.
10. Financial inclusion can improve the access to finance and the social quality (including gender equality) and cost of the service that small businesses receive from banks. These factors are a key to the profitability and prosperity of these businesses and that are the backbones of the growing economy. Therefore,

achieving greater financial inclusion and maintaining financial stability are now complementary policy compulsions in so far as India is concerned.

The global financial crisis has brought the need for financial inclusion into greater focus worldwide as it is believed that widespread incidence of financial exclusion was one of the factors that precipitated the financial crisis. Several countries across the globe now look at financial inclusion as the means for a more comprehensive growth, wherein, each citizen of the country is able to use his/her earnings as a financial resource that they can put to work to improve their future financial status and simultaneously contribute to the nation's progress.

Access to affordable financial services would lead to increasing economic activities and employment opportunities for rural households with a possible multiplier effect on the economy. It could enable a higher disposable income in the hands of rural households, leading to greater savings and a wider deposit base for banks and other financial institutions.

In majority of the developing countries, access to finance is now being perceived as a public good, such as access to safe drinking water, primary healthcare, or primary education. One of the important effects of financial inclusion is that the entire national financial system benefits by greater inclusion (and lesser exclusion), especially when promoted in the wider context of economic inclusion. Financial inclusion efforts do have multiplier effect on the economy as a whole through higher savings pooled from the vast segment of the *bottom of the pyramid population* by providing access to formal savings arrangement resulting in expansion in credit-base and investment by banks. Deeper engagements of the under-banked population in the economy through the formal financial system could lead to improvement of their financial conditions and living standards, particularly the poorer segments of the society, enabling them to create financial assets, generate income and build resilience to meet macro-economic and viable income-generating livelihood support systems. In this endeavour, the Government also immensely benefits from financial inclusion drives by way of efficient and leakage-proof transfer of vast amounts of social welfare benefits to the targeted and largely disadvantaged groups of population.

4.4 Strategies for Financial Inclusion

Financial inclusion strategies can be defined as road maps of actions, agreed and defined at the national or sub-national level that stakeholders follow to achieve financial inclusion objectives. Successful strategies coordinate efforts with the main stakeholders, define responsibilities among them, and state a clear planning of resources by, for example, prioritizing targets. A strategy can promote a more effective and efficient process to achieve significant improvements in financial inclusion, and is ideally prepared with the private sector in order to establish and achieve shared, achievable goals for financial inclusion. Strategies can integrate public and private sector actions to address different barriers to financial inclusion, and can also focus on high-impact, high-priority areas, such as SME finance or financial education action plans. Financial inclusion is interlinked with financial stability, financial integrity, market conduct, and the financial capability of consumers, and should be prepared with reference to analysis and objectives for those areas, irrespective of whether the financial inclusion strategy is a standalone document or a component of a broader financial sector development strategy for India.

Bringing the larger population within the structured and organised financial system has to be an important item on the development agenda of a government. While several central banks focus solely on inflation, many in developed and emerging economies alike, including India, also focus on growth. The RBI has, therefore, introduced various new measures to encourage the expansion of financial coverage in the country. Financial inclusion is considered essential for fostering economic growth in a more inclusive fashion.

In a fast growing economy, an important issue is how to sustain and diversify growth so that the risk to growth process is diversified across sectors. It is in this context that the search for potential sources of incremental growth, i.e. sectors that have difficulty in accessing financial services, assumes importance. Therefore, including such segments or sectors would, on the one hand, unleash their productive capacities, and on the other, would augment domestic demand on a sustainable basis driven by income and consumption growth from such sectors. This would also have strong inter-sectoral linkages.

The Reserve Bank of India (RBI) has, therefore, formulated the policy of financial inclusion with a view to provide banking services at an affordable cost to the disadvantaged and low-income groups. In view of the poor level of financial inclusion in India, RBI has accorded top-most policy priority to financial inclusion, by advising commercial banks, to formulate specific Board approved Financial Inclusion Plans (FIP) and to act on them on a mission mode. Banks were also advised by RBI to provide banking services in every village having a population of over 2000 by March 31, 2012, through bank branches as well as through various ICT-based models, including through business correspondents (BCs).

The broad strategy for financial inclusion in India in recent years comprises the following elements:

1. Encouraging penetration into unbanked and backward areas and encouraging agents and intermediaries such as non-governmental organizations (NGOs), micro finance institutions (MFIs), and business correspondents (BCs).
2. Focusing on a decentralized strategy by using existing arrangements such as state

level bankers' committee (SLBC) and district consultative committee (DCC) and strengthening local institutions such as co-operatives and regional rural banks (RRBs).
3. Using technology for furthering financial inclusion.
4. Advising banks to open a basic banking *no frills* account.
5. Emphasis on financial literacy and credit counselling.
6. Creating synergies between the formal and informal segments.

The overriding and most transformative driver would be the policy imperative to extend the reach of banking services and to provide fair, transparent and affordable products and services. Apart from the potential to expand banks' business manifold besides acquiring new customers for other value added services, they would have the satisfaction of contributing immensely to higher inclusive growth. This is an opportunity which will not present itself again. With the Government of India and the Reserve Bank prioritizing financial inclusion, banks have been encouraged to expand the network through setting up of new branches and also through the business correspondent model.

Improving the quality of life of the people of India by enabling them to have access to banking services could be the next big game changer as it could unlock the vast potential of rural India.

4.5 Barriers to Financial Inclusion

Access to financial products is constrained by several factors which include lack of awareness about the financial products, high transaction costs and products which are inconvenient, inflexible, not customized and of low quality. However, we need to understand here that apart from the supply side factors, demand side factors such as lower income and/or asset holdings, financial literacy/awareness issues, etc. also have a significant bearing on inclusive growth. Owing to difficulties in accessing formal sources of credit, poor individuals and small and micro enterprises usually rely on their personal savings and internal sources or take recourse to informal sources of finance to invest in health, education, housing and entrepreneurial activities. The mainstream financial institutions like banks have an important role to play in helping overcome this constraint, not as a social obligation, but as a business proposition.

A comprehensive strategy promotes not only the adoption of financial products and services, but also the ability of customers to take full advantage of them. Financial inclusion strategies can be broad in scope, covering public and private sector actions. They can stand alone, or can be a component of broader financial sector development strategies. Strategies can also focus on certain areas where the need for actions has been highlighted, such as SME finance (through a "compact," for example) or financial education action plans, or they can cover a broader set of actions to address different barriers to financial inclusion. Financial inclusion is interlinked with financial stability, financial integrity, market conduct, and the financial capability of consumers, and should be prepared with reference to analysis and objectives for those areas, even if the financial inclusion actions are not part of a broader financial sector strategy.

The major barriers that are to be seen to be potential constraints in extension of appropriate services to poor by financial service providers are the lack of reach, higher cost of transactions and time taken in providing those services, apart from attitudinal issues. In this regard, major barriers to financial inclusion require to be identified are as under:

4.5.1 Demand Side Barriers: These are as under:

1. Low literacy levels.
2. Lack of awareness and/or knowledge/understanding of financial products.
3. Irregular income.
4. Frequent micro transactions.
5. Lack of trust in formal banking institutions.
6. Cultural obstacles (e.g., gender and cultural values).

4.5.2 Supply Side Barriers: These are as follows:

1. Outreach (low density areas and low income populations are not attractive for the provision of financial services and are not financially sustainable under traditional banking business models).
2. Regulation (frameworks are not always adapted to local contexts).
3. Business models (mostly with high fixed costs); service providers (limited number and types of financial service providers).
4. Services (non-adapted products and services for low income populations and the informal economy).
5. Age factor (financial service providers usually target the middle of the economically active population, often overlooking the design of appropriate products for older or younger potential customers. There are hardly any policies or schemes for the younger lot or the old people who have retired, as the banks do not see any business from them).
6. Bank charges (in most of the countries, transaction is free as long as the account has sufficient funds to cover the cost of transactions made. However, there is a range of other charges that have a disproportionate effect on people with low income).

4.6 Measuring and Monitoring of Financial Inclusion Impact

The fact that financial inclusion concepts have different meanings in different parlance has often led to difficulty in using a standard yardstick for benchmarking its policy parameters. The associated difficulties are that the targeted variables used for financial inclusion may differ from one country or organization to another because of different institutional set-up as well as domestic rules and regulations implicit in the countries unique economic policy. Inherent weaknesses in the linkages between the financial inclusion database and welfare parameters of the society add to the complexity associated with precise measurement tools to be used for the purpose.

Moreover, there are no agreed composite measures of financial inclusion which could facilitate comparisons across time and geography; but then they also suffer from inherent operational and execution constraints to ensure proper governance at all levels. Therefore, to ensure consistency and accuracy in measurement of financial inclusion parameters, it is essential that the parameters concerned are objectively defined in the first stage of the measurement process. As a way forward, we need to assess financial behaviour and understand where the challenges and opportunities lie for the future in measuring and effectively monitoring the gains from various financial inclusion measures. To do that, we need high-quality, multi-dimensional, comparable financial inclusion data based on internationally standardized terms and concepts. As such, the measurement needs also include analytics for correct interpretation of data and establishment of international benchmarks; that can widely vary from country to country and certainly across regions.

One of the measures of the level of financial inclusion is the financial inclusion index. This index is based on three basic dimensions of an inclusive financial system—banking penetration, availability of the banking services and usage of the banking system. Banking penetration is definitely the most critical parameter for measuring the depth financial inclusion and is measured as a ratio of bank accounts to the total population. The second parameter, availability of banking services provides an indication to the number of bank outlets available per 1,000 people to deliver financial services. The bank outlets may include the brick and mortar branches, ATMs, business correspondents etc. The third parameter seeks to determine the usage of banking services going beyond mere opening of accounts. Therefore, this is evaluated on the basis of outstanding deposits and credits. Accordingly, the volume of outstanding deposit and credit as proportion on the net district domestic product is used for measuring this dimension.

In the Indian context, financial inclusion has also been a major policy objective since long though the term financial inclusion has come to the forefront only of late. In fact, the Reserve Bank of India (RBI) is perhaps the only central bank in the world which attempts to reach the remotest locations of the country in a bid to create awareness and promote inclusion. The objective of achieving greater financial inclusion in India has been pursued in a regulated space. The framework for financial inclusion has been bank-led to a large extent and banks are closely regulated and supervised entities in the Indian context. However, these initiatives for strengthening financial inclusion are yet to have a substantial impact on the lives of the excluded population, especially the economically vulnerable or disadvantaged lot.

There are several challenges that require concerted efforts from banks, the RBI and the Government to ensure convenient and cost-effective delivery of financial services to the public at large. In particular, the challenge is to introduce innovations in risk assessment, reduce transaction costs, devise new credit delivery channels, and use information technology to make financial inclusion a viable model.

Endnotes

1. United Nations Capital Development Fund (UNCDF), *Building Inclusive Financial Sectors for Development*, UNCDF, May 2006. UNCDF is the UN's capital investment agency for the world's 48 least developed countries. It creates new opportunities for poor people and their communities by increasing access to micro finance and investment capital.
   UNCDF focuses on Africa and the poorest countries of Asia, with a special commitment to countries emerging from conflict or crisis. It provides seed capital—grants and loans—and technical support to help micro finance institutions reach more poor households and small businesses, and local governments finance the capital investments—water systems, feeder roads, schools, irrigation schemes—that will improve poor peoples' lives.
   UNCDF works to enlarge peoples' choices. It believes that poor people and communities should take decisions about their own development. Its programmes help to empower women—over 50 percent of the clients of UNCDF-supported micro finance institutions are women—and its expertise in micro finance and local development is shaping new responses to food insecurity, climate change and other challenges. All UNCDF support is provided via national systems, in accordance with the Paris Principles. UNCDF works in challenging environments—remote rural areas, countries emerging from conflict—and paves the way for others to follow. Established by the General Assembly in 1966 and with headquarters in New York, UNCDF is an autonomous UN organization affiliated with UNDP.
2. Report of the Taskforce set up by the Centre for Global Development, October 2009.
3. G-20 Toronto Summit Declaration, June 26-27, 2010.

5

Recent Financial Inclusion Measures in India

5.1 Why Financial Inclusion?

It is a known fact that in India, while one segment of the population has access to assortment of banking services encompassing regular banking facilities and portfolio counselling, the other segment of underprivileged and lower income group is totally deprived of even basic financial services. Exclusion of large segments of the society from financial services affects the overall economic growth of a country. It is for this reason that financial inclusion is a global concern.

In Sweden and France, banks are legally bound to open an account for anybody who approaches them. In Canada, law requires banks to provide accounts without minimum balance to all Canadians regardless of employment or credit history. In the United States, the Community Reinvestment Act (1977) is intended to encourage depository institutions to help meet the credit needs of the communities in which they operate, including low and moderate income neighbourhoods, consistent with safe and sound operations.

Census 2011 estimated that out of 24.67 crore households in the country, 4.48 crore (58.7 percent) households had access to banking services. Of the 16.78 crore rural households, 9.14 crore (54.46 percent) were availing banking services. Of the 7.89 crore urban households, 5.34 crore (67.68 percent) households were availing banking services.

Despite various measures for financial inclusion, poverty and exclusion continue to dominate socio-economic and political discourse in India even after 67 years of Independence. Though economy has shown impressive growth during post-liberalization era (1991 onwards), impact is yet to percolate to all sections of the society and therefore, India is still home to 1/3rd of world's poor.

As on March 31, 2014, the banking network of the country comprised of a bank branch network of 1,15,082 and an ATM network of 1,60,055. Of these, 43,962 branches (38.2 percent) and 23,334 ATMs (14.58 percent) were in rural areas.

Indian economy in general and banking services in particular have made rapid strides in the recent past. However, a sizeable section of the population, particularly the vulnerable groups, such as weaker sections and low income groups, continue to remain excluded from even the most basic opportunities and services provided by the financial sector. Access to a well-functioning financial system, by creating equal opportunities, enables economically and socially excluded people to integrate better into the economy, so as to actively contribute to development and protect themselves against economic shocks.

Financial inclusion is new paradigm of economic growth which plays a major role in driving away the poverty. Lack of access to financial services in most of rural areas due to high informative barriers and low awareness, creates the need and scope of financial inclusion. Fruits of development have hardly reached to nearly half of Indian population because of lack of access to loans and insurance services. Financial inclusion is integral to the inclusive growth process and sustainable development of the country. It should, therefore, ideally be a policy of involving a much wider section of population deposit mobilization and credit intermediation.

Financial inclusion is the key to inclusive growth with its motto of empowerment of poor, underprivileged and low income/skilled rural/urban households. Financial inclusion is designed to bring about the capability to participate and contribute among the economically and socially excluded people by creating equal opportunities. Achieving sustainable financial inclusion will require a systemic effort which leverages technology, viable business models and appropriate regulatory framework cohesively.

India has several strategic assets providing favourable initial conditions for transformational change towards digital financial inclusion:

1. A strong banking network (1,15,000 branches) linked to eKuber (RBI's Core Banking Solution), now spreading into unbanked rural areas.
2. A significant outreach of India Post (1,55,000 outlets), PoS and ATM terminals which can facilitate a vibrant cash-in/cash-out network across the country.
3. A nationwide telecom network with 1048 million mobile connections and 81 percent mobile penetration.
4. A strong network of computer-based service providers in the form of Common Service Centres (CSC) promoted by the Department of IT.
5. A strong national payments infrastructure that includes an Inter-Mobile Payments Service/Immediate Payment System (IMPS) to transfer funds over mobile phones.
6. A world class national ID system covering the largest (650M) headcount and expanding by 30M citizens per month.

The banking sector—particularly the Reserve Bank of India (RBI) and National Bank for Agriculture and Rural Development (NABARD)—have taken a lead and proactive role in promoting financial inclusion through various carefully designed programme initiatives, blended with institutional support in a time-bound manner with fairly good response at various levels and segments of the economy. The systems developed so far are still evolving.

The foundation for promoting greater financial access in India can be traced to the findings of the All-India Rural Credit Survey in the early 1950s. In order to ensure financial inclusion various initiatives have been taken by the Government of India and the Reserve Bank of India (RBI) from time to time.

These have included nationalization of commercial banks in 1969 and 1980, establishment and expansion of rural credit co-operatives [1], regional rural banks (RRBs) [2], urban co-operative banks (UCBs) [3], micro finance and self-help groups (SHGs) [4], mutual funds [5], pension funds [6] and Pradhan Mantri Jan-Dhan Yojana (PMJDY), 2014. [7]

5.2 RBI Measures for Financial Inclusion

Given the socio-demographic complexities in India, the policy endeavour of the RBI has been to adopt a multi-institutional and multi-instrument approach to comprehensively address the issue of financial inclusion in all its dimensions, going beyond mere availability of credit to the masses. The term *financial inclusion* needs to be understood in a broader perspective to mean the provision of the full range of affordable financial services, viz. access to payments and remittance facilities, savings, loans and insurance services by the formal financial system to those who tend to be excluded from these services. The RBI, while recognising the concerns in regard to the banking practices that tend to exclude rather than attract vast sections of population, has been urging the banks to review their existing practices to align them with the objective of achieving greater financial inclusion. The RBI too has taken a number of measures with the objective of attracting the financially excluded population into the formalised financial system. Some of the measures taken in this direction are as follows.

5.2.1 No Frills Account: RBI vide Mid-term Review of Annual Policy Statement for the year 2005-2006, advised banks to align their policies with the objective of financial inclusion. Banks were advised to make available a basic banking *No frills* account either with *nil* or very minimum balances as well as charges that would make such accounts accessible to vast sections of population. Besides, it was emphasized upon by the RBI for deepening and widening the reach of financial services so as to cover a large segment of the rural and poor sections of population.

All the public and the private sector banks as well as the foreign banks, except those not having significant retail presence, are reported to have introduced the basic banking ‘no-frills’ account.

5.2.2 General Credit Card (GCC): With the objective of providing hassle-free credit to the banks’ constituents in rural and semi urban areas, the banks were advised in December 2005, to consider introduction of a *General Credit Card* (GCC) to such constituents. The card was to have a credit limit of up to ₹ 25,000, based on the assessment of income and cash flows of the household without insistence on security or purpose or end-use of credit. The credit facility was to be in the nature of revolving credit entitling the holder to withdraw up to the limit sanctioned. The banks are required to charge appropriate and reasonable Interest rate on the facility.

5.2.3 Business Facilitator and Business Correspondent (BC) Models: In January 2006, banks were permitted to utilise the services of non-governmental organisations (NGOs/SHGs), micro finance institutions and other civil society organisations as intermediaries in providing financial and banking services through the use of *business facilitator* and *business correspondent (BC) models*. The BC model allows banks to do *cash in-cash out* transactions at the location of the BC and allows branchless banking.

5.2.4 Passbook Facility: The matter of issuing passbooks to the small depositors has been a nagging issue for sometime past. Passbooks provide the account holders a ready reckoner of the transactions in their accounts and is a convenient reference document—which can not be substituted by periodical bank account statements, particularly by the small account holders. Since non-issuance of the passbooks to the small customers could indirectly lead to their financial exclusion, the RBI had advised the banks in October 2006 to invariably offer the passbook facility to all its savings bank account holders (individuals) and not to levy any charge on the customers thereof.

5.2.5 Simplified KYC Procedure: With a view to facilitating the opening of bank accounts by the common man through a simplified KYC procedure, in the Mid-Term Review of the Annual Policy of the RBI for the year 2006-07, it was announced that the "banks could open accounts of low balance/turnover (where the balance does not exceed ₹ 50,000 in all the accounts taken together and the total credit in all the accounts taken together is not expected to exceed rupees two lakh in a year) only with self certification of address by the customers and his photograph". However, this policy announcement is yet to be operationalised as the matter is under consideration of the Government in the light of the provisions of the Rules framed under Prevention of Money Laundering Act.

5.2.6 Credit Counselling and Financial Education: Promoting *credit counselling and financial education* of the clientele of the banks is also an area that deserves due attention of the banking community. Towards this objective, the banks were also advised by the RBI to make available all printed material used by retail customers in the concerned regional language. As far as RBI itself is concerned, it has launched on June 18, 2007, a multilingual website in 13 Indian languages on all matters concerning banking and the common person so that the language does not become a barrier to acquiring financial education by the public at large.

5.2.7 Use of Technology: Recognizing that technology has the potential to address the issues of outreach and credit delivery in rural and remote areas in a viable manner, banks have been advised to make effective use of information and communications technology (ICT), to provide doorstep banking services through the business communication (BC) model where the accounts can be operated by even illiterate customers by using biometrics, thus ensuring the security of transactions and enhancing confidence in the banking system.

5.2.8 Simplified Branch Authorization: To address the issue of uneven spread of bank branches, in December 2009, domestic scheduled commercial banks were permitted to freely open branches in tier III to tier VI centres with a population of less than 50,000 under general permission, subject to reporting.

5.2.9 Banking Services in Unbanked Villages: Banks were advised to draw up a road map to provide banking services in every unbanked village having a population of over 2,000 by March 2012. RBI advised banks that such banking services need not necessarily be extended through a bricks and mortar branch, but could also be provided through any of the various forms of ICT-based models. About 73,000 such unbanked villages were identified and allotted to various banks through state-level bankers' committees.

5.2.10 Financial Inclusion Plans of Banks for Three Years: RBI advised all public and private sector banks to submit a board-approved, three-year financial inclusion plan (FIP) starting April, 2010. These plans broadly include self-set targets in respect of rural bricks and mortar branches opened, BCs employed, coverage of unbanked villages with a population above 2,000 as also other unbanked villages with population below 2,000 through branches.

Government of India had set up the Financial Stability and Development Council (FSDC), which is mandated, *inter alia,* to focus on financial inclusion and financial literacy issues. In order to further strengthen the ongoing financial inclusion agenda in India, a high level Financial Inclusion Advisory Committee has been constituted by RBI. The Committee would pave the way for developing a viable and sustainable banking services delivery model focusing on accessible and affordable financial services, developing products and processes for rural and urban consumers presently outside the banking network and for suggesting appropriate regulatory framework to ensure that financial inclusion and financial stability move in tandem. India has, for a long time, recognized the social and economic imperatives for broader financial inclusion and has made an enormous contribution to economic development by finding innovative ways to empower the poor.

5.3 Financial Inclusion Measures by NABARD

Set up in 1982, National Bank for Agriculture and Rural Development (NABARD) is the apex institution accredited with all matters concerning policy, planning and operations in the field of credit for agriculture and other economic activities in rural areas in India.

NABARD serves as an apex refinancing agency for the institutions providing investment and production credit in rural areas.

NABARD has been instrumental in facilitating various activities under micro finance sector, involving all possible partners at the ground level in the field. NABARD has been encouraging voluntary agencies, bankers, socially spirited individuals, other formal and informal entities and also government functionaries to promote and nurture self-help groups (SHGs).

The focus in this direction has been on training and capacity building of partners, promotional grant assistance to self-help promoting institutions (SHPIs), revolving fund assistance (RFA) to MFIs, equity/capital support to MFIs to supplement their financial resources and provision of 100 percent refinance against bank loans provided by various banks for microfinance activities.

In view of the large outreach and pre-dominant position of the micro finance programme, it is important to keep a continuous track of the status, progress, trends, qualitative and quantitative performance comprehensively. To achieve this objective, Reserve Bank of India and NABARD issued guidelines in the year 2006-07 to commercial banks, regional rural banks and co-operative banks to furnish data on progress under micro finance.

The data so collected covers various parameters like savings of SHGs with banks, bank loan disbursed to SHGs, bank loan outstanding against SHGs, gross non-performing assets of bank loans to SHGs, recovery performance of loans to SHGs. Further, the banks also furnish the data regarding bank loans provided to micro finance institutions (MFIs). NABARD has been bringing out the consolidated document annually.

The data furnished by the banks have been analysed on a region-wise, state-wise, agency-wise, bank-wise and also for SHGs exclusively under Swarnajayanti Gram Swarojgar Yojana and exclusive women SHGs.

The major support provided by NABARD under Micro Finance Development and Equity Fund relates to promotion and nurturing of SHGs by self-help promoting institutions and training and capacity building of the stakeholders in the sector. NABARD is also experimenting innovative projects for further developing the micro finance through Joint Liability Groups.

Since 2006-07, NABARD has been compiling and analysing the data on progress made in micro finance sector, based on the returns furnished by commercial banks (CBs), regional rural banks (RRBs) and cooperative banks operating in the country. Most of the banks participating in the process of microfinance have reported the progress made under the programme.

5.4 Committee on Financial Inclusion

Committee on Financial Inclusion (Chairman: C. Rangarajan) [8] was constituted by the Government of India on June 26, 2006 to prepare a strategy of financial inclusion. The Committee submitted its Final Report on January 4, 2008.

As is evident from the preamble of the report, the Committee interpreted financial inclusion as an instrumentality for social transformation: "Access to finance by the poor and vulnerable groups is a prerequisite for inclusive growth. In fact, providing access to finance is a form of empowerment of the vulnerable groups. Financial inclusion denotes delivery of financial services at an affordable cost to the vast sections of the disadvantaged and low-income groups.

The various financial services included credit, savings, insurance and payments and remittance facilities. The objective of financial inclusion is to extend the scope of activities of the organized financial system to include within its ambit people with low incomes. Through graduated credit, the attempt must be to lift the poor from one level to another so that they come out of poverty".

The Report viewed financial inclusion as a comprehensive and holistic process of ensuring access to financial services and timely and adequate credit, particularly to vulnerable groups such as weaker sections and low income groups at an affordable cost.

Financial inclusion, therefore, according to the Committee, should include access to mainstream financial products such as bank accounts, credit, remittances and payment services, financial advisory services and insurance facilities.

The Report observed that in India, 51.4 percent of farmer households are financially excluded from both formal/informal sources and 73 percent of farmer households do not access formal sources of credit.

Exclusion is most acute in Central, Eastern and North Eastern regions with 64 percent of financially excluded farmer households. According to the Report, the overall strategy for building an inclusive financial sector should be based on the following policy measures:

1. Effecting improvements within the existing formal credit delivery mechanism.
2. Suggesting measures for improving credit absorption capacity especially amongst marginal and sub-marginal farmers and poor non-cultivator households.
3. Evolving new models for effective outreach.
4. Leveraging on technology based solutions.

Keeping in view the enormity of the task involved, the Committee recommended the setting up of a mission mode National Rural Financial Inclusion Plan (NRFIP) with a target of providing access to comprehensive financial services to at least 50 percent (55.77 million) of the excluded rural households by 2012 and the remaining by 2015. This would require semi-urban and rural branches of commercial banks and RRBs to cover a minimum of 250 new cultivator and non-cultivator households per branch per annum. The Committee also recommended that the Government should constitute a National Mission on Financial Inclusion (NaMFI) comprising representatives of all stakeholders for suggesting the overall policy changes required, and supporting stakeholders in the domain of public, private and NGO sectors in undertaking promotional initiatives.

The major recommendations relating to commercial banks included: (a) target for providing access to credit to at least 250 excluded rural households per annum in each rural/semi-urban branches, (b) targeted branch expansion in identified districts in the next three years, (c) provision of customised savings, credit and insurance products, (d) incentivising human resources for providing inclusive financial services, and (e) simplification of procedures for agricultural loans.

The major recommendations relating to regional rural banks (RRBs) included: (a) extending their services to unbanked areas and increasing their credit-deposit ratios, (b) no further merger of RRBs, (c) widening of network and expanding coverage in a time-bound manner, and (d) separate credit plans for excluded regions and strengthening of their boards.

In the case of co-operative banks, the major recommendations were: (a) early implementation of Vaidyanathan Committee Revival Package, (b) use of primary agricultural credit societies (PACS) and other primary co-operatives as business correspondents, and (c) co-operatives to adopt group approach for financing excluded groups.

Other important recommendations of the Committee included: (a) encouraging self-help groups (SHGs) in excluded regions, (b) legal status for SHGs, and (c) measures for urban micro-finance and separate category of micro finance institutions (MFIs).

The Committee recommended setting up of two funds: Financial Inclusion Fund (FIF) and Financial Inclusion Technology Fund (FITF). Each of the Funds shall consist of an overall corpus of ₹ 500 crore, with initial funding to be contributed by the Government of India, Reserve Bank of India (RBI) and NABARD in the ratio of 40:40:20.

The two funds have been established with NABARD which is the coordinating agency for financial inclusion initiatives with its Financial Inclusion Department (FID) as the nodal department. The core activities of the FID are to carry forward the agenda of financial inclusion of the excluded population at the national level as per the framework described by the Committee on Financial Inclusion in general and operationalising the Financial Inclusion Fund (FIF) and Financial Inclusion Technology Fund (FITF), in particular. The implementation is under the guidance of the two Advisory Boards set up for FIF and FITF respectively.

5.4.1 Financial Inclusion Fund (FIF): The objective of FIF is to support "developmental and promotional activities" with a view to securing greater financial inclusion, particularly among weaker sections, low income groups and in backward regions/hitherto unbanked areas.

A. Eligible Activities/Purposes: These are as under:

1. Funding support for capacity building inputs to business facilitators and business correspondents.
2. Providing promotional support to institutions, such as resource centres, farmers' service centres and rural development and self-employment training institutes to enable them to provide improved technical and financial services (including counselling) aimed at increasing technology adoption, effective management of assets, nurturing entrepreneurial capacity and increasing financial education and literacy.
3. Providing funding support for promotion, nurturing and credit linking of self-help groups (SHGs).
4. Capacity building of personnel of NABARD, banks, post offices, state government departments, micro finance institutions, NGOs, local level associations, members of SHGs/joint liability groups etc.
5. Defraying expenses of approved institutions for undertaking interventions for financial inclusion in Central, Eastern and North East Regions; Jammu and Kashmir, Himachal Pradesh and Uttarakhand.
6. Funding support for setting up of rural credit bureaus and credit rating of rural customers.
7. Supporting initiatives of local level associations/federations.
8. Supporting pilot projects for development of innovative products, processes and prototypes for financial inclusion.
9. Any other developmental and promotional interventions recommended by the advisory board for the FIF.

B. Eligible Institutions: These are as under:

1. Financial Institutions, viz. NABARD, commercial banks, regional rural banks (RRBs) and cooperative banks.
2. NGOs, MFIs, SHGs, farmers' clubs, local level associations etc.
3. Training and research organisations, academic institutions, universities.
4. Service providers like insurance companies (providing micro insurance services), post offices, railways etc.

5. Any other organisation whose objectives are in conformity with the overall objectives of the FIF and are approved by the advisory board from time to time.

5.4.2 Financial Inclusion Technology Fund (FITF): The objective of FITF is to enhance investment in information communication technology (ICT) aimed at promoting financial inclusion, stimulate the transfer of research and technology in financial inclusion, increase the technological absorption capacity of financial service providers/users and encourage an environment of innovation and cooperation among stakeholders.

A. Eligible Activities/Purposes: These are as follows:

1. Encouraging user-friendly technology solutions.
2. Providing financial support to technological solutions aimed at providing affordable financial services to the disadvantaged sections of the society.
3. Creating a common technology infrastructure with comprehensive credit information.
4. Funding support to technologies facilitating the documentation for processing of loans.
5. Providing viability gap/pilot project funding for unproven but potential technological interventions.
6. Conduct of studies, consultancies, research, evaluation studies relating to technological interventions for financial inclusion.
7. Promoting seminars, conferences and other mechanisms for discussions, dissemination relating to financial inclusion technological interventions.
8. Publication of financial inclusion technology literature, publicity material, etc.
9. Capacity building of personnel of banks, post offices, State Government Departments, MFIs, NGOs, and other stakeholders.
10. Any other activity as may be approved by the advisory board.

B. Eligible Institutions: These are as under:

1. Financial institutions, viz. NABARD, commercial banks, regional rural banks (RRBs) and cooperative banks.
2. NGOs, MFIs, SHGs, farmers' clubs, local level associations etc.
3. Technology service providers and other service providers like insurance companies (providing micro insurance services), post offices, railways etc.
4. Any other institution/organisation whose objectives are in conformity with the overall objectives of the FITF and are approved by the advisory board.

5.5 Committee on Comprehensive Financial Services for Small Businesses and Low-income Households (CCFS), 2014

The RBI set up the CCFS in September 2013 (Chairman: Nachiket Mor) which submitted its Report in January 2014. CCFS emphasized that in order to achieve the task of financial inclusion in a manner that enhances both financial inclusion and stability, there was need to move away from an exclusive focus on any one model to an approach where multiple models and partnerships were allowed to thrive, particularly between national full-service banks, regional banks of various types, non-banking financial companies (NBFCs), and financial markets. The common theme of all the recommendations made by the CCFS was that instead of focusing only on large generalist institutions, specialization and partnerships between specialists must be encouraged. Such an approach, in its view, would be far more effective at delivering high quality financial inclusion, without compromising financial stability or responsibility towards customers. Some of the key recommendations of the CCFS included the following:

- Universal Electronic Bank Account for every resident to be made available at the time of issuing the Aadhaar number.
- Licensing, with lowered entry barriers but otherwise equivalent treatment, more functionally focused banks, including payment banks, wholesale consumer banks, and wholesale investment banks.
- Developing risk-based supervision processes for regional banks and strengthening existing ones before creating new regional banks.
- Reorienting the focus of NABARD, SIDBI, and NHB to be market-makers and providers of risk-based credit enhancements.
- Consolidating NBFC definitions into two categories: core investment companies and other NBFCs.
- On priority sector lending, while the CCFS acknowledged that the current focus of the policy, on small farmers, small businesses, and weaker sections, was well placed, it recommended an approach that incentivizes each provider to specialise in one or more sectors of the economy and regions of the country. Government subsidies should be channelled as direct benefit transfers (DBTs) rather than as subventions or waivers.
- All financial firms regulated by the RBI should be required to have an internal process to assess suitability of products prior to advising clients with regard to them.

5.6 Recent Important Guidelines on Financial Inclusion

- **2006:** In January, banks were allowed to enlist non-profit *Bank Mitras* [Business Correspondents (BCs)] as agents for delivery of financial services, acting in the capacity of *last-mile infrastructure*.
- **2008:** In April, it was determined that BCs should be located not more than 15 kilometres from the nearest bank branch, so as to ensure their adequate

supervision. This was a very restrictive rule that severely limited the expansion of this model.

- **2008:** RBI issued operative guidelines for mobile banking and amended the same in December 2009 to ease the various transaction limits and security norms.
- **2009:** Kirana stores, gas stations, public call offices (PCOs) etc. were allowed to participate as BCs. Further, BCs were allowed to operate up to 30 kilometres from the nearest bank branches.
- **2009:** Banks were allowed to apply *reasonable* service charges from customers to ensure viability of the BC model, and to pay a *reasonable* commission/fee to the BCs to incentivize them.
- **2010:** In June the RBI and Telecom Regulatory Authority of India (TRAI) were able to reach an initial agreement regarding the rollout of mobile banking, whereby TRAI would deal with all interconnection issues and RBI would handle the banking aspects such as Know Your Customer (KYC) checks, transaction limits etc.
- **2010:** In September, all companies listed under the Companies Act (1956) were allowed to act as BCs, with the exception of non-banking financial companies.
- **2010:** The same directive determined that the distance rule was open to relaxation in certain cases, based on the decision of the State Level Bankers' Committees.
- **2011:** In January, TRAI announced its intent to fix mobile tariffs for financial services as against their current market pricing, with a view to ensuring affordability.
- **2011:** RBI issued guidelines for opening Aadhaar-enabled Bank Accounts to facilitate routing of MGNREGA wages and other social benefits into the accounts of beneficiaries.
- **2012:** RBI permitted Aadhaar letter as a proof of both identity and address for the purpose of opening of bank accounts.
- **2012:** Government of India introduced Sub-Service Area (SSA) approach for opening of banking outlet and for Direct Cash Transfer.
- **2012:** Aadhaar Payment Bridge System (APBS) was introduced for centralised credit of social benefits.
- **2013:** To ease the account opening process, RBI permitted the use of e-KYC.
- **2014:** RBI issued guidelines for scaling up of Business Correspondent model.

To sum up, the banking industry in India has grown both horizontally and vertically but the branch penetration in rural areas has not kept pace with the rising demand and the need for accessible financial services. Even after decades of bank nationalization—whose rationale was to shift the focus from class banking to mass banking—usurious money lenders in rural areas and urban slums continue to exploit the poor. After economic reforms initiated in 1991, the country can ill-afford not to include the poor in the growth paradigm. Financial inclusion of the poor will help in bringing them to the mainstream of growth and would also provide the financial institutions an opportunity to be partners in inclusive growth.

The Indian experience has proved that financial inclusion can work within the framework of financial stability given an enabling regulatory environment. A combination of viable business strategies targeted towards the population at the bottom of the pyramid, lower transactions costs with technological innovations and appropriate regulatory environment have helped foster greater financial inclusion with stability. The twin objectives of financial stability and financial inclusion are arguably two sides of a coin but it is imperative that a robust risk-mitigating framework which exploits their complementarities while minimizing the conflicts is adopted to ensure that they do not work at cross purposes. Looking to the immense potential lying ahead, rapid progress of financial inclusion efforts in India is the need of the hour. The stakeholders have come to realize the need for viable and sustainable business models which can sharply focus on accessible and affordable financial services, products and processes, synergistic partnerships with non-bank entities including the technology service providers.

There is substantial progress towards opening of accounts, providing basic banking services during the recent years. However, it is essential that all the sections be financially included in order to have financial stability and sustainability of the economic and social order. There is urgent need to push forward the financial inclusion agenda to ensure that people at the bottom of the pyramid join the mainstream of the formal financial system.

Endnotes

1. See chapter 6 of this book.
2. See chapter 7 of this book.
3. See chapter 8 of this book.
4. See chapter 9 of this book.
5. See chapter 10 of this book.
6. See chapter 11 of this book.
7. See chapter 12 of this book.
8. Government of India, Planning Commission, *Report of the Committee on Financial Inclusion* (Chairman: C. Rangarajan), 2008.

6

Rural Credit Co-operatives

India is a country with a population of 121 crore (2011 Census) of which around 70 percent resides in around 6 lakh villages. There were 92,432 primary agricultural credit societies (PACS) in the country as on March 31, 2012. On grounds of outreach, co-operatives cannot be ignored. The outreach is significant not merely in absolute numbers but also in terms of location of outlets. The number of PACS located in hilly terrains, deserts and other areas with poor access far exceed the number of rural branches of commercial banks and RRBs. Though the network of commercial banks and RRBs has spread rapidly, their reach in the countryside both in terms of the number of clients and accessibility to the small and marginal farmers and other poorer segments is far less than that of co-operatives.

The Government has taken many policy initiatives for strengthening farm credit delivery system for providing credit at affordable rates of interest to support the resource requirements of the agricultural sector. The emphasis of these initiatives has been on providing timely and adequate credit support to farmers with particular focus on small and marginal farmers and weaker sections of society to enable them to adopt modern technology and improved agricultural practices for increasing agricultural production and productivity. The policy essentially lays emphasis on augmenting credit flow at the ground level through credit planning, adoption of region specific strategies and rationalization of lending policies and procedures and bringing down the rate of interest on farm loan.

6.1 Credit Needs of the Indian Farmers

Need for agricultural credit arises because modern farm technology is costly and the personal resources of the farmers are inadequate. Provision of agricultural credit, as an input, is essential for widespread use of improved agricultural methods.

Credit requirements of the farmers may be classified: (a) on the basis of purpose, and (b) on the basis of time. They need credit for productive as well as for unproductive purposes. Productive purposes include all such activities which help in the improvement of agricultural productivity such as purchase of inputs and permanent improvements in land. Unproductive credit needs include celebration of marriages and other social and religious functions and litigation.

Finance required for productive purposes can be divided broadly into the following categories:

- Short-term (for periods up to 15 months).
- Medium-term (from 15 months up to 5 years).
- Long-term (above 5 years).

Short-term loans are required for purchasing seeds, manures and fertilizers or for meeting labour charges etc. These are expected to be repaid after the harvest.

Medium-term loans are granted for purposes such as sinking of wells, purchase of bullocks, pumping plants and other improved implements etc.

Loans repayable over a longer period (i.e. above 5 years) are classified as long-term loans. These are utilised for payment of old debts, purchase of the heavier machines, making permanent improvements and increasing the size of the holding.

6.2 Sources of Credit for the Farmers

Sources of micro credit for the poor are grouped into two categories: (a) institutional sources, and (b) non-institutional sources. Institutional sources include co-operative societies, commercial banks and other government agencies. Non-institutional sources comprise moneylenders, landlords, relatives etc.

6.2.1 Institutional (Formal) Sources: These are as under:

A. Member-owned Organizations: These include self-help groups, credit unions, and a variety of hybrid organizations like financial service associations. Like their informal cousins, they are generally small and local, which means they have access to good knowledge about each other's financial circumstances and can offer convenience and flexibility. Since they are managed by poor people, their costs of operation are low. However, these providers may have little financial skill and can run into trouble when the economy turns down or their operations become too complex. Unless they are effectively regulated and supervised, they can be *captured* by one or two influential leaders, and the members can lose their money.

B. Non-governmental Organizations (NGOs): NGOs have spread around the developing world in the recent past. They have proven very innovative, pioneering banking techniques like solidarity lending, village banking and mobile banking that have overcome barriers to serving poor populations. However, with boards that do not necessarily represent either their capital or their customers, their governance structures can be fragile, and they can become overly dependent on external donors.

C. Formal Financial Institutions: In addition to commercial banks, these include state banks, agricultural development banks, savings banks, rural banks and non-banking financial institutions. They are regulated and supervised, offer a wider range of financial services, and control a branch network that can extend across the country. However, they have proved reluctant to adopt social missions, and due to their high costs of operation, often cannot deliver services to poor or remote population.

In India, agricultural credit is disbursed through a multi-agency network comprising of commercial banks, regional rural banks and co-operatives. With their vast network (covering almost all the villages in the country), wider coverage and outreach extending to the remotest part of country, the co-operative credit institutions, both in short and long-term structure are the main institutional mechanism for dispensation of agricultural credit.

Agricultural growth is crucial for alleviating rural poverty. Access to institutional credit to more farmers and appropriate quantity and quality of agricultural credit are crucial for realising the full potential of agriculture as a profitable activity.

Provision of sufficient and timely credit at fair rates of interest has, therefore, to be considered as an integral part of agricultural development. Assistance rendered by way of credit has, however, to be related to specific items of productive work or of essential costs of cultivation.

6.2.2 Non-institutional (Informal) Sources: These include moneylenders, pawnbrokers, savings collectors, money-guards, input supply shops. Because they know each other well and live in the same community, they understand each other's financial circumstances and can offer very flexible, convenient and fast services. These services can also be costly and the choice of financial products limited and very short-term.

Till Independence in 1947, money lenders and the landlords were the principal sources of rural credit. Over the years, the operations of moneylenders have declined in view of debt relief legislations, the system of licensing moneylenders and restrictions on the use and transfer of land as security. Similarly, the abolition of all privileged tenures, both in zamindari and ryotwari areas, has discouraged investment by the landlords and larger cultivators.

Historically, moneylenders have played a significant role in meeting the credit needs of the rural producers. With stringent laws against money lending and the phenomenal growth of the formal credit delivery system, it was thought that money lenders would soon be out of business. Instead they have been in the business of lending in several disguises.

There are two types of moneylenders in rural areas: (a) agriculturist moneylenders who carry on the business of money lending along with farming, and (b) professional moneylenders whose only occupation is money lending. Although the relative importance of moneylenders has declined over the years, they are still an important source of credit for the rural people, particularly the small farmers and the artisans.

Moneylenders usually charge higher rates from poorer borrowers than from less poor ones. While moneylenders are often demonized and accused of usury, their services are convenient and fast, and they can be very flexible when borrowers run into problems. Moneylenders are popular because, unlike government agencies, they give credit for every purpose. They are easily approachable by the credit seekers and there are not many formalities in transacting a loan. However, the malpractices adopted by the moneylenders to exploit the needy farmers cannot be overlooked. These malpractices pertain to charging of high rate of interest and adopting unfair means in the maintenance of accounts.

Perhaps influenced by traditional Western views about usury, the role of the traditional moneylender has been subject to much criticism, especially in the early stages of modern micro finance. As more poor people gained access to loans from micro credit institutions, it became apparent that the services of moneylenders continued to be valued. Borrowers were prepared to pay very high interest rates for services like quick loan disbursement, confidentiality and flexible repayment schedules. They do not always see lower interest rates as adequate compensation for the costs of attending meetings, attending training courses to qualify for disbursements or making monthly collateral contributions. They also find it distasteful to be forced to pretend they were borrowing to start a business, when they were often borrowing for other reasons (such as paying for school fees, dealing with health costs or securing the family food supply). The more recent focus on inclusive financial systems affords moneylenders more legitimacy, arguing in favour of regulation and efforts to increase competition between them to expand the options available to poor people.

It is true that the institutional sources of credit have weakened the hold of moneylenders on the rural masses. However, the benefits of institutional credit have not percolated to all sections of rural population. Landless workers and marginal farmers have not benefited adequately due to their ignorance of new sources of credit and also on account of their weak repaying capacity. These underprivileged rural sections still depend on the moneylenders and suffer their exploitative practices.

6.3 Co-operative Credit Societies

These societies form an integral part of the rural credit system in India. They are the main source of institutional credit to the farmers. These societies are chiefly responsible for breaking the monopoly of moneylenders in providing credit to the agriculturists. There are around 1 lakh such societies in the country at present. In spite of their suitability and useful role in building up a just socio-economic rural life, co-operative societies suffer from various weaknesses. The heavy overdues of co-operative societies are a cause for concern. The rising overdues have reduced the borrowing and lending activities of these societies. Moreover, these societies have paid inadequate attention to the needs of landless workers and rural artisans. Influential people in the villages have been the main beneficiaries of co-operative credit. Of late, there has been a tendency on the part of political leadership to write-off loans of the farmers. The RBI has repeatedly expressed concern in this regard because non-repayment of loans by the existing borrowers can adversely affect recycling of funds and the credit chances of the prospective borrowers.

6.4 Co-operative Banks

Co-operative banks in India are more than 100 years old. These banks came into existence with the enactment of the Agricultural Credit Co-operative Societies Act in 1904. Co-operative banks form an integral part of the banking system in India. These banks operate mainly for the benefit of rural areas, particularly the agricultural sector. Co-operative banks mobilise deposits and supply agricultural and rural credit with a wider outreach. They are the main source of institutional credit to the farmers. Co-operative banks are chiefly responsible for breaking the monopoly of moneylenders in providing credit to agriculturists. They have also been an important instrument for various development schemes, particularly subsidy-based programmes for the poor. Co-operative banks operate for non-agricultural sector also but their role is small.

Though much smaller as compared to scheduled commercial banks, co-operative banks constitute an important segment of the Indian banking system. They have an extensive branch network and reach out to people in remote areas. They have traditionally played an important role in creating banking habits among the lower and middle-income groups and in strengthening the rural credit delivery system.

Unfortunately, financial reforms have not impacted the functioning of co-operative banks. This was brought out clearly in the following observation of the Reserve Bank of India, "Since the introduction of reforms, there has been very little perceptible improvement in either stability or efficiency of co-operative banks. In particular, the asset quality and profitability of scheduled urban co-operative banks (UCBs) showed some deterioration in the reform period. Positive impact of reforms, as has been witnessed in the case of commercial banking sector, may take longer to get manifested for co-operative banks given the late start of the reform process in this sector". [1]

The financial reforms process initiated in 1991 has tried to achieve regulatory convergence among various financial intermediaries in view of their systemic importance. Therefore, the basic objectives and instruments of reforms for co-operative banks have been the same as for state co-operative banks (SCBs). However, given the special characteristics of co-operative banks, they have been extended certain dispensations in terms of pace and sequencing of reforms.

6.4.1 Classification of Co-operative Banks: The co-operative banking structure in India comprises urban co-operative banks and rural co-operative credit institutions.

A. Urban Co-operative Banks (UCBs): UCBs consist of a single tier, *viz.* primary co-operative banks, commonly referred to as urban co-operative banks.

B. Rural Co-operatives: Based on the nature of their lending operations, rural credit co-operatives have traditionally been bifurcated into two parallel wings: short-term and long-term.

6.5 Rural Co-operatives

6.5.1 Short-term Rural Co-operatives: The short-term provide crop and other working capital loans to farmers and rural artisans primarily for short-term purposes. These credit institutions have a three-tier federal structure: (a) at the apex of the system is a state co-operative bank (SCB) in each State, (b) at the middle (or district) level, there are central co-operative banks (CCBs) also known as district co-operative banks, and (c) at the lowest (or village) level are the primary agricultural credit societies (PACS). The smaller States and Union Territories (UTs) have a two-tier structure with SCBs directly meeting the credit requirements of PACS.

A. State Co-operative Bank (SCB): SCB is the highest agency of the three-tier co-operative credit structure in a state. It serves as a link between RBI and the CCBs and PACS. The RBI provides credit to lower level co-operatives through the SCB. This function of the RBI has now been taken over by NABARD. The SCB also acts as a *balancing centre* for CCBs in the sense that surplus funds of some CCBs are made available to other needy CCBs. The SCB exercises general control and supervision over CCBs and PACS.

B. Central Co-operative Banks (CCBs): These banks act as a link between the SCB and the PACS. The main task of CCBs is to lend money to affiliated village primary societies. The CCBs are expected to attract deposits from the general public.

C. Primary Agricultural Credit Societies (PACS): These societies form the basic unit of the co-operative credit system in India. These voluntary societies based on the principle of one man one vote have posed challenge to the exploitative practices of the village moneylenders.

The farmers and other small-time borrowers come in direct contact with these societies. The success of the co-operative credit movement depends largely on the strength of these village level societies. There are around 92,000 such societies in the country at present.

As a result of the expansion of the activities of PACS, the role of moneylenders in providing credit to agriculturists has decreased over the years. A major objective of PACS is to serve the needs of weaker sections of the society. For this purpose, the people with limited means, particularly scheduled castes and scheduled tribes, are encouraged to become members of these societies. Government has promoted multi-purpose societies in tribal areas for the benefit of people living there.

6.5.2 Long-term Rural Co-operatives: The long-term provide typically medium and long-term loans for making investments in agriculture, rural industries and, in the recent period, housing. Generally, these co-operatives have two tiers, viz.:

A. State Co-operative Agriculture and Rural Development Banks (SCARDBs): These banks operate at the State level.

B. Primary Co-operative Agriculture and Rural Development Banks (PCARDBs): These banks operate at the *taluka/tehsil* level.

6.6 Rural Co-operatives: History and Recent Policy Measures

Rural credit co-operatives in India were originally envisaged as a mechanism for pooling the resources of people with small means and providing them with access to different financial services. Democratic in features, the movement was also an effective instrument for development of degraded waste lands, increasing productivity, providing food security, generating employment opportunities in rural areas and ensuring social and economic justice to the poor and vulnerable.

The history of the co-operative credit movement in India can be traced back to 1904 when the Co-operative Societies Act was passed. In 1919, *co-operation* became a provincial subject. The Co-operative Planning Committee, 1945 found that a large number of co-operatives were "saddled with the problem of frozen assets because of heavy overdues in repayment".

The co-operative banks in India play an important role in catering to the banking needs of the rural population. Soon after Independence in 1947, the inadequacy of rural credit engaged the attention of the Government of India and the RBI. The agricultural credit system as it has emerged over the years is the result of both evolution and intervention, and symbolises the nation's response to the dissatisfaction with the discredited colonial credit delivery system.

The Reserve Bank of India Act, 1934 has specific provisions relating to agricultural credit. Section 54 of the RBI Act specifically authorised the creation of an Agricultural Credit Department within the RBI to deal not only with the rural credit but also with the long-term finance including refinance. Section 17 of the Act empowered it to provide agricultural credit through state co-operative banks or any other banks engaged in the business of agricultural credit.

The foundation for building a broader credit infrastructure for rural credit was laid down by the All India Rural Credit Survey (1954). The Committee of Direction that conducted the survey recommended the creation of National Agricultural Credit Fund, which was subsequently created by the RBI. The Agricultural Refinance Corporation (ARC) set up by the RBI in 1963 provided funds by way of refinance, but credit co-operatives still did not function too well. Decentralised credit planning through the Lead Bank Scheme was also introduced to spearhead the credit allocation for, *inter alia*, agricultural lending. In order to emphasise the developmental and promotional role assigned to the ARC in addition to refinancing, the ARC was renamed as the Agricultural Refinance and Development Corporation (ARDC) in 1975.

Despite all these efforts, the flow of credit to the agricultural sector failed to exhibit any appreciable improvement as the co-operatives lacked resources to meet the expected demand. To solve these problems, the regional rural banks (RRBs) were set up in 1975. In order to strengthen the institutional credit for agriculture and rural development, National Bank for Agriculture and Rural Development (NABARD) was set up on July 12, 1982. On its establishment, NABARD took over the entire functions of the ARDC, the refinancing functions of the RBI in relation to co-operatives and regional rural banks (RRBs).

The rural credit co-operative system has served as an important instrument of credit delivery in rural and agricultural areas. The separate structure of rural co-operative sector for long-term and short-term loans has enabled these institutions to develop as specialised institutions for rural credit delivery. At the same time, their federal structure has helped in providing support structure for the guidance and critical financing for the lower structure. These institutions have wide outreach with as many as 92,432 primary agricultural co-operative societies (PACS), the grass root organisation of the rural co-operative banking structure, operating in the country at end-March 2012.

The rural co-operative credit institutions, however, are beset with many problems which include the following.

1. Low resource base.
2. High dependence on refinancing agencies.
3. Lack of diversification.

4. Huge accumulated losses.
5. Persistent NPAs.
6. Low recovery levels.
7. Various other types of organisational weaknesses.

NABARD and the RBI, therefore, have been taking several supervisory and developmental measures in consultation with the Government of India for the revival of weak institutions and orderly growth of this important segment of the financial sector.

6.7 Primary Agricultural Credit Societies (PACS)

Primary agricultural credit societies (PACS) are the foundation of the co-operative credit system on which the superstructure of the short-term co-operative credit system rests. It is the PACS which directly interface with individual farmers, provide short-term and medium-term credit, supply agricultural inputs, distribute consumer articles and arrange for marketing of produce of its members through a co-operative marketing society.

PACS continue to rely heavily on external support and have not yet been able to become self-reliant in respect of resources through deposit mobilisation and internal accruals, affecting their growth and expansion of business activities.

PACS need to function as viable units responsive to the needs, aspirations and convenience of its members, particularly those belonging to the more vulnerable sections of the society. They must function effectively as well-managed and multi-purpose institutions mobilising the savings of the rural people and providing a package of services including credit, supply of agricultural inputs and implements, consumer goods, marketing services and technical guidance with focus on weaker sections.

Some of the critical challenges facing primary level co-operative credit institutions, apart from improving resource mobilisation, are the following.

1. Increasing diversification in business portfolio.
2. Improving volume of business.
3. Arresting decline in membership by the borrowers.
4. Reducing cost of management.
5. Correcting imbalances in loans outstanding.
6. Improving skills of the staff and imparting professionalisation.
7. Strengthening management information system (MIS).
8. Reducing involvement in non/less profitable business.

6.8 Problems of Rural Co-operatives

Rural co-operatives form an integral part of the rural credit system in India. They are the main source of institutional credit to the farmers. These societies are chiefly responsible for breaking the monopoly of moneylenders in providing credit to the agriculturists.

Despite the phenomenal outreach and volume of operations, the financial health of a very large proportion of rural credit co-operatives has deteriorated significantly. The institutions are beset with problems like low resource base, high dependence on external sources of funding, excessive governmental control, dual control, huge accumulated losses, imbalances, poor business diversification, low recovery etc. These institutions do not, therefore, inspire confidence among their existing and potential members, depositors, borrowers and lenders. Thus, there is a need to find ways for strengthening the co-operative movement and making it a well-managed and vibrant medium to serve the credit needs of rural India, especially the small and marginal farmers.

Moreover, these societies have paid inadequate attention to the needs of landless workers and rural artisans. Influential people in the villages have been the main beneficiaries of co-operative credit. Of late, there has been a tendency on the part of political leadership to write-off loans of the farmers. The RBI has repeatedly expressed concern in this regard because non-repayment of loans by the existing borrowers can adversely affect recycling of funds and the credit chances of the prospective borrowers. A national approach on this issue is required so that co-operative credit system may fulfil the task assigned to it.

It is part of a historic policy infirmity which allowed co-operatives to be treated as *refinance windows* instead of incentivising them into becoming genuine thrift and credit institutions.

The rural co-operative credit institutions are beset with many problems which include the following:

1. Low resource base.
2. High dependence on refinancing agencies.
3. Lack of diversification.
4. Huge accumulated losses.
5. Persistent non-performing assets (NPAs).
6. Low recovery levels.
7. Various other types of organisational weaknesses.

NABARD and the RBI have been taking several supervisory and developmental measures in consultation with the Government of India for the revival of weak institutions and orderly growth of this important segment of the financial sector.

6.9 Task Force on Revival of Rural Co-operative Credit Institutions

The Government of India had constituted this Task Force (Chairman: A.

Vaidyanathan), 2005 to propose an action plan for reviving the rural co-operative banking institutions and suggest an appropriate regulatory framework for these institutions. The Task Force in its Report submitted to the Central Government on February 15, 2005 made several recommendations to strengthen the rural co-operative credit structure in the country.

The major recommendations of the Task Force were as under:

1. Co-operative credit structure (CCS) is impaired in governance, managerial and financial fronts and hence needs to be revived and restructured.
2. Financial restructuring should be contingent on commitment to and implementation of legal and institutional reforms by the State Governments.
3. Financial assistance should be made available for: (a) wiping out accumulated losses, (b) covering invoked but unpaid guarantees given by the State Governments, (c) increasing the capital to a specified minimum level, (d) retiring Government share capital, and (e) technical assistance.
4. Availability of financial assistance from the Government of India should be strictly subject to legal and institutional reforms in the co-operative sector to ensure that the co-operatives become truly democratic and member-driven. These reforms should include: (a) ensuring full voting membership rights on all users of financial services including depositors, (b) removing state intervention in administrative and financial matters in co-operatives, (c) removing provision for Government equity and participation in the Boards of Co-operatives, (d) withdrawing restrictive orders on financial matters, and (e) permitting co-operatives the freedom to take loans from any financial institution and not necessarily from only the upper tier and similarly place their deposits with any financial institution of their choice.
5. The Task Force also recommended certain major amendments to the provisions of the Banking Regulation Act, 1949 enabling removal of dual control and bringing the co-operatives under the regulatory control of the RBI. These included: (a) all co-operative banks should be on par with the commercial banks as far as regulatory norms are concerned (b) RBI should prescribe *fit and proper* criteria for election to the Boards of Co-operative Banks, (c) RBI should prescribe certain criteria for professionals to be on the Boards of Co-operative Banks, (d) CEOs of the co-operative banks should be appointed by the respective banks themselves, and (e) co-operatives, other than co-operative banks as approved by the RBI, should not accept non-voting member deposits. Such co-operatives should also not use words such as *bank*, *banking*, *banker* or any other derivative of the word *bank* in their registered name.
6. Total financial assistance was estimated tentatively at ₹ 14,839 crore. The Task Force, however, recommended a special audit to ascertain the exact

requirement of assistance. The financial assistance should be shared by the Government of India, State Governments and the CCS, based on the origin of losses within a flexible matrix.

7. NABARD should be designated as the nodal *implementing and pass through agency* to co-ordinate and monitor the progress of the programme representing the Government of India. NABARD should prepare model MoUs, model balance sheet proforma for PACS and CCBs.

6.10 NABARD and the Co-operative Sector

National Bank for Agriculture and Rural Development (NABARD) provides refinance to state co-operative agriculture and rural development banks (SCARDBs), state co-operative banks (SCBs), regional rural banks (RRBs) and other financial institutions approved by the RBI. The ultimate beneficiaries of refinance from NABARD could be individuals, partnership concerns, companies, State-owned corporations or co-operative societies.

6.10.1 Credit Extended by NABARD: NABARD provides short-term credit facilities to SCBs in respect of eligible CCBs for the following purposes:

1. Financing seasonal agricultural operations.
2. Marketing of crops.
3. Pisciculture activities.
4. Production and marketing activities of primary weavers/other industrial co-operative societies.
5. Labour contract/forest labour co-operative societies.
6. Individual rural artisans through PCS.
7. Procurement, stocking and distribution of chemical fertilisers.
8. Approved agricultural, allied and other marketing activities.

Besides short-term credit limits are also sanctioned to SCBs on behalf of apex/regional weavers/other industrial societies for financing procurement and marketing and trading-in-yarn.

Short-term limits are also provided to RRBs for financing seasonal agricultural operations, marketing of crops and pisciculture activities.

Medium-term facilities are also provided to SCBs and RRBs for converting short-term into medium-term loans and for approved agricultural investments.

Long-term loans are provided to the State Governments for contributing to the share capital of co-operative credit institutions.

In pursuance of the announcement made by the Finance Minister in June 2004 for enhancing the credit flow to the agriculture sector, NABARD advised SCBs, CCBs and RRBs on the measures to be taken under various schemes to give relief to farmers. It was apprehended that the implementation of these measures coupled with providing conversion/rescheduled loans to farmers may result in a liquidity problem for co-operative banks and RRBs, impairing their ability to provide fresh loans and achieve the desired growth rate during the year. In order to mitigate this, NABARD introduced a liquidity support scheme during 2004-05 for these institutions. SCBs were sanctioned a liquidity support of ₹ 1,770 crore during 2004-05. NABARD also sanctioned long-term loans to 9 State Governments amounting to ₹ 39 crore as contribution to the share capital of co-operative credit institutions.

6.11 Advisory Committee on the Flow of Credit to Agriculture and Related Activities from the Banking System, 2004

As indicated in its mid-term review of November, 2003, the RBI constituted an Advisory Committee on flow of Credit to Agriculture and Related Activities from the Banking System (Chairman: V.S. Vyas). The Advisory Committee submitted its interim report in April, 2004 and the final report in June, 2004. It made the following recommendations.

1. A review of mandatory lending to agriculture by commercial banks to enlarge direct lending programmes.
2. Public and private sector banks to increase their direct agricultural lending to 12 percent of net bank credit in the next two years and to 13.5 percent two years thereafter, within the overall limit of 18.0 percent of total agricultural lending.
3. Banks to increase their disbursements to small and marginal farmers under Special Agricultural Credit Plan (SACP) to 40 percent by March 2007.
4. SACP to be restricted to direct lending and extended to private sector banks.
5. Reduction in cost of agricultural credit by enhancing the cost effectiveness of agricultural loans.
6. NPA norms for agricultural credit to be aligned with crop seasons. Loans for allied activities to be classified as NPA after 180 days of default. Credit flow to small borrowers to be improved through reduction in cost of borrowing, revolving credit packages, procedural simplification, involvement of panchayati raj institutions (PRIs) and micro finance.
7. The SAA to be modified to remove rigidities. SAA to be mandatory only for Government sponsored programmes and the format of village surveys to be changed in view of current realities.

Based on the recommendations contained in the interim report of the Vyas Committee, the RBI, in its annual policy statement for 2004-05, announced a number of measures to improve credit delivery to agriculture. These included, treating loans to storage units designed to store agricultural products, irrespective of location, as indirect credit to agriculture, treating investment by banks in securitised assets representing direct (indirect) lending to agriculture as direct (indirect) lending to agriculture, and waiver of margin/security requirement for agricultural loans up to ₹ 50,000 and in case of agribusiness and agri-clinics for loans up to ₹ 5 lakh. In addition, RBI also aligned repayment dates with harvesting of crops by treating loans granted for short duration crops as an NPA, if the instalment of the principal or interest thereon remains unpaid for two crop seasons beyond the due date. Loans granted for long duration crops are treated as an NPA, only if the instalment of the principal or interest thereon remains unpaid for one crop season beyond the due date.

As recommended by the Vyas Committee, RBI announced that microfinance institutions would not be permitted to accept public deposits, unless they comply with the extant regulatory framework. The recommendation relating to service area approach (SAA) was accepted and an announcement to this effect was made in the RBI's mid-term review of annual policy statement for 2004-05.

Upon the instructions of the Government of India in 2013-2014, most of the PSBs, co-operative banks and RRBs had reduced the rate of interest on farm loans up to ₹ 3,00,000 and are being offered at 7 percent p.a. This has enabled the farmers to derive the benefit of falling interest rates and to improve their margins on farming and allied operations. Also, as a measure to minimise the incidence of under-financing, the scale of finance for crop loans and unit costs of farm investments have been further revised and made more realistic. Furthermore, to mitigate the risk of agriculture arising out of drought conditions, banks either postponed the recovery of loans or converted short-term credit into medium-term credit with appropriate rescheduling in repayment in the concerned areas. The norms of financing in the Rabi season have been liberalised taking into account the likely shortfall in Kharif output on account of deficient rainfall.

In connection with the implementation of the recommendations of the Vyas Committee, the *Economic Survey, 2005-06* observed, "Continuing its endeavour to enhance the flow of credit to agriculture by removing delivery bottlenecks, the RBI, together with NABARD, implemented most of the recommendations of the Advisory Committee on Flow of Credit to Agriculture and Related Activities from the Banking System (Chairman: V.S. Vyas). Out of 99 recommendations made by the Committee, 33 were accepted and implemented by October 2005. These related to the following matters.

1. Procedural modifications and rationalisation of systems and procedures.
2. Tie-ups with related farm machinery manufacturers by banks.
3. Co-opting joint liability group (JLG) and self-help group (SHG) approaches in addressing issues relating to financing oral lessees.

4. Addressing delays/refusal in opening savings bank accounts of SHGs.
5. Improving staffing in the rural areas to promote retail lending to agriculture.
6. Use of individual volunteers, farmers' clubs or NGOs/SHGs as direct selling agents.
7. Building synergy between good working primary agricultural credit societies and commercial banks.
8. Use of IT in rural branches.
9. Working out appropriate incentive structure for prompt repayment.
10. Making the rates of interest on small loans reasonable.
11. Improving the efficiency of credit delivery to small borrowers and association with contract farming.

Furthermore, some of the recommendations, viz., stepping up credit for marketing and introduction of negotiable warehousing receipt system, support of State Governments for collecting dues, reduction of stamp duty on agricultural loans, legal amendments to Agricultural Produce Marketing Committee (APMC) Act by the State Governments, amendment to NABARD Act for operational autonomy, which were referred to the Government of India for examination, have been accepted". [2]

6.12 Expert Group on Investment Credit in Agriculture, 2005

With a view to increasing the flow of credit to agriculture, the RBI set up this Expert Group (Chairman: Y.S.P. Thorat) to formulate a strategy for increasing investment credit in agriculture. The Group in its Report submitted in June 2005 identified several factors which constrain growth in investment in agriculture. These included the following.

1. Meagre growth in minor irrigation and farm mechanization.
2. Declining public sector investment.
3. Limited credit absorptive capacity.
4. Lack of effective mechanism for technology transfer and poor extension services.
5. Inadequate extension services.
6. Limited infrastructure for agro processing, storage, warehousing, value addition and marketing.
7. Restrictions on purchases outside the *mandis.*
8. Weather aberrations and output price fluctuations.
9. Inadequate risk mitigation mechanism.
10. Non-availability of land records.

The Group emphasised the need to accelerate investment in agriculture in order to achieve the desired level of growth. It also highlighted the need for investments to be appropriately structured, timed and well implemented in order to attain maximum effectiveness.

Major recommendations of the Group are set out below.

1. In view of various changes in the Indian rural canvas over the past few years, there is need for a shift in the thrust areas for investment credit to agriculture. Apart from the traditional investments such as land development and irrigation, increased focus needs to be accorded to the entire supply chain management of agriculture products, reform of agriculture markets and public management in agricultural infrastructure.
2. State Governments need to lay emphasis on legal provisions/computerisation of land records, legal support for recovery, reforms in agricultural marketing, improving credit absorptive capacity through supporting infrastructure, strengthening infrastructure, improving extension network and developing marketing links.
3. NABARD should take special steps to facilitate capacity building of credit institutions in appraisal skill, particularly in North Eastern States, and design appropriate products for financing rural infrastructure projects outside the RIDF by mobilising resources from the market or banks at competitive rates of interest.
4. Water management policies and investment in water conservation be designed jointly by the State Governments and banks for improving productivity in agriculture.
5. The State Governments and NABARD should make investments in participatory community projects and in soil treatment to make wasteland and fallow land cultivable.
6. With a view to strengthening the institutional credit mechanism, short-term credit be integrated with term credit and efforts be made to reach the 'unreached' areas, promote supplementary credit delivery channels, outsource monitoring services, provide loan support for diversified agriculture, review HR policies, share the pool of technical expertise and make use of the model bankable projects prepared by NABARD.
7. The RBI along with banks could adopt agency models for credit delivery.
8. Government of India/State Governments and organisations engaged in agricultural research and development (R&D) to reorient R&D activities.
9. To mitigate the risk in financing of agriculture, the Group suggested several measures. These included:

- developing suitable financial products and commodity exchanges;
- allowing banks to operate on behalf of farmers and participate in commodity futures;

- establishing a risk fund for fragile agriculture;
- designing special risk mitigation packages for low asset-based borrowers;
- using warehousing receipts with price hedging instruments;
- adopting technology for dissemination of market intelligence;
- sharing borrower information; and
- financing value chain by banks/through RIDF.

6.13 Working Group on Warehouse Receipts and Commodity Futures, 2005

In pursuance of the announcement made in the Mid-term Review of Annual Policy Statement for the year 2004-05, the RBI constituted this Working Group (Chairman: Prashant Saran) with a view to examining the role of banks in providing loans against warehouse receipts and evolving a framework for participation of banks in the commodity futures market. The Working Group in its Report submitted in April 2005 recommended that banks may be permitted to offer futures-based products to farmers in order to enable them to hedge against price risk.

The Working Group was entrusted with the task of evolving broad guidelines, criteria, limits, risk management system as also a legal framework for facilitating participation of banks in commodity (derivative) market and use of warehouse receipts in financing of agriculture. The major recommendations of the Group are set out below.

1. As banks at present are not allowed to deal in goods, the Central Government may issue a Notification under clause (o) of sub-section (1) of Section 6 of the Banking Regulation Act, 1949 permitting banks to deal in the business of agricultural commodities, including derivatives.
2. Considering the experience that banks already have in dealing with agricultural commodities, it would be prudent at the current stage to permit banks to deal with derivatives in agricultural commodities only.
3. A system needs to be evolved by which warehouse receipts become freely transferable between holders as it would reduce transaction costs and increase usage.
4. An umbrella structure, which may act as a closed user group (CUG) for everyone engaged in the agricultural commodities business, be created. The umbrella structure is envisaged as an electronic platform that would offer straight through processing for everyone connected with commodities. There can be more than one CUG which would be subject to regulation and supervision by a regulatory authority such as Forward Markets Commission (FMC).
5. Proprietary positions in agricultural commodity derivatives could be used by

banks to mitigate their risk in lending to farmers. To achieve this, they will have to buy options on futures.

6. The Forward Contracts (Regulation) Act, 1952 be amended and the FMC should evolve a framework for introducing "options" trading in agricultural commodities in India.
7. Banks may be permitted to have independent proprietary position in commodity futures linked in a macro way to their credit portfolio. However, suitable risk control measures may have to be adopted by banks.
8. At present, purely cash-settled contracts are not available in India. The banks trading or dealing in commodity contracts should, therefore, be prepared to make or accept delivery of physical goods. While no restriction may be placed in this regard, banks may be persuaded to preferably close their positions and cash settle the contracts.
9. Banks may be granted general permission to become professional clearing members of commodity exchanges subject to the condition that they do not assume any exposure risk on account of offering clearing services to their trading clients. At least for the present, banks may not be permitted to act as trading members in the commodity exchanges.
10. While banks may continue to hold their equity stake in the commodity exchanges in order to provide them financial strength and stability, they may reduce/divest their equity holding to a maximum permitted level of 5 percent over a period of time so as to avoid any conflict of interest.

6.14 Regulatory Framework and Supervision

6.14.1 Asset Classification for State Government Guaranteed Advances: Revised guidelines on asset classification norms for State Government guaranteed exposures (i.e. advances and investments), as applicable to commercial banks, were issued to SCBs and CCBs on January 20, 2005 which are to be implemented in a phased manner. Accordingly, it was decided to delink the asset classification and provisioning requirements in respect of State Government guaranteed loans and advances from invocation of State Government guarantee and treat such exposures for asset classification purpose in the same manner as applicable to exposures not guaranteed by the State Governments. However, with a view to enabling banks to have a smooth transition in the matter, the revised prudential norms in respect of State Government guaranteed exposures (i.e. both advances and investments) will be implemented in a phased manner in two stages.

With effect from the year ending March 31, 2006, State Government guaranteed advances and investments in State Government guaranteed securities would attract asset classification and provisioning norms, if interest and/or instalment of principal or any other amount due to the bank remains overdue for more than 180 days. In the second stage, which would begin from the year ending March 31, 2007, State Government guaranteed advance and investment in State Government guaranteed securities would attract asset classification and provisioning norms, if interest and/or instalment of principal or any other amount due to the bank remains overdue for more than 90 days.

6.14.2 Additional Provisioning Requirement for NPAs: For the sake of convergence in policies governing all banks, guidelines for additional provisioning for all advances classified as *doubtful for more than three years* were issued on March 1, 2005, to be implemented in a phased manner from April 1, 2007.

In terms of the guidelines, for the unsecured portion of the advance, which is not covered by the realisable value of tangible security to which the bank has a valid recourse and the realisable value is estimated on a realistic basis, provision will be to the extent of 100 percent, as hitherto. The secured portion, on the other hand, would be divided into two categories. Outstanding stock of NPAs classified as *doubtful for more than three years* as on March 31, 2007 would need to be provided for in a phased manner up to 100 percent till March 31, 2010. Also, 100 percent provisioning would need to be made for the advances classified as *doubtful for more than three years* on or after April 1, 2007.

6.14.3 Prudential Guidelines on Agricultural Advances: As mentioned in the Annual Policy Statement of the RBI for the year 2004-05, prudential norms on income recognition, asset classification and provisioning with respect to agricultural advances were modified on July 12, 2004 with a view to aligning the repayment dates with harvesting of crops. Accordingly, effective September 30, 2004 a loan granted for short duration crops is required to be treated as NPA if the instalment of the principal or interest thereon remains unpaid for two crop seasons beyond the due date. A loan granted for long duration (with crop season longer than one year) crops is required to be treated as NPA, if the instalment of principal or interest thereon remains unpaid for one crop season beyond the due date.

6.14.4 Inspections: NABARD undertakes inspection of RRBs, SCBs and CCBs in accordance with the powers vested under Section 35(6) of the Banking Regulation Act, 1949 (AACS). Besides, NABARD conducts voluntary inspection of SCARDBs, Apex Weavers' Co-operative Societies and State Co-operative Marketing Federations. The frequency of statutory/voluntary inspections by NABARD was increased from 2005-06. The statutory inspections of CCBs and RRBs with positive net worth as also the voluntary inspections of Apex Co-operative Societies/Federations would continue to be conducted once in two years. With the introduction of annual inspections, the system of conducting quick inspections has been dispensed with.

The Board of Supervision (BoS) constituted by NABARD in 1999 to provide guidance and direction on matters relating to supervision of SCBs, CCBs and RRBs meets periodically and deliberates on such issues as listed below.

1. Review of insolvent SCBs and CCBs.
2. State-wise review of the functioning of co-operative credit institutions.
3. Review of off-site supervisory system (OSS).
4. Review of frauds, misappropriation, embezzlements, and defalcations.
5. Review of progress in implementation of the recommendations of the Advisory Committee on Flow of Credit to Agriculture and Related Activities (Chairman: V.S. Vyas).
6. Review of functioning of StCBs and SCARDBs based on inspection findings.
7. Procedure for receipt and follow-up of compliance reports on inspection findings.
8. Risk management systems in co-operative banks and RRBs.
9. Review of financial position of RRBs with deposit erosion of 25 percent or more.
10. Making applicable the revised prudential norms to SCARDBs and PCARDBs.

The Board has often expressed concern over: (a) deterioration in the financial position of many co-operative banks, (b) non-compliance by several banks with the provisions of Section 11(1) of the Banking Regulation Act, 1949 (AACS), relating to minimum capital requirement, and (c) absence of penal provision against the banks not adhering to the RBI's guidelines for asset classification and provisioning norms.

6.15 Problem of Triangular Regulation of Rural Co-operatives

In the case of the rural banking sector, apart from the presence of the Registrar of Co-operative Societies for incorporation/registration-related regulation, banking regulation is further split between the RBI, which has the regulatory powers, and NABARD which is vested with the supervisory responsibility. The shortcomings of this segregation of regulatory and supervisory roles is compounded by the fact that NABARD has limited powers of enforcement of its supervisory findings, for which it has to depend on either its own persuasiveness or seek action through interventions by the RBI or the State Government.

The *duality of control* over the co-operative institutions is a contentious issue. The Task Force on Co-operative Credit System (Chairman: Jagdish Capoor), 1999 addressed the issue of duality of control over co-operative credit institutions and suggested to remove the overlap of controls and endowing functional autonomy and operational freedom to co-operatives. The Task Force was suggested to draw an Action Plan to redefine the roles and responsibilities and areas of regulation through delegation of powers in respect of all the players in the field, *viz.* the State Government, RBI, NABARD and co-operative institutions. In view of the weaknesses persisting in the co-operative banks, a system of preparation of institution-specific development action plans and execution of Memorandum of Understanding have been initiated since 2003-04.

6.16 Agricultural Credit: Recent Policy Announcements

Concerned over the slower growth of agriculture credit, the Government announced a comprehensive policy on June 18, 2004. The policy envisaged a 30 percent increase in credit to agriculture sector in 2004-05 over an estimated credit flow of ₹ 80,000 crore in 2003-04. The implementation of the policy was entrusted to public sector banks, private sector banks, regional rural banks (RRBs) and co-operative banks. The policy indicated that each rural and semi-urban branch of commercial banks, on an average, would take up at least two to three new investment projects in the area of plantation and horticulture, fisheries, organic farming, agro-processing, livestock, micro irrigation, sprinkler irrigation, watershed management, village pond development and other agricultural activities. NABARD was asked to advise District Level Technical Committees to review the scales of finance to meet the realistic credit needs of farmers, especially for capital intensive agricultural operations.

The Budget for 2004-05, presented in the Parliament on July 8, 2004, proposed doubling of credit to agriculture in three years and announced further measures to achieve the target growth in agricultural credit. These measures included holding the sponsor bank of each RRB squarely responsible for the performance of RRB under its control and an incentive scheme under which RRBs, adopting new governance standards and abiding by prudential regulations, qualified for receiving funds from the Government for their restructuring. The Budget proposed setting up of a Task Force to examine the reforms required in the co-operative banking system including the appropriate regulatory regime.

Consequent upon above mentioned policy measures, the flow of institutional credit to the agricultural sector has increased significantly in recent years (Table 6.1).

6.16.1 Agricultural Debt Waiver and Debt Relief Scheme, 2008: In the wake of suicides by farmers in some parts of the country, indebtedness of the farmers was high on the agenda of the Government. The Government had appointed a Committee (Chairman: R. Radhakrishna) to examine all aspects of agricultural indebtedness. The Committee in its report made a number of recommendations but stopped short of recommending waiver of agricultural loans.

Table 6.1: Flow of Institutional Credit to Agriculture and Allied Activities

(₹ crore)

Agency	2008-09	2009-10	2010-11	2011-12^	2012-13*
Co-operative Banks	46,192 (15)	63,497 (17)	78,121 (17)	87,963 (17)	64,664 (27)
Regional Rural Banks	26,765 (9)	35,218 (9)	44,293 (10)	54,450 (11)	32,127 (13)
Commercial Banks	2,28,951 (76)	2,85,799 (74)	3,45,877 (74)	3,68,616 (72)	1,42,838 (60)
Total	3,01,908	3,84,514	4,68,291	5,11,029	2,39,629

^ Provisional; * Up to September 2012

Figures in parentheses indicate percentage of total flow of institutional credit.

Source: Government of India, *Economic Survey*, 2012-13, p. 111, Table 5.7.

However, Government was conscious of the problems being faced by the farmers, especially the small and marginal farmers. Having carefully weighed the pros and cons of debt waiver and having taken into account the resource position, the Finance Minister announced the following scheme of debt waiver and debt relief for farmers:

1. All agricultural loans disbursed by scheduled commercial banks, regional rural banks and cooperative credit institutions up to March 31, 2007 and overdue as on December 31, 2007 were covered under the scheme.
2. For marginal farmers (i.e. holding up to 1 hectare) and small farmers (1-2 hectare), there was a complete waiver of all loans that were overdue on December 31, 2007 and which remained unpaid until February 29, 2008. In respect of other farmers, there was a one time settlement (OTS) scheme for all loans that were overdue on December 31, 2007 and which remained unpaid until February 29, 2008. Under the OTS, a rebate of 25 percent was given against payment of the balance of 75 percent.
3. Agricultural loans were restructured and rescheduled by banks in 2004 and 2006 through special packages. These rescheduled loans, and other loans rescheduled in the normal course as per RBI guidelines, were also eligible either for a waiver or an OTS on the same pattern.
4. The implementation of the debt waiver and debt relief scheme was to be completed by June 30, 2008. Upon being granted debt waiver or signing an agreement for debt relief under the OTS, the farmer was entitled to fresh agricultural loans from the banks in accordance with normal rules.
5. Government estimated that about 3 crore small and marginal farmers and about 1 crore other farmers would benefit from the scheme. The total value of overdue loans waived was estimated at ₹ 50,000 crore and the OTS relief on

the overdue loans at ₹ 10,000 crore.

In addition to above, Government has initiated several measures to galvanize the institutional credit system to make it more responsive to the needs of farmers. Some of the important measures initiated in this regard are as under:

1. Banks have been advised to simplify procedures for documentation for agricultural loans.
2. As part of the measures announced by the RBI for financial inclusion, banks have been advised to open *no frills* accounts and issue simple overdraft facility against such accounts. Banks have also been advised to issue General Credit Cards up to ₹ 25,000 without insisting on security and end use of funds.
3. Banks have been advised to undertake, on a pilot basis, 100 percent financial inclusion in at least one district in each State. Based on the success of the pilot, the State Level Bankers Committee in the States will draw a time-bound plan for achieving 100 percent financial inclusion in other districts of the State.

To sum up, historically, rural co-operative credit institutions (or simply rural co-operatives) have played an important role in providing institutional credit to the agricultural and rural sectors. The structure of rural co-operative banks is not uniform across all the States of the country. Some States have a unitary structure with the State level banks operating through their own branches, while others have a mixed structure incorporating both unitary and federal systems.

Rural indebtedness is noted as a major reason for the spurt in farmer suicides during recent times across a number of states. In most, if not all, such cases, the economic status of the suicide victim was very poor, being small and marginal farmers. After the Green Revolution, agricultural activities have become cash-based individual enterprises requiring high investment in modern inputs and wage labour. This is evident from the list of states with high incidence of farmer suicides, which are not necessarily backward or predominantly agrarian or with low income. Increased liberalization and globalisation have in fact led to a shift in cropping pattern from staple crops to cash crops like oilseeds and cotton, requiring high investment in modern inputs and wage labour, and increasing credit needs but when the prices decline farmers have no means to supplement their incomes.

In spite of their suitability and useful role in building up a just socio-economic rural life, co-operative societies suffer from various weaknesses and their performance has been far from satisfactory in certain respects. The heavy overdues of co-operative societies are a cause for concern. The rising overdues have reduced the borrowing and lending activities of these societies. The increasing incidence of defaulting has brought bad name to these societies.

Co-operative societies have paid inadequate attention to the needs of landless workers and the rural artisans. The influential people in the villages have been the main beneficiaries of co-operative credit. Of late, there has been a tendency on the part of political leadership to write off the loans of the farmers. The RBI has repeatedly expressed concern in this regard because the non-repayment of loans by the existing borrowers adversely affects recycling of funds and the credit chances of prospective borrowers. A national approach on this issue is required so that co-operative credit system may fulfil the task assigned to it.

Positive impact of reforms, as has been witnessed in the case of commercial banking sector, may take longer to get manifested for co-operative banks given the late start of the reform process in this sector. Unless such a positive scenario evolves for the co-operative banking sector in the near future, the financial health of many of these banks would continue to remain a cause of concern.

It is imperative that the government takes initiatives to expand the network of institutional credit facilities in the rural areas and that the credit needs of the small and marginal farmers are met through earmarking credit for the group. Extension and marketing initiatives need to focus on this segment. At the same time, group initiatives need to be encouraged and awareness among the group has to be increased. The procedural formalities also have to be made less stringent to make the system more user-friendly for the largely illiterate group.

Given the distress among the farmers, it is important that a safety-net programme is introduced to ensure a minimum income for the farmers. Also the risk factor has to be mitigated through adequate insurance and credit facilities. At the same time, the outreach and efficiency of the institutional credit sources have to be improved. This is important to protect the small and marginal farmers who still heavily rely on private moneylenders who charge high interest rates and follow unscrupulous means to perpetuate indebtedness.

Endnotes

1. Reserve Bank of India, *Report on Currency and Finance,* 2001-2002, p. VI-18.
2. Government of India, *Economic Survey,* 2005-06, p. 63.

7

Regional Rural Banks (RRBs)

Regional rural banks (RRBs) were introduced and promoted by the Government of India with the noble objective of promoting savings habits and providing credit delivery mechanism to the rural India. The target groups were small and marginal farmers, agricultural labourers, artisans and small entrepreneurs for development of agriculture, trade, industry and other commercial activities in rural India. RRBs have wide reach in rural India and with their region-centric banking activities and closer relationship with the local authorities and population, they were expected to provide necessary banking infrastructure. They have been successful in mobilizing small savings in the rural sector.

RRBs form an important segment of the rural financial sector. They were conceived as institutions that combine the local feel and familiarity of the co-operatives with the business capabilities of commercial banks. This sector has an exclusive role in improving financial inclusion and catering to vital sectors like agriculture and allied economic activities. Public policy, therefore, aims at keeping this sector viable and strong through various forms of active intervention.

7.1 Nature and Objectives of RRBs

Agriculture and rural sectors play an important role in India's overall development strategy in terms of income and employment generation and poverty alleviation. Great significance has, therefore, been accorded to developing appropriate institutions and mechanisms for catering to the credit requirements of these sectors.

Despite the measures taken by the Government of India and the RBI—including nationalisation of 14 major commercial banks in 1969—a large proportion of the rural poor continued to be outside the banking fold. A Working Group (Chairman: M. Narasimham) was set up in 1975 to explore the possibilities of evolving an alternative rural credit agency to benefit the rural poor. The Group recommended formation of a new set of regionally-oriented rural banks which would combine the local feel and familiarity of rural problems characteristic of cooperatives and the professionalism and large resource base of commercial banks. RRBs were set up as a sequel to this recommendation.

RRBs have a special place in the multi-agency approach adopted to provide agricultural and rural credit in India. These banks were established under the Regional Rural Banks Act, 1976 "with a view to developing the rural economy by providing, for the purpose of development of agriculture, trade, commerce, industry and other productive activities in the rural areas, credit and other facilities, particularly to small and marginal farmers, agricultural labourers, artisans and small entrepreneurs, and for matters connected therewith and incidental thereto".

The capital of RRBs is contributed by the Union Government, concerned State Government and a sponsor bank in the ratio 50:15:35. RRBs have played a key role in rural institutional financing in terms of geographical coverage, clientele outreach, business volume and contribution to the development of the rural economy.

As in February 2014, the number of RRBs in the country stood at 57. The number of branches of RRBs increased to 17,856 as on March 31, 2013 from 16,909 as on March 31, 2012.

Besides the RRBs, commercial and co-operative banks have been catering to the credit requirements of the rural sector. While the commercial banks, with their focus on profitability had certain limitations in accelerating agricultural credit, the cooperative banks efforts were also hampered by several financial weaknesses. Though over the years the RRBs have been able to expand their outreach and business and meet the credit requirements of the poor, several weaknesses have emerged, eroding their profitability and viability. The recent focus of the Government of India on doubling the flow of credit to the agricultural sector has warranted a re-look at the relative roles of co-operative banks, RRBs and commercial banks.

As the very objective of setting up RRBs was to extend adequate credit to the rural borrowers and particularly the economically weaker sections, owing to their rural orientation, there is a growing realization that RRBs could be used as an effective vehicle for credit delivery in the rural areas. There is, therefore, a need to devise ways and means to improve the health and viability of RRBs so as to reposition them in the credit delivery mechanism in India.

7.2 Amalgamation of RRBs

RRBs have been in sharp focus over the last few years with several measures initiated towards strengthening them and making them vibrant channels of credit delivery, particularly for the rural sector. The most prominent of these has been the process of state-wise amalgamation of RRBs sponsored by the same sponsor bank. As a result of the process of amalgamation, initiated in 2005, the number of RRBs in the country declined from 196 to 96 at the end of March 2007 and further to 57 at the end of March 2014. The Gross NPAs of RRBs stood at ₹ 7,907 crore as on March 31, 2013.

The structural consolidation of RRBs has resulted in formation of new RRBs, which are financially stronger and bigger in size in terms of business volume and outreach. They will thus be able to take advantages of the economies of scale and reduce their operational costs. With the advantages of local feel and familiarity acquired by the RRBs, they would now be in a better position to achieve the objectives of rural development and financial inclusion.

7.3 Autonomy for RRBs

Further, measures have been taken to provide greater autonomy to RRBs and enlarge their business activities. A majority of the recommendations of the Task Force on Empowering RRB Boards for Operational Efficiency (Chairman: K.G. Karmakar) have already been implemented. RRBs have also been allowed to open currency chests, conduct State government business as sub-agents of sponsor banks, take up corporate agency business without risk participation for distribution of all types of insurance products and open foreign currency non-resident (FCNR) accounts, subject to certain conditions. The branch licensing procedure for RRBs has been simplified with powers now delegated to the Regional Offices of Reserve Bank of India. The branch licensing policy has also been liberalised and the norms for opening new branches in hitherto uncovered districts have been relaxed. As a result, there has been a rapid increase in the number of branches of RRBs. The spread of RRBs has also increased and at the end of March 2013, they covered 635 districts of the country.

7.4 RRBs as Vehicles of Financial Inclusion

RRBs have the potential to play a greater role in financial inclusion primarily because of their strategic geographical location in remote places in the country. In certain parts of the country, e.g. in the states of UP, Bihar and North Eastern regions, the banking system mainly exists in the form of RRBs. Recognising the importance of achieving inclusive growth in the country, the RBI has permitted banks to utilise the services of non-governmental organizations (NGOs), self-help groups (SHGs), micro finance institutions (other than non-banking financial companies) and other civil society organisations as intermediaries to provide financial and banking services through the use of business facilitator and business correspondent (BC) models. The BC model allows banks to do 'cash-in-cash-out' transactions at a location much closer to the rural population, thus addressing the last mile problem. However, customers in many parts of the country have to travel long distances, spend on transportation costs besides sacrificing their daily wages to visit the banks for doing their routine banking transactions and such inaccessibility contributes to the dormancy of many accounts in RRBs as well.

The objective of financial inclusion would be fully achieved if RRBs are able to bring banking to the door step of the customers just as the commercial banks have started taking such initiatives. It is here that the large scale usage of information and communication technology (ICT) solutions lends support. RRB presence in rural areas leveraged by ICT would considerably enhance their reach, and delivery of banking services to the remote corners of the country.

The Committee on Financial Inclusion (Chairman: C. Rangarajan), also emphasised the role of IT and banking correspondents on a larger scale for achieving financial inclusion. The Committee envisaged that RRBs may extend services to unbanked areas and increase their credit to deposit ratio. The need for setting target for microfinance and financial inclusion was also envisaged. The Committee also recommended 100 percent financial inclusion of the large number of hitherto excluded farm households in order to reduce their indebtedness to the unregulated/informal sector.

The Committee estimated that 51.4 percent of the farm households do not get any credit from formal or informal sources. The North Eastern Region, Eastern Region and Central Region taken together, account for 68 percent of the farm households having no access to credit.

The reach of RRBs particularly in regions and across population groups facing the brunt of financial exclusion is impressive. In rural areas, RRBs account for a substantial 37 percent of total offices of all scheduled commercial banks. In semi-urban areas, their share comes to 15 percent. With the process of merger strengthening, to some extent, the viability of the RRBs and also because of the local feel and familiarity they command, RRBs are in a unique position to play a very useful role in financial inclusion.

The RRBs need to be encouraged and supported in their financial inclusion initiatives for, *inter alia*, the following reasons:

1. Have presence in most of districts of the country.
2. Stronger presence in NER, ER and Central Regions.
3. Essential particularly for the areas where the financial exclusion rate is quite high.
4. Higher concentration of rural and semi-rural branches.
5. Have potential for intake of many more small accounts.
6. Though there are 56 RRBs with relatively reasonable performance, their net worth is not high and thus majority of RRBs are not financially very sound.

7.5 Factors Influencing the Performance of RRBs

Since their inception, the financial health of RRBs has been indifferent. A host of factors, both internal and external, have had a bearing on the performance of RRBs. Some of the major factors that had a bearing on the performance of RRBs are as follows.

7.5.1 Area of Operation and Clientele Base: The RRBs are constrained in their operations by their limited area of operation. This coupled with their narrow base of business activities and the low clientele base, has resulted in high risk exposure of RRBs. The customers of RRBs comprise small and marginal farmers, small-scale sector, small transport operators, SHGs, etc., whose credit requirements are mostly small. RRBs are unable to cross-subsidise their lending business as they do not generally provide credit to wealthy borrowers with large needs, thereby affecting their capacity to earn higher incomes.

There has been an uneven growth of RRBs due to the diffusion in the perceived objectives of RRBs over time. Despite the pressures of credit expansion, improvement in recovery performance, profit orientation and strict compliances to banking norms, the general perception has been that RRBs have got only social objectives, without any viability consideration, which has to be changed.

7.5.2 Capital Base and Organisational Structure: RRBs as a group have a low capital base, and their authorised capital of ₹ 1 crore places serious limitations on their business size. Furthermore, in the case of some of the RRBs their deposit liabilities are very large compared to their capital base. In view of their low capital base, in the event of inefficient use/misuse of funds resulting in a financial problem, the stakeholders would have to bail out the bank.

The size of financial assets, as well as linkages which are necessary for effective banking services has been limited by the small organizational structure of RRBs. This has also come in the way of growth in business volumes and garnering a larger share of the rural financial market.

7.5.3 Loan Delinquencies: RRBs loan recovery rates have declined over the years, resulting in a large over hang of NPAs which has come in their way of recycling funds and increasing the flow of credit to the rural sector. The directed lending policy for RRBs has resulted in low quality of assets. This coupled with high cost of funds and below cost interest rates on loans has led to high accumulated losses and piling up of bad assets in the case of many RRBs.

It is noteworthy that the target rural group has been one of the weaker and lowest strata of the Indian society. Smaller and marginal farmers and agricultural labourers always run short of money even for meeting their daily needs of life. Given the fact that most the villages in India still does not have clean drinking water and sanitation facilities, top it with lack of basic health facilities, makes them one of the most vulnerable groups in India. In any nature-made or man-made calamities, they are the most affected. Thus, credit facilities taken by the rural poor are mostly not utilized for specified productive objective for which it was made available. For instance, when an agricultural labourer takes a small loan from an RRB for the purpose of buying a cow and small portion of it only being utilized for the stated purpose, with the remaining amount used for household needs or for tending the sick. Such misappropriation seems very common and ultimately the labourer who took the loan would be unable to repay it. This naturally leads to substantial non-performing and lost assets in RRBs.

7.5.4 Cost Structure and Poor Financial Management Skills: RRBs are characterized by high cost of servicing numerous small accounts and high wage cost. Furthermore, RRBs get credit from sponsor banks and refinance from NABARD at rates of interest higher than the market rates. This places limitations on their ability to reduce the rates they charge to their ultimate borrowers, although they are compelled to do so on account of competition from banks.

Poor financial management skills, coupled with pressures from various quarters (like sponsor banks) appears to have resulted in inefficient allocation of resources by RRBs which in turn is reflected in the high incidence of NPAs and parking of large funds with sponsor banks.

7.5.5 Staff Structure: Limited exposure and lack of appropriate training, has resulted in RRBs staff lacking the necessary skills and capacity to cater to the changing requirements of the rural sector. Furthermore, the ban on recruitment has also resulted in ageing staff structure constraining efficiency in operations. Uniform norms and personnel policies have been applied to RRBs through out the country ignoring local touch thereby causing staff unrest, poor industrial relations, innumerable litigations and lowering of staff morale as also their involvement with the development tasks.

The chairmen of most of the RRBs are from sponsor banks, which limits the freedom and decision making capacity of the RRBs. Even for small matters RRBs have to refer to their sponsor banks, which leads to delay in decision-making and reduces efficiency. Furthermore, the board of directors of RRBs may not always function effectively as some of the members do not have necessary skills and expertise to take important financial decisions.

7.5.6 Dependence on Sponsor Banks: Another weakness observed in the case of RRBs is their failure to adequately integrate with the financial markets of the country due to their heavy dependence on sponsor banks for financial/ business initiatives. RRBs are also some times perceived as potential competitors, due to the presence of the sponsor banks in the same area of operation. Despite the best intentions at the policy levels in sponsor banks, the RRBs have suffered at the ground level wherever there has been any conflict of business interests of RRBs and their sponsor banks. RRBs have therefore, not been able to establish systems and procedures required for providing efficient services to their clients, as also for efficient management of their financial resources.

Besides the above, functioning of RRBs has also been affected by certain legacy problems and policy constraints. The administered interest rate regime prevalent in the system for a considerably long time influenced the performance of RRBs. These banks were required to lend at low interest rates as they were financing the weaker sections and at the same time allowed to pay a slightly higher rate of interest on deposits.

The RRBs were required to maintain their local character or flavour with a view to identifying more with the rural populace. This was initially embedded in the wage structure designed for these banks. However, thc change in the wage structure of RRBs by bringing them on par with the commercial banks led to higher wage costs, thereby affecting the performance of these banks.

7.6 Restructuring of RRBs

In order to reposition RRBs as an effective instrument of credit delivery in the Indian financial system, an Internal Working Group on RRBs (Chairman: A.V. Sardesai) was set up by the RBI in February 2005 to examine various alternatives available within the existing legal framework for strengthening the RRBs and making them viable rural financial institutions. The Group, in its final report submitted in June 2005, made several recommendations for restructuring the RRBs. The main recommendations of the Working Group related to restructuring options, change of sponsor banks, minimum capital requirements, governance and management, regulation and supervision.

The major recommendations of the Group were as follows:

1. To improve the operational viability of RRBs, the route of merger/amalgamation of RRBs may be considered along two lines: (a) merger between RRBs of the same sponsor bank in the same State, and (b) merger of RRBs sponsored by different banks in the same State.
2. A change in sponsor banks may, in some cases, help improve competitiveness, work culture and efficiency of concerned RRBs for which new banks, both public and private sector, could be considered.
3. Merged entities and existing RRBs that have accumulated losses can be capitalised to wipe out the losses and satisfy minimum capital requirement. The CRAR may initially be kept at 5 percent.
4. For those RRBs which may not turn around within a specified time limit, say 3 to 5 years, an exit route may be considered subject to extant legal provisions.

5. Process of appointment of Chairmen of RRBs may be re-examined to explore the possibility of appointing them from the open market through a transparent process.
6. Boards of RRBs may be strengthened by making them broad-based through inclusion of professionals such as agricultural experts, bankers etc.
7. An appropriate recruitment policy, providing for greater flexibility and freedom, may be required for RRBs.
8. An appropriate incentive structure, career planning, relevant training, especially in skill upgradation and information technology, be evolved for employees of RRBs.
9. It would be appropriate if both the regulatory and supervisory functions relating to RRBs are exercised by the RBI.
10. RRBs may be encouraged to actively consider distribution of products of mutual fund/insurance companies, rationalisation of branch network, participate in consortium lending within their areas of operations.
11. RRBs may be considered for currency chest facility and empowered to collect taxes by the State Governments.

7.7 Manpower Challenges of RRBs

Measures have also been taken to address the manpower challenges in the RRBs. It is known that RRBs do not have their own training establishments so far. The existing training facilities available for RRB staff are Bankers Institute for Rural Development, Lucknow, College of Agricultural Banking, Pune, regional training colleges of NABARD at Mangalore and Bolpur, and the sponsor bank training institutes. However, all these institutions (other than sponsor bank training institutes) provide training only to officers and not to clerical or subordinate staff.

The Committee to Formulate a Comprehensive Human Resource Policy for RRBs (Chairman: Y.S.P. Thorat), had, in its report recommended that RRBs should have an exclusive training cell within the Personnel Department at Head Office and bestow more attention to the training function. It also recommended that sponsor banks can consider earmarking in any one training institute in a state, at least one channel to cater to the training requirements of all RRBs within the state and/or the adjoining states.

7.8 Computerisation in RRBs

The need for computerisation in RRBs had been felt since long and some RRBs had been taking some steps in that direction. In July 2001, Government of India and NABARD advised the RRBs to initiate immediate steps so that head office, area office and a minimum of 50 percent of the branches were computerised in a phased manner in the next 5 years. Sponsor banks were also advised to formulate RRB-wise Action Plans, keeping in view the financial position of RRBs, infrastructure facilities available in their command area and the business potential of the RRB branches. Necessary support to implement the programme was also required to come from the sponsor bank.

NABARD made a beginning by extending support to select RRBs by providing PCs, peripherals, standard software packages as also customised MIS package and training inputs under its Swiss Agency for Development and Cooperation (SDC) programme. A review made by NABARD in respect of 152 RRBs in 2005 indicated that only 9 banks had reported achieving 100 percent computerisation. Most of the RRBs were lagging behind the target of computerising 50 percent of their branches.

The Task Force on Empowering RRBs for Operational Efficiency (Chairman: K.G. Karmakar) had made the following observations regarding the computerisation scenario in RRBs:

1. Level of computerisation is far behind schedule.
2. Even RRBs of same sponsor banks although following the same technology, are at different levels of computerisation due to varied financial health, environment, local conditions which has become a problem when such RRBs have been amalgamated.
3. Computerisation needs both capital and recurring expenses which are beyond the capability of some of the banks.
4. RRBs, which have progressed well, have adopted a particular technology mainly of the sponsor bank and invested sizeable amounts.
5. A few RRBs reaped the benefit of hosting their own website by way of mobilisation of deposits from non traditional segments.
6. A few of them established direct links with money market operators for investments.
7. Internet facilities have been used for faster communication with techno savvy customers and other agencies.

These observations highlighted the varying status of RRBs with regard to computerisation.

The status of computerisation at the end of March 2007 as reported by 76 of the 96 RRBs to the Committee to Formulate a Comprehensive Human Resource Policy for RRBs (Chairman: Y.S.P. Thorat) indicated that 35 of the reporting banks had achieved 100 per cent computerisation while 25 banks had achieved 50 to 100 per cent computerisation.

7.8.1 Working Group on Technology Upgradation of Regional Rural Banks, August 2008: In RBI's Mid-term Review of Annual Policy for 2007-08, it was stated that in order to prepare RRBs to adopt appropriate technology and migrate to core banking solutions (CBS) [1] for better customer services, it was proposed to constitute a Working Group with representatives from RBI, NABARD, sponsor banks and RRBs for preparing a road-map for migration to core banking solutions by RRBs.

Accordingly, a Working Group (Chairman: G. Srinivasan) was set up with the following terms of reference:

1. To determine the nature of core banking solutions required for RRBs having regard to the range of their business and customer service;
2. To examine various options including extending core banking solutions of the sponsor banks to their RRBs with necessary modifications and firewalls;
3. To estimate the likely costs involved and funding and training arrangements that may be necessary; and
4. To draw out a time-bound road map for implementation.

The Working Group was also requested to examine the possibility of using solar power generating devices for meeting the power requirements of RRBs, especially in remote areas.

The Working Group was of the opinion that RRBs cannot afford to remain isolated from the technological developments sweeping the banking sector. With the commercial banks racing towards a higher degree of technological sophistication, the RRBs would be required to adopt technology for improving the quality of their customer service. However, given the different levels at which the different RRBs are presently placed in regard to their status of computerisation, a "one strategy fits all" approach may not be workable.

The Working Group was of the view that as a matter of policy, all RRBs should begin moving towards CBS. The CBS in RRBs should be geared towards better management control and monitoring, wider range of services offered and enhanced level of customer satisfaction. Adoption of CBS would lead to uniformity in work environment, more informed decision-making, centralised processing and better MIS and reporting and improved regulatory compliance.

The Working Group also examined the use of solar power devices such as solar photovoltaic cells [2] for RRBs, particularly in respect of branches located in remote areas which are not assured of continuous power supply. In this context, the experience of one of the RRBs in Uttar Pradesh, which has made a beginning in this direction, was also studied.

Funding the cost of moving towards CBS is an important issue for RRBs, particularly as several RRBs continue to incur operating losses. Further, many RRBs still continue to have accumulated losses and even negative net worth. Despite this position, there are RRBs which are healthy and making sustained profits. The Working Group considered this aspect and was of the view that funding support may be provided to all RRBs in the matter of adopting CBS, irrespective of their financial position. This would enable the entire sector to move uniformly towards adopting CBSs.

A summary of the recommendations of the Working Group is given below.

1. The significant differences in the level of computerisation between different RRBs need to be taken into account while preparing any plan for further technology upgradation of RRBs.
2. As a matter of policy, all RRBs should begin moving towards CBS. The CBS in RRBs should be geared towards better management control and monitoring, wider range of services offered and enhanced level of customer satisfaction. Adoption of CBS would lead to uniformity in work environment, more informed decision making, centralised processing and better MIS and reporting and improved regulatory compliance.
3. The respective sponsor banks may be given the option of selecting the service provider for their RRBs. This provider may be same as for the sponsor bank or different as per the requirement of the RRBs. In case a sponsor bank has developed its own software, it may consider making the same available to its RRBs.
4. Any technology platform for CBS needs to be reliable, scalable, easily available, manageable and secure. For this, the background, credentials and experience of the vendor are extremely important. It would therefore be prudent to rely on the trusted and established vendors to provide services to RRBs.
5. Sponsor banks must own major responsibility in taking RRBs on the path to CBS. However, the requirements of the RRBs have to be borne in mind as these banks may not require the full suite of services that are available in sponsor banks and hence a plain vanilla tailored to their needs should be provided.
6. RRB branches in remote areas where power is a serious problem may take recourse to powering their branches through solar power in a CBS scenario.
7. Funding support may be provided to all RRBs in the matter of adopting CBS, irrespective of their financial position. This would enable the entire sector to move uniformly towards adopting CBS.
8. While sponsor banks may contribute 25 percent of the cost required for taking their RRBs to CBS, the remaining cost may be borne by Reserve Bank through Institute for Development and Research in Banking Technology (IDRBT). The IDRBT, in turn would provide necessary funds to the sponsor banks for their sponsored RRBs. The support could be in the form of interest free loans, repayable in three years.

9. The training requirements of staff of RRBs on account of moving towards CBS would have to be met by sponsor banks through their training establishments. The sponsor banks should also meet the costs incurred in this regard.
10. The roll-out of the road map for implementation of CBS in RRBs should start at the earliest. RRBs in which 100 per cent branches are computerised, should implement CBS in all their branches by September 2009.
11. The remaining RRBs may also start the process of moving their branches to CBS at the earliest. Such RRBs should implement CBS in at least 25 percent of their branches by September 2009 and at least 50 percent of their branches by September 2010. The remaining branches may be endeavoured to be covered by September 2011. By that date, at least 90 percent of the business of the banks should be on CBS.
12. The responsibility of ensuring that the time frame suggested is adhered to would be that of the sponsor bank.
13. All new branches opened after September 2009 may be made CBS compliant from day 1.

To sum up, in spite of the various measures taken by the Government and the RBI through social control and the nationalisation of major commercial banks in 1969, a large proportion of the rural poor remained outside the banking fold. Therefore, the Government of India promoted regional rural banks (RRBs) through the RRBs Act of 1976 to bridge the gap in the flow of credit to the rural poor. The RRBs have a special place in the multi-agency approach adopted to provide agricultural and rural credit in India. These banks are state-sponsored, regionally based and rural-oriented.

Setting up of RRBs in the mid-1970s was a major initiative to meet credit requirements of rural people. The RRBs are specialized rural financial institutions for developing the rural economy by providing credit to small and marginal farmers, agricultural labourers, artisans and small entrepreneurs. During the 45 years of existence of RRBs, several Working Groups and Committees were set up at various points of time to deliberate on issues relating to RRBs and suggest measures to address the same. The focus has varied over time depending on the immediate concerns and the prevailing policy regime. While some of the issues relating to RRBs have lost their significance over time, others have become more relevant.

RBI has been initiating several measures from time to time for facilitating better access to financial services and credit for the rural population. The regional rural banks (RRBs), since their inception, have played a vital role in taking banking to the rural masses, making available credit to weaker sections of society, mobilising and channelising rural savings towards productive activities and in generating employment opportunities in rural areas. During the last few years, RRBs have been provided greater flexibility in operations. Branch licensing norms have been made liberal and powers are delegated to the Regional Offices of the Reserve Bank. Further, the process of mergers of all RRBs of the same sponsor bank in the same State has been effected and the RRBs with negative net-worth are in the process of being re-capitalised.

RRBs, with their wide outreach in rural India, region-centric banking activities and close relationship with the local authorities and population, were expected to cater to the credit requirements of the rural areas and provide necessary banking infrastructure. Though the RRBs have been able to mobilize small savings of the rural sector, they have been relatively less successful in enhancing the flow of credit to the targeted rural poor.

With their increasing strength and spread, RRBs would have to enlarge their client base and become the principal vehicles for financial inclusion and rural banking in the country. However, technological changes are sweeping the banking sector. In order to survive effectively in the present scenario, the RRBs would require to be adequately equipped in terms of technology to provide efficient customer service to their clientele. While the commercial banks have gone ahead in computerisation of their operations and most banks are in an advanced stage of implementing total core banking solutions (CBS), the RRBs are lagging behind in this area.

The expectations of the Central and the State Governments from the RRBs are also increasing. It is envisaged that RRBs are able to render the same quality of service that commercial banks are able to give to their clients. Further, the Government, in order to reduce intermediation and reach out directly to the beneficiaries under several of its programmes, proposes to reach these persons through the electronic mechanisms. It is thus becoming imperative for RRBs to become increasingly technologically sound so as to offer competitive services to their clients.

The renewed emphasis on agricultural and rural development by the Government of India would lead to a growing demand for different types of financial services in the rural areas, as financial needs of the rural economy becomes diversified. The present structure of rural credit may not be able to cater to the same. RRBs would be called upon to play a greater role in providing such services due to their rural character and feel. RRBs have to take over a larger share of credit disbursements calling for much larger resource mobilization, as also greater efforts for their institutional strengthening.

Endnotes

1. Although there is no formal definition of CBSs, the term has been in use during the last few years. The advancement in technology, especially internet and information technology, has led to a new way of doing business in banking. The technologies have cut down time, working simultaneously on different issues and increased efficiency. The platform where information and communication technology are merged to suit core needs of banking may be referred to as CBS. In CBS, computer software performs the core operations of banking like handling and recording of transactions, maintenance of passbooks, interest calculations on deposits and loans, maintaining customer records and generating reports and statements. The software is installed at bank branches and then interconnected by means of communication lines telephone, internet and satellite communication. It allows customers to transact with the bank from any branch if it has installed CBS. This new platform has changed the way of working of banks.

   In an ideal CBS scenario, all products, processes, channels and customer relationship management tools are integrated and administered via a central database of the bank with branches and channels as delivery points. This enables data integration for various purposes including regulatory reporting and internal MIS all at considerably lower cost. The new generation private sector banks were the first to adopt CBS technologies in India followed by a few public sector banks. Gradually, the same were adopted by most of the commercial banks as part of their computerisation processes.

   As per the Report on Trend and Progress of Banking in India, 2006-07, the process of computerisation in commercial banks was now reaching near completion for most of the banks. Public sector banks continued to expend large amounts on computerization and development of communication networks.
2. Solar photovoltaic cells convert the sun's energy into DC electricity using silicon cells called solar cells. When sunlight falls on the solar cells, a DC voltage is generated across the cell. The solar cell is connected to a battery through a charge controller and electrical energy is stored in the battery. From the energy stored in the battery, either a DC load or an AC load through inverter is operated.

8

Urban Co-operative Banks (UCBs)

Co-operative banks in India are more than 100 years old. These banks came into existence with the enactment of the Agricultural Credit Co-operative Societies Act in 1904. Co-operative banks form an integral part of the banking system in India. These banks operate mainly for the benefit of rural areas, particularly the agricultural sector. Co-operative banks mobilise deposits and supply agricultural and rural credit with a wider outreach. They are the main source of institutional credit to the farmers. Co-operative banks are chiefly responsible for breaking the monopoly of moneylenders in providing credit to agriculturists. They have also been an important instrument for various development schemes, particularly subsidy-based programmes for the poor. Co-operative banks operate for non-agricultural sector also but their role is small.

8.1 Importance of UCBs

The co-operative banking system forms an integral part of the Indian financial system. It comprises urban cooperative banks and rural co-operative credit institutions. Urban co-operative banks (UCBs) have a single-tier structure whereas rural co-operatives have a two- or three-tier structure. As on March 31, 2014, there were 1,538 non-scheduled UCBs in India.

The single tier urban co-operative banks (UCBs)—also referred to as primary cooperative banks—play an important role in meeting the growing credit needs of urban and semi-urban areas of the country. The UCBs, which grew rapidly in the early 1990s, showed certain weaknesses arising out of lack of sound corporate governance, unethical lending, comparatively high levels of non-performing loans and their inability to operate in a liberalised environment. Accordingly, some of the weak UCBs have been either liquidated or merged with other banks.

Though much smaller as compared to scheduled commercial banks, co-operative banks constitute an important segment of the Indian banking system. They have an extensive branch network and reach out to people in remote areas. They have traditionally played an important role in creating banking habits among the lower and middle-income groups and in strengthening the rural credit delivery system.

Urban co-operative banks play an important role in meeting the growing credit needs of urban and semi-urban areas. UCBs mobilise savings from the middle and lower income groups and purvey credit to small borrowers, including weaker sections of the society. Scheduled UCBs are under closer regulatory and supervisory framework of the RBI.

Unfortunately, financial reforms have not impacted the functioning of co-operative banks. This was brought out clearly in the following observation of the Reserve Bank of India, "Since the introduction of reforms, there has been very little perceptible improvement in either stability or efficiency of co-operative banks. In particular, the asset quality and profitability of scheduled urban co-operative banks (UCBs) showed some deterioration in the reform period. Positive impact of reforms, as has been witnessed in the case of commercial banking sector, may take longer to get manifested for co-operative banks given the late start of the reform process in this sector". [1]

The financial reforms process initiated in 1991 has tried to achieve regulatory convergence among various financial intermediaries in view of their systemic importance. Therefore, the basic objectives and instruments of reforms for co-operative banks have been the same as for state co-operative banks (SCBs). However, given the special characteristics of co-operative banks, they have been extended certain dispensations in terms of pace and sequencing of reforms.

UCBs have grown rapidly since the early 1990s. During the phase of rapid expansion, however, the sector showed certain weaknesses arising out of: (a) lack of sound corporate governance, (b) unethical lending, (c) comparatively high level of loan defaults, and (d) inability to operate in a liberalised and competitive environment. The RBI, therefore, has been striving to harness the growth of UCBs with appropriate application of prudential regulation and supervision to safeguard the interests of depositors.

Keeping in view the weak financial position of many UCBs, the RBI has undertaken a series of measures directed towards strengthening of the UCBs. Since March 31, 1993, the UCBs have been advised to adhere to the prudential norms which include, *inter alia*, the following.

1. Applying capital adequacy standards.
2. Prescribing an asset-liability management framework.
3. Enhancing the proportion of holding of Government and other approved securities for the purpose of statutory liquidity ratio (SLR) stipulation.
4. Restriction on bank finance against the security of corporate shares and debentures.
5. Limiting the exposure to capital market investment.

In view of the challenges arising from the functioning of the UCBs for the financial system, the RBI appointed a High Power Committee (Chairman: K. Madhava Rao), 1999 to review the performance of UCBs and to suggest necessary measures to strengthen this sector. Based on the recommendations of this Committee, measures have been initiated to strengthen the existing urban banking structure.

8.2 Vision Document and Medium-Term Framework (MTF) for UCBs

Various entities in the urban co-operative banking sector display a high degree of heterogeneity in terms of deposits/asset base, areas of operation and nature of business. In view of its importance, it is imperative that the sector emerges as a sound and healthy network of jointly owned, democratically controlled and professionally managed institutions. In order to achieve these objectives, the RBI has taken a series of policy initiatives in recent years. The most significant initiative in this regard was the Vision Document and Medium-Term Framework (MTF) for UCBs. With a view to protecting depositors' interests on the one hand, and enabling UCBs to provide useful service to local communities on the other, the medium-term framework (MTF) seeks to achieve the following objectives.

1. To rationalise the existing regulatory and supervisory approach keeping in view the heterogeneous character of the entities in the sector.
2. To facilitate a focused and continuous system of supervision through enhancement of technology.
3. To enhance professionalism and improve the quality of governance in UCBs by providing training for skill upgradation and also by including large depositors in the decision making process/management of banks.
4. To put in place a mechanism that addresses the problems of dual control, given the present legal framework and the time-consuming process in bringing requisite legislative changes.
5. To put in place a consultative arrangement for identifying weak but potentially viable entities in the sector and provide a framework for nursing them back to health including, if necessary, through a process of consolidation.
6. To identify the unviable entities in the sector and provide an exit route for such entities.

The above framework is implemented through the following measures:

1. A differentiated regulatory regime as opposed to a *one-size-fits-all* approach.
2. A two-tier regulatory regime: (a) simplified regulatory regime for unit banks and single district banks with deposits less than ₹ 100 crore, and (b) regulation for all other banks on the lines of commercial banks.
3. As the strategy to deal with UCBs may need to be State-specific, a State Level Task Force for Urban Co-operative Banks (TAFCUB) is to be constituted comprising senior officials from the RBI, State Governments and

local/central co-operative Federations.

4. TAFCUB would be responsible for: (i) identifying weak but viable UCBs and devise a time-bound programme for revival; and (ii) recommending: (a) the nature and extent of financial support, (b) future set up of unlicensed banks, and (c) the manner and timeframe for exit of unviable banks.
5. To address issues/difficulties relating to dual control within the existing legal framework, it has been proposed to evolve a working arrangement in the form of memorandum of understanding (MoU) between the RBI and the State Government.

8.3 Regulation and Supervision of UCBs: Strengthening Measures

The regulation and supervision of the urban co-operative banks (UCBs) was brought within the ambit of the RBI's statutory control under the Banking Laws (as Applicable to Cooperative Societies) Act, which came into force from March 1, 1966. The regulatory powers conferred on the RBI with regard to co-operative banks are limited. While the principles of supervision with regard to co-operative banks have been formulated and implemented by the RBI in respect of UCBs under the Banking Regulation Act, 1949, the Act does not apply to primary agricultural credit societies and land development banks, thus leaving them under the regulatory purview of the State.

Instances such as the Madhavapura Mercantile Co-operative Bank's failure brought to the fore the need to have stringent regulatory control over the co-operative banking system. In order to strengthen the supervisory mechanism, the RBI extended the off-site surveillance system (OSS) to all non-scheduled UCBs having deposit size of ₹ 100 crore and above. A supervisory reporting system was introduced for the scheduled UCBs from March 2001 as a first step towards setting up of OSS for all UCBs. The capital adequacy norms were introduced in a phased manner from March 2002. Better risk management through avoidance of concentration of credit risk, off-site surveillance for non-scheduled UCBs and following up of know your customer (KYC) guidelines have also been introduced to strengthen the UCBs.

A total ban has been imposed since October 2003 on grant of loans and advances to directors of UCBs, their relatives and concerns in which they have interest with a view to preventing certain irregularities. The RBI has also directed that UCBs should undertake usual due diligence in respect of investments in non-SLR securities. The RBI introduced a new system of grading of UCBs in April 2003, which is based on their CRAR, level of net NPAs, record of losses and compliance with regulatory environment. Similarly, a system of supervisory rating for UCBs under the CAMELS model has also been introduced. Initially, it was implemented for scheduled UCBs but subsequently its simplified version was extended to non-scheduled UCBs in March 2004.

Despite the structural and cultural differences between UCBs and commercial banks, the above measures suggest that the RBI has been exercising its regulatory and supervisory powers to ensure that the co-operative credit structure is strengthened on the lines similar to the regulation and supervision of commercial banks.

The RBI is entrusted with the responsibility of regulation and supervision of the banking-related activities of UCBs under the Banking Regulation Act, 1949 As Applicable to Co-operative Societies (AACS). Other aspects such as incorporation, registration, administration, management and winding-up of UCBs are supervised and regulated by the respective State Governments through Registrars of Co-operative Societies (RCS) under the Co-operative Societies Acts of the respective States. UCBs with a multi-state presence are registered under the Multi-State Co-operative Societies Act, 2002 and are regulated and supervised jointly by the Central Government through Central Registrar of Co-operative Societies and the RBI.

Thus, current legislative framework provides for dual control over UCBs. For resolving problems arising out of dual control regime, a draft legislative bill proposing certain amendments to the Banking Regulation Act, 1949 (AACS), based on the recommendations of the High Powered Committee on UCBs, was forwarded to the Government. Pending the amendment to the Act, the RBI is entering into a regulatory arrangement with the State Governments through memorandum of understanding (MoU) to facilitate proper and coordinated regulation and supervision of UCBs. MoUs have already been signed between the RBI and three States that have a large network of UCBs, viz. Andhra Pradesh, Gujarat and Karnataka. As a follow-up to the signing of MoUs, the RBI constituted State Level Task Force for Urban Co-operative Banks (TAFCUBs) in these States.

8.3.1 Memorandum of Understanding (MoU) with the State Governments: The MoUs contain the following commitments by the State Government and the RBI.

The State Governments, through the MoU, agree to:

- Introduce long form audit report for statutory audit and modify their audit rating models to bring them in alignment with the gradation system adopted by the RBI for UCBs.
- Provide for statutory audit by chartered accountants (CAs) for UCBs with deposits over ₹ 25 crore and special audit by CAs, if required by the RBI, for any UCB.
- Put in place *fit and proper* criteria for chief executive officers (CEOs), based

on guidelines of the RBI.

The RBI, as a signatory to the MoU, is committed to:

- Constitute a State Level TAFCUB, comprising regional director of the RBI, Registrar of Co-operative Societies (RCS) of the State, a representative of central office of Urban Banks Department of the RBI, a representative of the State Government and a representative each from the State and National Federation of UCBs. TAFCUBs would identify and draw up time bound action plans for the revival of potentially viable UCBs and recommend non-disruptive exit for non-viable ones.
- Facilitate human resources development and IT initiatives in UCBs.

MoUs signed between the RBI and the respective State Governments also envisage the signing of another MoU between the Registrars of Co-operative Societies of the States and respective Regional Directors of the RBI. This MoU stipulates the broad measures to be taken by the signatories for implementing the recommendations of the TAFCUB for each of the potentially viable/non-viable UCBs that are placed for consideration of TAFCUB.

The MoU, *inter alia,* also provides that the RBI would consult RCS before cancelling or refusing licence under the Banking Regulation Act, 1949, of a UCB covered by the MoU, i.e. in States with which MoUs have been signed. The RCS would comply without delay any requisition by the RBI for supersession of the Board or for winding up of any UCB.

8.3.2 Licensing of New Banks/Branches: Consequent upon the easing of licensing norms in May 1993, more than 800 licences were issued for setting up urban cooperative banks. However, close to one-third of these newly licensed UCBs became financially weak within a short period. There was, thus, a need to moderate the pace of growth of this sector, particularly given the vexatious issue of dual control over UCBs. The RBI proposed certain amendments to the Banking Regulation Act, 1949 (AACS) to overcome the difficulties arising out of dual control. Pending enactment of these amendments, it was announced in the Annual Policy Statement for 2004-05 that issuance of fresh licences would be considered only after a comprehensive policy on UCBs, including an appropriate legal and regulatory framework for the sector, is put in place and a policy for improving the financial health of the urban cooperative banking sector is formulated. Accordingly, at present, applications for banking licence, including licence for opening of new branches, are not considered.

8.3.3 Income Recognition, Asset Classification and Provisioning Norms: In line with the international best practice and extant practices in commercial banks in India, the RBI decided to reduce the time period for reckoning an advance as non-performing from the existing 180 days to 90 days with effect from March 31, 2004. However, subsequently keeping in view the representations received from co-operative federations/banks, small loans up to ₹ 1 lakh were exempted from the purview of the 90 days norm and continued to be governed by 180 days norm. This exemption was granted only up to March 31, 2006. It was also decided to grant additional time of two years, in comparison with commercial banks, to meet the 100 percent provisioning required for advances identified as doubtful for more than three years.

Further, taking into consideration representations received from UCBs, it was decided to permit certain categories of UCBs to classify loan accounts as NPAs based on 180 days delinquency norm instead of 90 days norm. These included unit banks, i.e. banks having a single branch/HO and banks having multiple branches within a single district with deposits up to ₹ 100 crore. The relaxation was given up to the financial year ending March 2007 and banks were advised to build up adequate provisions to comply with the 90 days delinquency norm after the stipulated date.

The RBI also decided to delink the asset classification and provisioning requirements in respect of State Government guaranteed advances and investments from the invocation of the State Government guarantee. Accordingly, asset classification and provisioning norms on State Government guaranteed advances were made applicable in the same manner as exposures not guaranteed by the State Governments from the year ending March 31, 2006.

8.3.4 Exposure Norms: With a view to avoiding concentration of credit risk, UCBs were advised to fix the prudential exposure limits at 15 percent and 40 percent of the *capital funds* in the case of a single borrower and a group of borrowers, respectively. Banks were also advised that *capital funds* for the purpose of prudential exposure norms would be in relation to bank's total capital funds and the exposure for the purpose includes both credit and investment exposure (non-SLR).

8.3.5 Off-site Surveillance: The on-site financial inspection carried out by the RBI continues to be one of the main instruments of supervision over UCBs. The off-site surveillance system (OSS) for supervision was made applicable to all scheduled UCBs from March 2001. The returns for OSS were reviewed by the RBI and a revised set of 8 returns was prescribed from March 2004. The OSS returns of UCBs are designed to monitor compliance and obtain information from them on areas of prudential regulation. The main objective of the OSS returns is to obtain relevant information on areas of prudential interest, address the management information needs, strengthen the management information system (MIS) capabilities within the reporting institutions and to sensitise bank managements about concerns of the supervisory authority.

Compliance monitored through these returns covers assets and liabilities, earnings, asset quality, sector/segment-wise analysis of advances, concentration of exposures, connected or related lending and capital adequacy. These concerns earlier were being addressed through periodical on-site inspections of banks undertaken at intervals ranging from one to two years. The OSS system was extended to non-scheduled banks with deposit base of over ₹ 100 crore from June 2004.

8.3.6 Know Your Customer (KYC) Guidelines: Know your customer (KYC) guidelines were issued to UCBs by the RBI in the context of the recommendations made by the Financial Action Task Force (FATF) on anti-money laundering (AML) standards and combating financing of terrorism (CFT). UCBs were advised to ensure that a proper policy framework on KYC and also AML measures is formulated and put in place with the approval of their Boards. UCBs were also advised to ensure full compliance with the provisions of these guidelines before December 31, 2005.

8.3.7 Priority Sector Lending: UCBs are required to lend 60 percent of their total loans and advances to the priority sector of which 25 percent should go towards weaker sections. Housing loans come under the priority sector. In order to improve flow of credit to the housing sector, it was decided that UCBs with the approval of their Boards may extend direct finance to the housing sector up to ₹ 15 lakh per beneficiary of a dwelling unit, irrespective of location, against the earlier limit of ₹ 10 lakh, as part of their priority sector lending.

8.3.8 Disclosure Norms: In consonance with the best practices and in the interest of the members and depositors, it was decided that disclosure of the details of the levy of penalty on a bank would be put in public domain through a press release by the RBI. The UCBs were also advised that the penalty should be disclosed in the *Notes on Accounts* to their balance sheets in their next annual reports.

With a view to indicating the exact status of co-operative banks as also to avoid confusion among members of public, all UCBs were advised to display their full name on stationery item, publicity material and name board in the form in which it appears in the certificate of registration issued by the Registrar of Co-operative Societies and the licence granted by the RBI.

8.4 Mergers/Amalgamations of UCBs

With a view to encouraging and facilitating consolidation and emergence of strong entities and as well as for providing an avenue for non-disruptive exit of weak/unviable entities in the co-operative banking sector, guidelines were issued to facilitate merger/amalgamation in the sector. The RBI, while considering proposals for merger/amalgamation, confines its approval to the financial aspects of the merger taking into consideration the interests of depositors and financial stability. The RBI considers proposals subject to the post-merger entity meeting the prescribed following prudential norms.

1. When the net worth of the acquired bank is positive and the acquirer bank assures to protect entire deposits of all the depositors of the acquired bank.
2. When the net worth of acquired bank is negative but the acquirer bank, on its own, assures to protect deposits of all the depositors of the acquired bank.
3. When the net worth of the acquired bank is negative and the acquirer bank assures to protect the deposits of all the depositors with financial support from the State Government extended upfront as part of the process of merger.

8.5 Relaxation of Investment Portfolios of UCBs

UCBs were given some relaxation in the prudential norms for their investment portfolio in September 2004. They were allowed to exceed the limit of 25 percent of total investment under held till maturity (HTM) category provided: (a) the excess comprises only SLR securities, and (b) total SLR securities held in HTM category are not more than 25 percent of their net demand and time liabilities (NDTL) as on the last Friday of the second preceding fortnight.

Taking into account the difficulties faced by UCBs in meeting the provisioning requirements, it was further decided, as a special case, to consider relaxing the provisioning requirements both for scheduled UCBs and non-scheduled UCBs. Accordingly, scheduled UCBs were advised that they may crystallise the provisioning requirement arising on account of shifting of securities from HFT/AFS categories to HTM category consequent to the issue of guidelines dated September 2, 2004 and amortise the same over a maximum period of five years commencing from the accounting year ended March 31, 2005, with a minimum of 20 percent of such amount each year.

As regards non-scheduled UCBs, they were allowed to shift securities from HFT/AFS categories to HTM category at book value, subject to the following conditions. First, in case the book value is higher than the face value, the difference between the book value and the face value, i.e. the premium may be amortised in equal instalment over the remaining period to maturity. If the security was obtained at a discount to face value, the difference should be booked as profit only at the time of maturity of the security. Second, the securities transferred under this special dispensation should be kept separately under HTM category and should not be transferred back to the HFT/AFS category in future in terms of the existing instruction of transfer of securities from HTM category.

Third, in normal course, such securities under HTM category should not be sold in the market and redeemed on maturity only. However, in exceptional circumstances, if such securities are to be sold, profit on sale of investments in this category should be first taken to the *profit and loss account* and thereafter be appropriated to the *capital reserve*. Loss on sale will be recognised in the *profit and loss account* in the year of sale.

8.6 Restructuring of Scheduled UCBs with Negative Net Worth

A policy regarding restructuring of scheduled UCBs with negative net worth has also been formulated by the RBI. The RBI has begun a consultative process with a few scheduled UCBs with negative net worth by involving officials of the concerned State Governments and banks with a view to revitalising and rehabilitating them. The emphasis is on a time-bound programme by identifying the contours of their rehabilitation plan and setting up monitorable milestones. The RBI will be closely monitoring the achievements of the banks *vis-à-vis* the targets set at regular intervals and initiate appropriate action with a view to protecting depositors' interest and avoiding systemic problems.

Issues relating to large depositors, part conversion of deposits into equity, reduction of non-performing assets, human resources and technological development and the support from the State Governments would be examined. The option of merger/amalgamation could also be explored, wherever necessary. The RBI would limit its examinations and approvals to the banking and regulatory issues to satisfy itself that the restructuring package is in the interests of the depositors and the public at large. The RBI would also take into account various other parameters such as infusion of funds, sacrifice by stake holders, restructuring of liabilities, recovery of NPAs, regulatory support and forbearance, governance, business plan, and filing of applications and documents.

8.7 Problem of Dual Control in Co-operative Banking

The single most important regulatory and supervisory weakness that persists in the co-operative banking sector is the prevalence of dual control. While incorporation/registration and management-related activities are regulated in the states by the Registrar of Co-operative Societies or the Central Registrar of Co-operative Societies (for multi-state co-operative banks), banking-related activities are under the regulatory/supervisory purview of the Reserve Bank of India (RBI) or NABARD. The basic issue is that co-operation is a state subject under the Indian Constitution and as such co-operatives as a form of organisation are governed by the State Co-operative Societies Act, irrespective of whether they are banks or other forms of co-operative entities.

This duality of control and the absence of a clear demarcation of functions between the regulators have engaged the attention of a number of committees in the past. While in the case of commercial banks the RBI has the powers under the Banking Regulation Act, 1949 to deal with crucial aspects of functioning such as supersession of the board of directors, appointment of liquidators, initiating action for removal of the CEO/Chairman of a bank, instituting special audits, and conducting statutory audit through external chartered accountants. In the case of co-operative banks, these powers are subordinated in a way by the requirement that all such actions would require the intervention/approval of the Registrar of Cooperative Societies of the respective State Governments or the Central Registrar of Co-operative Societies, as the case may be.

This duality of control affects the quality of supervision and regulation, and it also affects the functioning of co-operative banks. The regulatory weaknesses foster inefficiency and impede the development of governance principles. Moreover, it burdens the banks with multiple levels of compliance and reporting requirements.

8.7.1 Impairment in Governance and Management: A unique feature of the co-operative banking system in India is that borrowers have a significant say in the management of the bank. This follows from the fact that only borrowers of the co-operative bank are eligible to be its members, contributing to share capital. As the Board Members of the bank are elected by borrowers, it results in the policies of the bank not always being in congruence with the interests of depositors. In view of the propensity of these banks to pursue borrower-oriented policies rather than policies that should be in favour of protecting interest of depositors, it has often been suggested that the involvement of depositors in the management of these banks should be enhanced by encouraging membership of depositors on par with borrowers.

Another reason for impairment of governance in the co-operative banking structure is attributed to interference in matters related to appointment of directors on the basis of political affiliations rather than on merit. This manifests itself in lack of professional expertise at the board level and interference in decision-making, particularly in respect of loan sanctions. This impairs the financial health of co-operative banks.

8.8 IT Support for Urban Co-operative Banks

In today's financial systems, usage of information technology is fundamental to the survival and growth of the institutions. Current regulatory and supervisory compliance demands that the institutions have a very sound usage of IT systems for their operations.

The Vision Document for Urban Cooperative Banks (UCBs), released in March 2005, proposed signing of memorandum of understanding (MoU) between RBI and Central and respective State governments for establishing a consultative approach to supervision and regulation of UCBs. The Reserve Bank has so far signed such MoUs with 16 State Governments and the Central Government.

In terms of the MoUs, the RBI is committed to facilitate IT initiatives in UCBs. In furtherance of the commitment made under the MoUs, Governor announced in the Mid-term Review of the Annual Policy 2007-08, that 'a working group comprising representatives of the Reserve Bank, State Governments and the UCBs sector' would be constituted 'to examine the various areas where IT support could be provided by the Reserve Bank'. Accordingly, the RBI constituted a Working Group on IT Support for Urban Cooperative Banks (Chairman: R. Gandhi) on December 19, 2007 with the following terms of reference:

1. To review the current level and use of IT infrastructure in UCBs.
2. To structure a model/benchmark level of IT infrastructure for UCBs in general or for identified sub-groups of UCBs.
3. To prepare a roadmap of building such an infrastructure by the UCBs.
4. To identify areas and ways in which IT support may be provided by the RBI.
5. To make recommendations on the nature, scope and delivery mechanism for IT support to UCBs by the RBI.

8.8.1 Findings of the Working Group: There exists a wide disparity with regard to the usage of information technology by the urban co-operative banks. As on March 31, 2007, 16 out of 1853 banks had implemented core banking solutions, while about 50 banks did not even have computers. The remaining banks exist somewhere along the continuum between those that had CBS on the one hand, and those without even PCs on the other.

Most banks have solutions based on total branch automation. Several banks have implemented locally developed and customised application solutions. While some big UCBs have in-house IT wings to take care of development and maintenance of systems, most banks have outsourced these services.

Anecdotal evidences are there about the problems faced by these banks because of their small size, lack of adequate IT knowledge, lack of adequate IT savvy manpower and small time vendors.

They had suffered because small vendors could not provide satisfactory AMC and adequate post-implementation support for making changes in the software on account of their inability to retain skilled staff or sometimes because of the small scale of their operations, which rendered them unviable. Moreover, such legacy systems, set up by small vendors, were not standardized and therefore made migration to new systems more cumbersome and expensive than even acquiring a new one.

The acquisition of non-standardized software developed by local/regional level vendors is fraught with the following risks:

1. **Vendor Disappearance:** Vendors who developed software for small banks are often small-time operators and are not available for support, modifications and change management subsequently. Their mortality rate is often high. Eventually, the software became obsolete and redundant.
2. **Loss of Key Personnel by Vendor:** Some times, the vendor is available but the key personnel, who were involved in the development of software, are no more with the vendor. The vendor finds it difficult to extend the required level of the support without its skilled personnel as being small it has little flexibility in the absence of backup staff. As they often also do not follow standard practice of software development and documentation, the maintenance and updation of source-codes becomes difficult for the new personnel.
3. **Lack of Regulatory Compliance Modules:** Almost all the small-vendor developed software systems do not contain important regulatory provisions such as compliance to KYC norms etc.

The Group also observed that there were several large banks which had their own data centres and were offering core banking solutions to the smaller banks and that a few successful cases of sharing of data centre facilities among banks were also known. However, as awareness of IT among UCBs was not pervasive, several banks seemed reluctant to keep their data in the data centres owned by other bank/banks.

8.8.2 Problem Analysis and Possible Solutions: Considering the increasing penetration of commercial banks in what till recently were the niche areas of UCBs (such as middle and low income housing finance/retail loans etc.), the need to computerize the operations of even the smallest UCBs has become imperative to improve customer service and ensure survival. While deliberating upon the level of computerization of UCBs, the Group noted that in a country like China, all the two-lakh odd branches of all the banks had been computerized.

The Group, while noting with satisfaction that the front line UCBs have taken advantage of what the ICT can offer, also observed that a very large proportion of UCBs have not done the same. Among UCBs, considering the high concentration of very small banks, lack of uniformity in the levels of computerization and inadequate awareness about effectiveness of computers in enhancing competitiveness, the Group felt that it is necessary to articulate the minimum IT infrastructure which should exist in each UCB regardless of its size, location or profitability. This minimum level of IT infrastructure, the Group felt should include the following:

1. Computerized front-end i.e. customer interface.
2. Automatic backend accounting (through software).
3. Computerized MIS reporting.
4. Automated regulatory reporting.

The above minimum benchmark for computerization does not include 'networking' among branches, since the sector is largely dominated by unit banks or banks with only a few branches.

The Group then discussed about various methods by which a bank can create IT infrastructure for its use. In view of the variance in size, financial strength and IT capabilities of UCBs, the Group also considered the possibility of sharing of IT infrastructure at the state level as state was operationally a logical unit for UCBs which are under the regulation of state governments and RBI.

While an arms' length distance between banks owning the data centre and the database of other UCBs using the facility is technologically feasible, it also needs to be recognized that the long-term sustainability of such an arrangement is an issue, as banks are essentially in the business of banking and activities like development and maintenance of data centres and providing software support to financial institutions are focussed functions of IT firms.

8.8.3 Issues in Computerization and Support

A. Desired Level of IT in a Bank, Irrespective of Size, Location and Profits: The Group opined that the minimum level of IT infrastructure in a bank should be a computerized front office services, back-office accounting, MIS and regulatory reporting.

B. Available Solutions: Several solution providers from big firms to middle range players and banks etc., existed in the market. Peer group banks working jointly for developing facilities like data centre for use by group members could also come together to provide solutions for the smaller banks. Even local developers were offering inexpensive solutions to banks which were workable in the short/medium term. However, choosing standardized products was essential for ensuring reliability and continued support.

C. Cost Factor: Costs of the ASP models have been discussed earlier. However, the costs mentioned above were the 'list costs' of the firms and would be negotiable, particularly if banks got together and bulk orders were to be placed. Different payment terms were also available which included a small charge every month combined with per transaction fee which could possibly be of interest to the smaller banks. In addition to the ASP model, the outright purchase offering also existed.

D. Approach to be Adopted: In respect of the small banks, particularly the unit banks, it was felt that the best method for computerization could be through the ASP model wherein a few software vendors could be short-listed by an agency like IDRBT and the banks could select the vendor from out of the list, based on their geographical location and convenience. There was another view, however, that the independent application model might also be considered, should a bank be capable and desirous.

E. Who Should be Supported and How? The Group deliberated upon the need for mandating the minimum level of IT usage by UCBs. It was observed that so far, mandates had been given by the Reserve Bank for regulatory purposes only, but if necessary, Reserve Bank could explore the possibility of laying down prescriptions for business purposes too.

Prima facie banks that were making losses or very meagre profits or those that are very small in size and therefore do not have the financial strength to acquire the IT infrastructure set by RBI, require support. However, in case support is extended only to the weak or small banks, the better performing or growing banks may tend to interpret that they were indirectly suffering because of their good performance or growth as RBI was not extending support to them for their IT efforts. Even though, in fact, the better performing banks may not be needing support, this approach of providing support to only those which are loss making or small may give a wrong and unintended signal to better performing banks.

This dilemma can therefore be addressed by ensuring that the support is not seen as a grant from Reserve Bank. Instead it could be in the form of, say, an interest free conditional loan. The repayment could be structured for different categories of banks. For loss making banks, for example, there could be a moratorium on repayment till the bank turned around. RBI could also attach conditions and link declaration of dividend to the repayments. In such a case, while the loss making banks would not have any problem in accepting the loan, the profit making banks that avail of it would have an incentive to pay back quickly so that they can declare dividend.

F. Routing the Financial Support: On the issue of strategy for routing financial support to UCBs, the Group discussed the pros and cons of the following options:

1. Providing funds directly to banks for outright purchase of customised software and hardware.
2. Paying the vendors who provide the software, on behalf of the UCB.
3. Funding a national-level institution and routing the support through it.

8.8.4 Recommendations: Usage of information technology for financial systems in the modern world is fundamental to the survival and growth of the institutions. IT usage not only helps banks hold and reduce their cost of operations, several developments in the information and communication technology (ICT) enable the institutions to proffer highly profitable products and services to their constituents. IT has become not just an enabler, but also the distinguishing factor and differentiator. It also provides competitive advantage and edge to its users. Further, current regulatory and supervisory compliance demands that the institutions have a very sound usage of IT systems for their operations.

A. Minimum Information Technology Infrastructure in UCBs: Considering the concentration of small UCBs, the lack of uniformity in the levels of computerization and inadequate awareness about the efficacy of computers in enhancing competitiveness, the Group felt it necessary to articulate the minimum IT infrastructure which should exist in each UCB regardless of its size, location or profitability. This minimum level of IT infrastructure should include the following:

1. Computerized front-end i.e. customer interface.
2. Automatic backend accounting (through software).
3. Computerized MIS reporting.
4. Automated regulatory reporting.

B. UCBs to be Supported: While maximum support is required for the small/weak banks, if support is extended only to the weak or small banks, the better performing or growing banks may tend to interpret that they were indirectly suffering because of their good performance or growth as RBI was not extending support to them for their IT efforts. As such, the group felt that support should be structured in such a way that it can be offered to all.

C. Nature of Support: In order to implement the minimum level of IT infrastructure by the UCBs, core banking solutions (CBS) would be required to be adopted by the banks. The model of CBS may be according to the size and spread of the banks.

The models for acquiring the IT infrastructure could be one of the following:

(a) Application Service Provider (ASP) Model: In respect of the small banks, particularly the unit banks, it was felt that the best method for computerization could be through the ASP model as the problems of software development and maintenance, training and retention of IT professionals, installation and maintenance of complex and costly hardware and other logistics like data centres etc would be addressed by the service provider without need for much initiative or involvement of the UCB. An agency could short-list/select one/few vendors and be the conduit and service quality assuror to the banks. The payment model for the ASP option includes a one time payment and a small charge every month combined with per transaction fee, which could also be suitable for the smaller banks. Moreover, in ASP model, initial investment would be less and by combining the requirements of a large number of banks the cost could be further reduced.

(b) Outright Purchase Model: If banks seek to go for outright purchase of the Core Banking, including data centre, the cost would be in the range of ₹ 1.5 crore to ₹ 2 crore for 5-10 branches per bank. Further, availability and retention of IT savvy professionals are also to be ensured. Besides, the bank should be strong enough to enforce service quality by the vendor. The Group feels that only those banks which are well capitalised and with good track record, on whom we have confidence and comfort that the end use of funds are assured, and that they have IT savvy personnel to implement/oversee and deal with the vendors and for whom investing in an outright purchase option is financially a preferable option should be given the option to choose this model. As such, banks which have a business of more than ₹ 100 crore, capital to risk-weighted assets ratio (CRAR) of over 9 percent and have been profit making for the past 3 years could be provided support for outright purchase.

(c) Delivery Mechanism: As indicated above, the support will be available for all UCBs. However, it should not be given in the form of a grant; support may be in the form of a loan and not subsidy.

Experience shows that subsidy tends to reduce seriousness regarding the end use of funds. Financial support may be extended as follows:

1. Support could be in the form of interest free loan, repayable in 7 years, with one year moratorium. UCBs would be eligible for loan for software as also for purchase of hardware.
2. In the case of big banks preferring to go for outright purchase of software and hardware, interest free with only service charge of ½ percent to 1 percent to be charged by the SCB routing the loan may be considered.
3. In respect of weak/sick banks, the 'moratorium' may be for two years. In case the UCB defaults on its repayment obligations even after that, a view may be taken at that point regarding other options like continuation of management, non-disruptive exit of the bank etc.
4. For the banks which have to adopt ASP Model, routing of the interest-free loan by the Reserve Bank could be through some agency, which could prepare systems requirement specifications, select vendors, prepare development/testing and implementation plans, and vetting the SLA (service level agreement) between users i.e. UCBs and the service providing entity, to ensure smooth implementation and post-implementation support by the vendor.
5. For the banks which elect to have outright purchase of the application system, the Group felt that the Reserve Bank may not be able to extend direct loans

due to monetary policy implications. However, NABARD has a separate fund for IT usage in co-operative sector, a portion of which can be routed to UCBs.

(d) Conditionality:

1. The aforementioned facilities will be made available only for UCBs located in the MoU states.
2. Even if the UCB is a loss-making one, it would still have to honour repayment obligations in respect of the interest-free loan/loan from NABARD.
3. In case of banks which already have software in their existing branches, interest-free loan would be available for meeting cost of upgradation and/or expansion, under the same terms and conditions.
4. A bonus could be considered for the banks which repay the instalments on time and/or earlier. The bonus could be in the form of waiving the last instalment.

8.9 Working Group on Umbrella Organization and Revival Fund for Urban Co-operative Banks

There are a large number of urban co-operative banks (UCBs) in the country forming a heterogeneous group in terms of size and spread. Many of these banks are very small in size and reach. They compete with larger participants in the same banking space. Over the years, a number of UCBs have become weak and non-viable thus posing systemic risk to the UCB sector. They lack avenues for raising capital funds since they cannot go in for public issue of shares nor can they issue shares to members at a premium. At the same time, there are a number of UCBs in the sector that are financially strong and viable. Some sort of cooperative bonding and mutual support system could make the sector strong and vibrant. Looking at various successful federal models internationally, especially in Europe and USA, a need was felt for an umbrella organization that would be in a position to channelize their resources, aggregate their needs and also lend credibility through mutual support in the financial market.

In this backdrop, RBI constituted a Working Group (Chairman: V.S. Das) on May 28, 2008 to suggest measures including the appropriate regulatory and supervisory framework, to facilitate emergence of umbrella organization(s) for the UCB sector in the respective states. Further, the Standing Advisory Committee for UCBs opined that the Working Group may also look into the issues concerning creation of revival fund for the sector.

8.9.1 Terms of Reference of the Working Group:

1. To study the regulatory and supervisory structure of umbrella organizations of financial co-operative institutions/banks, as prevalent in other parts of the world, especially in relation to raising of capital and intra co-operative group

support system.

2. To study the existing structure and legal framework for UCBs in India and to examine the need and scope for a federated structure/umbrella organization for UCBs at the state level.
3. To suggest appropriate supervisory and regulatory framework to facilitate emergence of such umbrella organisation(s) for UCBs, taking into consideration the international experiences and systems.
4. To study and suggest modalities for setting up an appropriate mutual assistance/revival fund for urban co-operative banks and the nature of support that could be provided by such fund.

8.9.2 Recommendations:

A. Need for Umbrella Organization: Urban cooperative banks in India cater to the financial needs of the middle and lower middle class people in metropolitan, urban and semi-urban centres. They operate on a standalone basis, unlike rural cooperatives in India, which have a three tier structure. These banks are large in number, though of varied asset size, ranging from small to medium. Although they compete with commercial banks, their share in total deposits is barely 4 percent. There is a significant part of the UCB sector that lacks professionalism and is unable to keep pace with rapid advancements in IT, modern banking systems and financial products. The sector also has significant number of banks which are weak and need financial support. There have been occasions when, due to contagion effect, banks have encountered liquidity problems. Being in the nature of cooperative societies, the UCBs' ability to augment their capital is also restricted, thereby hindering their growth.

The organizational structure of UCBs, their small size and limited area of operation add to their vulnerability. Further, in the wake of advances in information and communication technology, payment and settlement systems and services, they need to widen their range of services to run on professional lines and match the services provided by commercial banks.

Internationally, cooperative banks, popularly called Credit Unions, operate in networks and have an entity which provides a wide range of services to them, such as, fund management services, lines of credit, asset management, payment and settlement system gateway, ATM networks, credit card, investment, securitisation, capital raising and other financial services. These entities act as umbrella organizations and the networks provide cooperative solidarity. International experience has shown that the presence of such an umbrella organization has contributed towards the member Credit Unions being stable, sound and efficient entities.

B. Umbrella Organization at the National Level: The Working Group carefully went into the important issue of whether in India we should have an umbrella organization at the national level or whether each state should have its own umbrella organization. While countries such as Canada and USA have provincial umbrella organizations, Australia and European countries have preferred to consolidate and have national level organizations.

UCBs in India are not evenly spread across the country. They have predominant presence in five states, viz. Andhra Pradesh, Gujarat, Karnataka, Maharashtra and Tamil Nadu accounting for about 89 percent of the total business of the sector. Further, UCBs in Maharashtra alone had about 64 percent of the total business. In contrast, their presence was minimal in many states. Considering the regional spread and market share of UCBs, the Working Group is of the opinion that having multiple umbrella organizations for UCBs in India or state-wise umbrellas may be neither feasible nor desirable. Therefore, the Working Group recommended that there should be one umbrella organization at the national level for the entire UCB sector.

C. Functions of the Umbrella Organization: The umbrella organization should act as a central credit institution for UCBs, like similar organizations abroad for Credit Unions. It should provide a wide range of services such as providing loans and advances, refinance, payment and settlement services, IT services, ATM network services, investment banking, fund management, management consultancy, capacity building services and even capital support. The UCB sector was found to be particularly keen that the organization provides payment and settlement services and liquidity assistance. This may possibly be emanating from the concern arising in the context of implementation of the new eligibility norms for MICR clearing, RTGS, SGL/CSGL accounts and making them out of reach for a large number of UCBs and lack of avenues for temporary liquidity assistance (even against SLR securities) in case of need and urgency; more so in case of run like situations. Similarly, many small UCBs are looking forward to a centralized agency for buying, selling and managing Government securities on their behalf in view of their lack of skill and expertise in the areas. The Working Group recommended that the umbrella organization should provide a whole range of services to member UCBs, as described above.

D. Form of Organization of the Umbrella Organization: The Working Group observed that non-banking financial companies (NBFCs) could perform most of the functions of umbrella organization. The minimum start-up capital for such companies has been stipulated at ₹ 2 crore, for the present, as per the Reserve Bank's policy for issue of certification for registration. The Working Group was of the view that even though contribution to share capital of the umbrella organization would be voluntary, the initial start-up capital could easily be garnered from UCBs. It would be better to build the edifice, brick by brick, with low start-up capital and augment the capital funds over the years, rather than to commit huge capital funds from the cooperative sector, which itself is facing difficulties in raising capital. Further, the Reserve Bank has been vested with adequate power to regulate and supervise NBFCs. The current RBI regulations, however, do not permit NBFC to undertake certain activities and place restrictions on certain others; more importantly, the Payment and Settlement services.

Considering that access to payment and settlement gateways and dealing platforms for securities through umbrella organization are the most sought after services, the Working Group was of the view that it would be within the powers of the Reserve Bank to grant regulatory permissions/forbearances wherever necessary, depending upon the type of functions. NBFCs may be broadly divided into deposit taking and non-deposit taking. The term "deposit", however, does not include amount of money received from banks and financial institutions and further, the term "public deposit" excludes certain categories of deposits. The NBFCs that are authorized to accept/hold public deposits need to have minimum net owned funds and they are required to maintain certain specified percentage (15 percent) of the public deposits in liquid assets in the form of approved securities and unencumbered term deposits with scheduled commercial banks. These NBFCs should achieve minimum investment grade credit rating for accepting public deposits. The regulations for the deposit taking NBFCs are tighter than that of non-deposit taking.

On the contrary, a non-deposit taking NBFC enjoys more freedom in undertaking its business, more particularly deployment of its funds. Keeping in view the extant regulations applicable and the relative merits of deposit taking and non-deposit taking NBFCs, the Working Group was of the opinion that to start with, a non-deposit taking NBFC may be the most suitable form of organization and recommended that umbrella organization may be initially set up as a non-deposit taking NBFC. The umbrella organization in the form of a non-deposit taking NBFC would, however, access money from UCBs and others, which are not treated as public deposits. The conversion of the umbrella organization to a banking company could be considered in due course in the light of experience gained.

E. Authorized Capital, Subscribed/Paid up Capital: The Working Group deliberated at length on the modus operandi of raising share capital for the umbrella organization. It was felt that share capital of the umbrella organization should be closely held by the UCBs and subscription should be voluntary.

However, some members strongly felt that contribution to the share capital of the umbrella organization should be made compulsory for UCBs and the Reserve Bank could consider issuing direction to UCBs in this regard. The Group discussed on the pros and cons of the proposal and was of the view that though equity participation by all UCBs should be encouraged; there could be constraints to make it compulsory for UCBs. The Group was of the view that both the options should be kept open. The National and State Federations should educate UCBs about the benefits of having an umbrella organization and also play a big role for its set up and raising of capital.

F. Sources of Working Capital: To begin with, the capital funds would normally go to finance fixed assets of umbrella organization and the balance amount could be used for financing activities. Umbrella organization would also need some source of working capital. Being a non-deposit taking NBFC, it would have access to the following sources for its working capital:

1. Borrowings from banks/financial institutions.
2. Deposits, i.e. term deposits from UCBs.
3. Debt instruments, i.e. bonds/debentures.
4. Refinance against financial assets (loans and advances) including securities.
5. Other miscellaneous sources.

The umbrella organization would need to have access to deposits from UCBs, which could be a major source of working capital for carrying out its business. A significant number of UCBs have low credit deposit ratios and they park their surplus funds with DCCB/SCB and commercial banks. Umbrella organization, being the central credit institution for UCBs, may be able to tap these deposits for its financing and investment activities.

G. CRR and SLR: The Working Group felt that it would be attractive for UCBs to place deposits with umbrella organization if these deposits are treated as CRR/SLR. The umbrella organization would definitely need such deposits to meet its working capital requirements. The Working Group, therefore, recommended that RBI may consider exempting UCBs placing term deposits with the umbrella organization from maintenance of SLR in the form of Government and other approved securities up to 15 percent of their NDTL. The Working Group also felt that this would serve as an incentive for UCBs to take up membership of the umbrella organization. The Working Group felt that RBI which has been instrumental in promoting several developmental and financial institutions should consider the recommendation positively and favourably as the umbrella organization is being conceptualized to provide the much needed stability to the UCB sector that would also contribute to financial stability.

H. Business Profile and Sources of Income: Profitability of the umbrella organization's operations is very crucial and, therefore, in most countries, the central credit institutions have a significant asset portfolio outside the captive business. Further, its ability to raise capital and debt in the market would also depend upon the strength of its balance sheet. The Working Group, therefore, recommended that umbrella organization should delicately balance its commitment towards UCB sector and the need to keep its asset portfolio strong and healthy.

As the umbrella organization would function as a central credit institution, it would orient its business to provide various services to the member UCBs (loans and advances, refinance, payment and settlement services, IT services, ATM network services, investment banking, fund management and capital support). This would fetch it revenue in the form of interest, commission, exchange, etc. It was felt that the income derived from services extended to the UCB sector may not be sufficient to sustain the umbrella organization. The large and strong UCBs may not avail some of the services. However, small and medium sized UCBs are expected to avail most services for their clients and for themselves, as they may not be eligible for carrying out such activities on their own. The umbrella organization's asset portfolio would predominantly comprise loans and advances, which would involve more than the normal risk as many of the UCBs are small entities and have local operations. The umbrella organization could also lend to non-UCBs. It would also need to have a healthy investment portfolio.

I. Management: It goes without saying that an umbrella organization should be run on thoroughly professional lines and observe the best practices insofar as corporate governance is concerned. The Working Group recommended that the memorandum and articles of association of the company (umbrella organization) should specifically provide for appointment of independent directors. In order to achieve this objective, the fit and proper criteria for the board of directors and executive board/CEO may be prescribed either in the memorandum and articles of association, or by the regulators.

CEO should be a professional of repute, with deep knowledge and understanding of the UCB sector, combined with business acumen of a finance company to inspire confidence in the umbrella organization. The Working Group left it to RBI for putting in place a suitable system, standards and stringent fit and proper criteria to ensure that the position of CEO is held by a competent person. The Working Group was also of the considered view that RBI should nominate on the Board a suitable officer, at least during the initial formative years of the umbrella organization. Subsequently, RBI may have an observer on the board. This would not only lend the umbrella organization greater credibility, but its nominee's guidance would also be useful in adherence to best corporate governance practices, regulations and formulation of appropriate business strategies and products.

J. Emergency Liquidity and Solvency Support: Occasionally, UCBs confronted by financial distress, caused by temporary liquidity problems, need emergency liquidity support systems to come to their rescue. Similarly, UCBs with meagre or entirely eroded net worth need solvency support for their revival. The Working Group, while appreciating the need for evolving a mechanism to address this issue, was of the view that it should not be the mandate of the umbrella organization to provide such emergency liquidity and solvency support to UCBs as it may be difficult for it to meet the quantum of financial assistance that may be required in this regard. Further, solvency support is subject to high risk and low or nil return and envisages a fairly long period of pay back. Neither the sector, nor the umbrella organization, being a non-deposit taking NBFC, would be in a position to fund the recapitalization needs of problem UCBs. However, arrangements need to be put in place to address and resolve these problems.

K. Emergency Liquidity Support: The Working Group believed that due to lack of homogeneity, uneven geographical spread of UCBs, cultural differences, affinity to state federations and state laws on cooperation, the bonding of UCBs at the State level is strong. Empirical evidence also demonstrates that the contagion effects are localized and solidarity amongst the cooperatives at the State level is far greater than at the national level. The emergency liquidity supports need to be provided to UCBs in financial distress and, in most cases, such facility would be without collateral and for a short-term. The uncollateralized emergency liquidity support would carry more than the normal counter party credit risk. Therefore, a thorough understanding of the local polity, the management and operations of the distressed UCB, its problems and prospects would be necessary. The Working Group was of the view that a State level institution would not only have better appreciation of the financial needs of the distressed UCB, but also pull resources for supporting the UCB concerned. Therefore, the Working Group recommended State-specific Emergency Fund Facility Schemes.

L. Revival Fund: The presence of a large number of weak and sick UCBs, which need solvency support, call for an urgent need for creation of a Revival Fund. If UCBs with negative net worth were to be brought to positive net worth, an enormous sum of about ₹ 2,500 crore may be required. While RBI may pursue a menu of options, including mergers, and financial restructuring for turn around of these banks, possibly, an amount of ₹ 2,000 crore may still be necessary.

However, such a fund could only be raised out of contribution from the net profits of UCBs. The total net profit of the sector being about ₹ 1,000 crore, mobilization of this magnitude of resources from the sector may not be feasible. The Working Group observed that though the Central/State Governments have been supporting the revival of the rural cooperatives, such support was not extended to UCBs. Therefore, in the absence of capital contribution from the Central/State Governments, the Revival Fund for solvency support to UCBs would not be feasible. The Working Group also believed that providing solvency support to UCBs from contributions from the profits may be resisted by the sector and the contribution would be too little to rescue sick UCBs. Therefore, it would be more appropriate to provide both short and medium term finance from the Emergency Fund.

To sum up, the financial sector reforms have been components of the overall economic reforms undertaken in a phased manner from 1991 by the Government of India. A look has to be taken at the reform process and what it means to the co-operative credit institutions. These reforms also envisaged improving the efficiency and productivity of the co-operative credit delivery system which in turn would accelerate the requisite credit flow to the productive sectors of the economy.

The major objectives of these reforms in the cooperative sector were as under:

1. To make the institutions competitive by removing external constraints having a bearing on their operations.
2. To improve their financial health.
3. To ensure transparency in their business operations.
4. To improve their profitability.
5. Institutional building and strengthening.

Positive impact of reforms, as has been witnessed in the case of commercial banking sector, may take longer to get manifested for co-operative banks given the late start of the reform process in this sector. Unless such a positive scenario evolves for the co-operative banking sector in the near future, the financial health of many of these banks would continue to remain a cause of concern.

It is significant to note that introduction of reforms and the consequent increase in competition has resulted in some convergence in operations of commercial banks and co-operative banks, especially scheduled UCBs. Furthermore, while most of the loss-making commercial banks are relatively small, in the case of UCBs some of the large banks are incurring losses and this has increased the vulnerability of the whole segment. Detection of irregularities in a few UCBs in the recent past has raised concerns about the conduct of the management in co-operative banks. For this purpose, the RBI has suggested the establishment of a unified supervisory authority for UCBs and the related amendment to the Banking Regulation Act, 1949.

Endnote

1. Reserve Bank of India, *Report on Currency and Finance,* 2001-2002, p. VI-18.

9

Micro Finance and Self-help Groups (SHGs)

9.1 Micro Finance

Micro finance is a movement whose objective is a world in which as many poor and near-poor households as possible have permanent access to an appropriate range of high quality financial services, including not just credit but also savings, insurance, and fund transfers. Many of those who promote micro finance believe that such access will help poor people get out of poverty. For others, micro finance is a way to promote economic development, employment and growth through the support of micro entrepreneurs and small businesses.

9.1.1 Micro Finance Defined: Micro finance is the provision of a diverse range of financial services and products including small loans (micro credit), savings accounts, insurance, pensions and money transfers. These are designed to assist people living in poverty who are not able to access financial services in the mainstream banking sector because they have no collateral, formal identification or steady income.

Poor people borrow from informal moneylenders and save with informal collectors. They receive loans and grants from charities. They buy insurance from state-owned companies. They receive funds transfers through formal or informal remittance networks. It is not easy to distinguish micro finance from similar activities. It could be claimed that a government that orders state banks to open deposit accounts for poor consumers, or a moneylender that engages in usury, or a charity that runs a heifer pool are engaged in micro finance. Ensuring financial services to poor people is best done by expanding the number of financial institutions available to them, as well as by strengthening the capacity of those institutions. In recent years there has also been increasing emphasis on expanding the diversity of institutions, since different institutions serve different needs.

9.1.2 Role of Micro Finance: Micro finance is the provision of financial services to low-income clients or solidarity lending groups including consumers and the self-employed, who traditionally lack access to banking and related services.

A. Micro Finance and Individuals/Households: Micro finance is the provision of financial services to people who would not usually qualify for traditional banking services because they have no form of collateral or formal identification. Even a small loan of ₹ 5,000 can help someone living in poverty to start or grow his own small business. This enables them to earn an income so they no longer have to struggle to afford food, clean water, healthcare and an education for their children.

By helping a mother buy a sewing machine to start a tailoring business or a father buy seeds to plant a vegetable garden, small loans enable people in poverty to earn an income and provide for their families. As each business grows, loans are paid back and lent out again. With loans repaid, the cycle continues, year after year. Each successful business can feed a family, employ more people and eventually help empower a whole community.

Various studies of the impact of micro finance have been carried out over the past 20 years, including large-scale studies by the World Bank. These studies have established that micro finance can improve the living standards of poor households and the communities in which they live. The benefits of micro finance include:

1. Higher and more reliable income and savings.
2. Improved access to healthcare and better nutrition.
3. Greater female empowerment.
4. Better housing.
5. More children being placed in school.

These studies provide good evidence that micro finance projects can indeed be effective.

Experience shows that micro finance can help people living in poverty to increase their income, build viable businesses and reduce their vulnerability to external shocks. It can also be a powerful instrument for self-empowerment by enabling the poor, especially women, to become agents of change, not just economically, but also socially as they emerge as influential leaders in their community.

Income generation from a business helps not only the business activity expand, but also contributes to household income, resulting in better food, shelter, education, sanitation, healthcare and so on.

Families living in poverty are often vulnerable to shocks such as the illness of a wage earner, extreme weather, theft or other such events. These shocks place a huge burden on the limited financial resources of a family, and can drive a family deeper into poverty if they do not have access to financial services like credit, insurance and savings.

It should be noted that although a large number of studies undertaken so far on the impact of micro credit programmes on household income show that participants of such programmes usually have higher and more stable incomes than they did before they joined the programmes, some practitioners still have reservations about the findings of these studies. Moreover, not many micro credit programmes can afford to undertake impact assessments because they are generally expensive and time-consuming. There are serious disagreements among experts on the validity of methodologies used in some of the published studies. In some cases, even the more rigorous studies have produced inconclusive results. Some studies show that there are limits to the use of credit as an instrument for poverty eradication, including difficulties in identifying the poor and targeting credit to reach the poorest of the poor. Added to this is the fact that many people, especially the poorest of the poor, are usually not in a position to undertake an economic activity, partly because they lack business skills and even the motivation for business.

B. Micro Finance and Women: Micro finance experts generally agree that women should be the primary focus of service delivery. Evidence shows that they are less likely to default on their loans than men. Because operating margins become tighter the smaller the loans delivered, many MFIs consider the risk of lending to men to be too high.

Women are typically poorer than men and have fewer options for earning a livelihood to provide adequate food, housing and education for their children. They are also the *change agents* of the family. Women are more likely to invest their earnings into improving the lives of the families. By encouraging women to take charge of their futures, MFIs can impact families and whole communities.

In developing countries, more women are involved in the informal labour sector. Men are more likely to be employed in contract work as labourers or overseas workers. Women are often left to support their families or supplement their husband's income by using any skills they possess. With limited resources to start or expand a small business, micro finance is attractive to women who are prepared to work hard to give their children a brighter future.

Micro finance generally targets poor women because they have proven to be reliable credit risks and when they have the financial means, they invest that money back into their families, resulting in better health and education and stronger local economies.

C. Micro Finance and Social Interventions: There are currently a few social interventions that have been combined with micro finance to increase awareness of HIV/AIDS, and gender equity. Such interventions educate on different gender roles, gender-based violence, and HIV/AIDS infections to strengthen the communication skills and leadership of women. Micro finance has also been combined with business education and with other packages of health interventions.

Micro finance programmes have been instrumental in generating employment, income and enhancing living standards of poor in underdeveloped and developing countries. They have good potential for uplifting the economic conditions of assetless poor people through group approach. Micro finance through self-help groups ensures active participation and involvement of the beneficiaries in effective implementation of the programmes for socio-economic development.

In India, micro finance programme has a crucial role to play in uplifting people living below poverty line. Poor people have less access to financial services because of their inability to provide collateral security which is demanded by the banks.

D. Micro Finance and the Economy: Micro finance is a form of financial services for entrepreneurs and small businesses lacking access to banking and related services. The two main mechanisms for the delivery of financial services to such clients are: (a) relationship-based banking for individual entrepreneurs and small businesses, and (b) group-based models, where several entrepreneurs come together to apply for loans and other services as a group. There is a rich variety of financial institutions in India which serve micro entrepreneurs and small businesses.

A significant proportion of the working population in many developing countries survives through involvement in the informal sector. By offering people a means to grow their small businesses to the point where many employ other people, micro finance has flow-on effects for local economies, decreasing unemployment and providing incomes for other poor families in the community.

With an increased income and therefore more money spent on items such as food, clothing and transport, micro finance clients become active participants in their local economies, also benefiting the providers of those products and services. By boosting local economies, micro finance benefits the developing world.

9.1.3 Micro Finance Institutions (MFIs): In India micro finance operates through the following two channels:

1. Micro finance institutions (MFIs).
2. Self-help Group (SHG)-Bank Linkage Programme (SBLP).

Those institutions which have micro finance as their main operation are known as micro finance institutions. Micro finance institutions (MFIs) offer financial services to underprivileged and impoverished communities. A micro finance institution (MFI) is a registered organisation that offers financial services to people living in poverty. Within the micro finance industry, the term *micro finance institution* has come to refer to a wide range of organisations dedicated to providing these services, such as non-governmental organisations (NGOs), credit unions, cooperatives, private commercial banks and non-banking financial institutions.

Not all MFIs are socially motivated, i.e. with the aim to help people out of poverty above all else. Some MFIs primarily exist to make a profit and seek commercial returns over social outcomes.

Clients of MFIs are typically self-employed, often household-based entrepreneurs, who do not have access to financial services in the traditional banking sector.

Forbes magazine named 7 micro finance institutions in India in the list of world's top 50 micro finance institutions. These are as under:

1. Bandhan.
2. Micro Credit Foundation of India.
3. Saadhana Microfin Society.
4. Grameen Koota.
5. Sharada's Women's Association for Weaker Section.
6. Asmitha Microfin Ltd.
7. SKS Microfinance Private Ltd.

To administer these services, MFIs need to develop and grow so that funds can be effectively managed on an on-going basis. MFIs need to develop strong leadership, train and equip staff, build new branches, and create efficient systems and processes that meet the needs of clients. Instead of funds having a one-time impact as with many humanitarian aid groups, MFIs leverage and recycle funds over and over, having a greater impact over a longer period of time.

Most MFIs lend on the basis of the past record of the group, i.e. self-help group (SHG) or joint liability group (JLG) and also on the individuals repayment performance. In the absence of a decent past record, members are deprived of getting bigger loan amounts and additional services.

MFIs also provide non-financial services such as business development to strengthen enterprises, and financial literacy training to empower families to look after their own finances. Access to these kinds of services helps empower families to become active participants in society, building self-confidence and dignity.

NABARD has been supporting the SHG-Bank Linkage Programme since 1992. In the context of growing demand for micro finance by self-help groups, RBI made linkage of self-help groups with banks as a priority sector activity in 1996. The Government of India has been supporting the programme by making special budgetary provision for promotion of self-help groups since 1999.

9.1.4 Legal Status: A number of organizations with varied size and legal forms offer micro finance service. MFIs in India exist as NGOs (registered as societies or trusts), Section 25 companies and non-banking financial companies (NBFCs) [Table 9.1]. Commercial banks, regional rural banks (RRBs), cooperative societies and other large lenders have played an important role in providing refinance facility to MFIs. Banks have also leveraged the self-help group (SHG) channel to provide direct credit to group borrowers.

Table 9.1: Legal Pattern of Micro Finance Institutions (MFIs) in India

Type of MFI	Legal Registration
MFIs Not-for profit	
Non-governmental Organizations (NGOs)	Society Registration Act, 1860 Indian Trust Act, 1882
Non-profit Companies	Section 25 of Indian Companies Act, 1956
MFIs for Mutual Benefits	
Mutually-aided Co-operative Societies (MACS)	Mutually-aided Co-operative Societies (MACS) Acts enacted by State Governments
MFIs for Profit	
Non-banking Financial Companies (NBFCs)	Indian Companies Act, 1956 Reserve Bank of India Act, 1934

A non-banking financial company (NBFC) in India is a company registered under the Companies Act, 1956. It engages in the business of loans and advances, acquisition of shares, stock, insurance business, and chit fund business. NBFCs perform functions similar to that of banks. However, there are a few differences: (a) an NBFC cannot accept demand deposits, (b) an NBFC is not a part of the payment and settlement system and as such, an NBFC cannot issue cheques drawn on itself, and (c) deposit insurance facility of the Deposit Insurance and Credit Guarantee Corporation is not available for NBFC depositors, unlike banks.

Although the SHG-Bank Linkage model is well managed in India by NABARD, currently there is no proper regulatory body for the supervision of MFIs. The presence of institutions with a variety of legal forms makes it difficult for the regulation of all such institutions by a single regulatory body in the current Indian legal structure. Though NBFCs, which cover the major part of the outstanding loan portfolio by the micro finance channel, are regulated by Reserve Bank of India, other MFIs like societies, trusts, Section 25 companies and cooperative societies fall outside the purview of RBI's regulation.

The Micro Finance Institutions (Development and Regulation) Bill, 2011 is a major step taken by the Government of India in the micro finance sector. The proposed bill clarifies all doubts pertaining to regulation of the MFIs by appointing RBI as the sole regulator for all MFIs.

9.1.5 Problem Areas of Micro Finance: While much progress has been made in developing a viable, commercial micro finance sector in the last few decades, several issues remain that need to be addressed. The obstacles or challenges to building a sound commercial micro finance industry include the following.

A. High Cost of Loans: Providing small loans at an affordable cost is one of the principal challenges of micro finance movement. The reason for the high interest rates is not primarily cost of capital. Rather, the main reason for the high cost of micro finance loans is the high transaction cost of traditional micro finance operations relative to loan size.

Micro finance practitioners have long argued that such high interest rates are simply unavoidable, because the cost of making each loan cannot be reduced below a certain level while still allowing the lender to cover costs such as offices and staff salaries. Credit risk for micro finance institutes is very high, because costumers need years to improve their livelihood and face many challenges during this time. Financial institutes often do not even have a system to check the person's identity. Additionally they are unable to design new products and enlarge their business to reduce the risk. The result is that the traditional approach to micro finance has made only limited progress in resolving the problem it purports to address: that the world's poorest people pay the world's highest cost for small business growth capital. The high costs of traditional micro finance loans limit their effectiveness as a poverty-fighting tool.

In recent years, the micro finance industry has shifted its focus from the objective of increasing the volume of lending capital available, to address the challenge of providing micro finance loans more affordably.

The answer to providing micro finance services at an affordable cost may lie in rethinking one of the fundamental assumptions underlying micro finance, i.e. micro finance borrowers need extensive monitoring and interaction with loan officers in order to benefit from and repay their loans.

In places with lower population densities, meeting the operating costs of a retail branch by serving nearby customers has proven considerably more challenging.

There has been a long-standing debate over the sharpness of the trade-off between *outreach*—the ability of a micro finance institution to reach poorer and more remote people—and its *sustainability*—its ability to cover its operating costs and possibly also its costs of serving new clients—from its operating revenues. Although it is generally agreed that microfinance practitioners should seek to balance these goals to some extent.

B. Repayment Problems: Major factors which adversely influence repayment are as under:

1. Environmental factors—which include natural disasters and adverse weather conditions like drought and floods—can disrupt a client's business,

particularly if it is related to agriculture.

2. Social factors—such as religious festivals, political elections and social unrest —can disrupt normal business operations and cause income to fluctuate.
3. Major events in a client's life—like the birth of a child, a family wedding or the death of a family member—can also affect their ability to operate their business and increase their daily expenses.

C. Financial Illiteracy: One of the major hindrances in the growth of the micro finance sector is the financial illiteracy of the people. This makes it difficult in creating awareness of micro finance and even more difficult to serve them as micro finance clients.

D. Inability to Generate Sufficient Funds: Inability of MFIs to raise sufficient funds remains one of the important concerns in the micro finance sector. Though NBFCs are able to raise funds through private equity investments because of the for-profit motive, such MFIs are restricted from taking public deposits.

Not-for-profit companies which constitute a major chunk of the MFI sector have to primarily rely on donations and grants from Government and apex institutions like NABARD and SIDBI. In the absence of adequate funding from the equity market, the major sources of funds for MFIs are the bank loans.

MFIs receive debt from banks against their equity and in order to increase their portfolio size they need to increase their debts for which they further need to increase their equity. The problem of inadequate funds is even bigger for small and nascent MFIs as they find it very difficult to get bank loans because of their small portfolio size and so they have to look for other costlier sources of fund.

E. Dropouts and Migration of Group Members: Majority of the micro finance loans are disbursed on group lending concept and a past record of the group plays an important role in getting new loans either through SHG-Bank Linkage or through MFIs. The two major problems with the group concept are dropouts (when one or more members leave the group) and migration (when one or more members move to another group).

F. Non-transparent Pricing: Though the concern about the transparent pricing in the micro finance sector has been an older one, it is gaining significance with the growing size and the increasing competition in the sector. Non-transparent pricing by MFIs confines the bargaining power of the borrowers and their ability to compare different loan products, because they do not know the actual price. In the absence of the proper understanding of the pricing, clients end up borrowing more than their ability to payback which results in over-indebtedness of the borrower.

It has been observed that MFIs are employing different patterns of charging interest rates and a few are also charging additional charges and interest free deposits (a part of the loan amount is kept as deposit on which no interest is paid). All this make the pricing very confusing and hence the borrower feels incompetent in terms of bargaining power. So a common practice for charging interest should be followed by all MFIs so that it makes the sector more competitive and the beneficiary gets the freedom to compare different financial products before buying.

G. Cluster Formation to Grab Established Market: MFIs' drive to grab an established market and reduce their costs is resulting in formation of clusters in some areas leaving the others out of the micro finance outreach. By getting an established micro finance market, MFIs reduce their initial cost in group formation of clients, educating them and creating awareness about micro finance.

This cluster formation is restricting MFIs from reaching to rural areas where there is the actual need for micro finance. People in urban and semi-urban areas are already having access to micro finance through SHG-Bank Linkage or individual lending, but in rural areas people do not have access to banks and so SBLP is not much active in such areas. Because of the initial cost involved in serving a new location, MFIs are not willing to go to such remote locations. This is the reason most of the MFIs have their branches in urban and semi-urban areas, resulting in a very low rural penetration of micro finance.

H. Multiple Lending and Over-Indebtedness: Both of these are outcome of the competition among the MFIs. Micro finance is one such sector where the Neo-liberal theory of free market operation fails, at least to some extent. Though competition is good for many sectors but in this case it is going against both the parties. In order to eat away each others' market share, MFIs are ending up giving multiple loans to same borrowers which in some cases is leading to over-indebtedness (a situation where the borrower has taken loans more than her/his repaying capacity) of the borrower. MFIs are getting affected because borrowers are failing to make payments and hence their recovery rates are falling, while over-indebtedness is making the borrowers slip into depression and in some cases forcing them to commit suicide.

I. Poor Regulation and Supervision: The regulation was not a major concern when the micro finance was in its nascent stage and individual institutions were free to bring in innovative operational models. However, as the sector completes almost two decades of age with a high growth trajectory, an enabling regulatory environment that protects interest of stakeholders as well as promotes growth, is needed.

In addition to proper regulation of the micro finance sector, field visits can be adopted as a medium for monitoring the conditions on ground and initiating corrective action if needed. This will keep a check on the performance of ground staff of various MFIs and their recovery practices. This will also encourage MFIs to abide by proper code of conduct and work more efficiently. However, the problem of feasibility and cost involved in physical monitoring of this vast sector remains an issue in this regard.

It has been seen that in lieu of reducing the initial cost, MFIs are opening their branches in places which already have a few MFIs operating. Encouraging MFIs for opening new branches in areas of low micro finance penetration by providing financial assistance will increase the outreach of the micro finance and check multiple lending. This will also increase rural penetration of micro finance in the state.

J. Incomplete Range of Products: Many MFIs provide only credit facilities. MFIs should provide complete range of products including credit, savings, remittance, financial advice and also non-financial services like training and support. As MFIs are acting as a substitute to banks in areas where people do not have access to banks, providing a complete range of products will enable the poor to avail all services.

In spite of above limitations, micro finance has come to occupy centre stage as a promising conduit for extending financial services to unbanked sections of population.

9.1.6 Micro Finance and Central Government: It was announced in the Union Budget for 2005-06 that the Government of India intends to promote micro finance institutions (MFIs) in a big way. For this purpose, the Micro-Finance Development Fund (MFDF) was re-designated as Micro-Finance Development and Equity Fund (MFDEF) and the corpus of the fund was increased from ₹ 100 crore to ₹ 200 crore. MFDEF is expected to play a vital role in capitalising the MFIs and thereby improving their access to commercial loans.

The Central Government is considering the need to identify and classify the MFIs and rate such institutions to empower them to intermediate between the lending banks and the clients. To facilitate the process of rating of MFIs, NABARD has decided to extend financial assistance to commercial banks and RRBs by way of grant to enable them to avail the services of credit rating agencies for rating of MFIs.

A. Micro Finance Development and Equity Fund (MFDEF): Recognising the need for up-scaling the micro finance interventions in the country, the Union Finance Minister, while presenting the budget for the year 2000-01, had created Micro Finance Development Fund (MFDF) with an initial contribution of ₹ 100 crore, to be funded by Reserve Bank of India, NABARD and commercial Banks in the ratio of 40:40:20. In the Union Budget for 2005-06, the Government of

India decided to re-designate the MFDF into MFDEF and raised its corpus from ₹ 100 crore to ₹ 200 crore.

To strengthen the efforts of NABARD towards promotional support for micro finance, the Government of India in the Union Budget for 2010-11 further increased the corpus of MFDEF to ₹ 400 crore.

The MFDEF is managed and administered by NABARD under the guidance of an MFDEF Advisory Board. The objective of MFDEF is to facilitate and support the orderly growth of the micro finance sector through diverse modalities for enlarging the flow of financial services to the poor, particularly for women and vulnerable sections of society consistent with sustainability.

The Fund is utilised to support interventions to eligible institutions and stakeholders. The major components of the assistance include promotional grant assistance to self-help promoting agencies, training and capacity building for microfinance clients and stakeholders of SHG-Bank Linkage Programme, funding support to MFIs, management information system (MIS) for microfinance, research, studies and publications.

9.1.7 Micro Finance and Reserve Bank of India (RBI): The RBI has been taking a pro-active role in promoting micro-finance. It set up four Groups in 2002 to look into various aspects of micro-financing. Based on the recommendations made by these Groups, the RBI announced that banks should provide adequate incentives to their branches in making the procedures for financing the SHGs simple and easy.

Based on the recommendations of the Vyas Committee, the RBI, in its annual policy statement for 2004-05, indicated that micro finance institutions would not be permitted to accept public deposits, unless they comply with the extant regulatory framework.

In view of the new paradigm shift in micro finance, the RBI is reviewing the issue of micro finance in a comprehensive manner. Accordingly, several initiatives have been taken in the recent period.

A Technical Paper on Policy relating to Development, Regulation and Supervision of Micro finance Services was prepared and discussed with the representatives of MFIs on July 18, 2005. Similarly, an Internal Group of the RBI on Rural Credit and Micro-Finance (Chairman: H.R. Khan) was set up to examine the issues relating to micro-finance. The final version of the Report was released to the public in July 2005.

The SHG-Bank linkage programme is now considered by the banking system as a commercial proposition, with advantages of lower transaction cost, near zero NPAs and coverage of maximum number of the rural clientele by the bank branches. It has also led to other quantifiable benefits in business expansion.

A. Priority-sector Status for Bank Loans to Micro Finance Institutions (MFIs): The RBI set up a committee to study issues and concerns in the micro-finance sector (Chairman: Y.H. Malegam). Based on its recommendation, all SCBs have been advised by the RBI that bank credit to MFIs extended on, or after April 1, 2011 for on-lending to individuals and also to members of SHGs/joint-liability groups (JLGs) will be eligible for categorization as priority-sector advance under the categories agriculture, MSE, and micro credit (for other purposes), as indirect finance, provided not less than 85 percent of total assets of the MFI (other than cash balances with banks and financial institutions, government securities, and money market instruments) are in the nature of 'qualifying assets'. In addition, the aggregate amount of loan, extended for income-generating activity, should not be less than 75 percent of the total loans given by MFIs.

B. Exemptions Granted to NBFCs Engaged in Micro Finance Activities: The Task Force on Supportive Policy and Regulatory Framework for Micro finance set up by NABARD in 1999 provided various recommendations. Accordingly, it was decided to exempt NBFCs which are engaged in micro financing activities, licensed under Section 25 of the Companies Act, 1956, and which do not accept public deposits, from the purview of Sections 45-IA (registration), 45-IB (maintenance of liquid assets) and 45-IC (transfer of profits to the Reserve Fund) of the RBI Act, 1934.

Hence, an increasing number of micro finance institutions (MFIs) is seeking non-banking finance company (NBFC) status from RBI to get wide access to funding, including bank finance.

RBI has been playing a supportive role for strengthening micro credit movement in India. As per notification issued by the RBI dated January 13, 2000, relevant provisions of RBI Act, 1934 as applicable to NBFCs do not apply to NBFCs: (i) licensed under section 25 of Companies Act, 1956, (ii) providing credit not exceeding ₹ 50,000 for a business enterprise and ₹ 1,25,000 for meeting the cost of a dwelling unit to any poor person, and (iii) not accepting public deposits. This provision certainly encourages NBFCs to participate in micro finance programme.

9.2 Self-help Groups (SHGs)

Micro finance is routed through self-help groups (SHGs). Over the years, SHG–Bank Linkage Programme—which includes commercial banks, regional rural banks and co-operative banks—has emerged as the major micro finance programme in the country. The focus under SHG-Bank Linkage Programme is largely on those rural poor who have no sustainable access to the formal banking system. The target groups, therefore, broadly comprise small and marginal farmers, agricultural and non-agricultural labourers, artisans and craftsmen and other poor engaged in small businesses like vending, and hawking.

The programme has been providing the rural poor access to the formal banking system and has achieved several milestones in terms of gender sensitisation, empowerment and poverty alleviation. The programme provides thrift linked credit support to the members of SHGs. While the programme directly benefits the members, it also helps banks in reducing their transaction costs as well as risk in delivering small loans.

The programme has now assumed the form of a micro finance movement in many parts of the country and has started making inroads in the resource poor regions of the country as well.

9.2.1 Self-help Group (SHG) Defined: A self-help Group (SHG) is a small voluntary association of 10-20 poor people from the same socio-economic background who come together for the purpose of addressing their common socio-economic problems through self-help and mutual-help. They collect small savings (thrift) on regular basis. Out of the pooled money, small interest bearing loans are given to the members and some amount is deposited with a bank regularly. The bank lends money for economic activities of the group without collateral security and at market rates. The savings of poor members are pooled resources saved with great difficulty. This hard-earned money is termed as *warm money.* The money obtained by the group from outsiders, i.e. banks, MFIs is termed as *cold money.*

Most self-help groups are located in India, though SHGs can also be found in other countries, especially in South Asia and Southeast Asia.

Members make small regular contributions over a few months until there is enough capital with the group to begin lending. Funds may then be lent back to the members or to others in the village for any purpose. In India, many SHGs are *linked* to banks for the delivery of micro credit.

SHGs are started by non-governmental organizations (NGOs) that generally have broad anti-poverty agendas. SHGs are seen as instruments for a variety of goals including empowering women, developing leadership abilities among poor people, increasing school enrolments, and improving nutrition and the use of birth control. Financial intermediation is generally seen more as an entry point to these other goals, rather than as a primary objective.

Self-help groups (SHGs) have been instrumental in initiating micro entrepreneurial activities among those poor people who have been neglected so far and far away from the process of social as well economic development. Self-help groups-bank linkage programme is responsible for developing banking habits among the poorest of the poor people.

The basic objective of self-help group is upliftment of poor people by means of micro economic activities so that the members get job opportunities, sustainable income and some assets for generation of regular income. There is tremendous enthusiasm in formation of the groups but care is not taken for their proper growth and survival.

The most significant contribution of SHGs is that they have been instrumental in building up enough confidence among the poor people and now they are ready to participate in the process of development. Many of these have been running fair price shops very successfully. A sizable number of the groups are working as caterers for the State Government-sponsored Mid-Day Meal Scheme. It is noteworthy that a good number of the SHGs have been marketing successfully the products of domestic as well as multinational corporations in remote rural areas.

9.2.2 Benefits of SHGs: There are many advantages of financing through SHGs: (a) an economically poor individual gains strength as part of a group, (b) financing through SHGs reduces transaction costs for both lenders and borrowers, (c) Lenders have to handle only a single SHG account instead of a large number of small-sized individual accounts, and (d) borrowers, as part of an SHG, cut down expenses on travel (to and from the branch and other places) for completing paper work and on the loss of workdays in canvassing for loans.

A. Benefits of SHG to the Members: A self-help group benefits its members in a number of ways.

1. Members are benefited with regular saving habits.
2. Easy availability of micro credit.
3. Creation of productive assets.
4. Financial discipline.
5. Status as an economic person.
6. Unity, fraternity and co-operation.
7. Development of entrepreneurship and leadership.
8. Employment to self and others.
9. Joint action for education, health, drinking water, housing, rural roads, family welfare and planning, sanitation, village cleanliness etc.
10. Exposure to the schemes for development, awareness about environment protection, prevention of social evils such as alcoholism, dowry, child marriages.

B. Benefits of SHGs to Banks: Due to group deposits and finance there is benefit of less paperwork and naturally it results in reduction of transaction cost. Loan recovery improves due to peer pressure. The banks have a huge scope for expansion of their business because of fast growing SHG-Bank Linkage Programme.

SHGs are seen as an effective tool for eradicating poverty. It is noteworthy that the SHG-Bank Linkage Programme in India is the fastest and largest micro finance initiatives in the world having participation of Government organisations, Non-government organizations, social workers, health workers and village level workers. NABARD, RBI, commercial banks, regional rural banks, co-operative banks and other financial institutions provide institutional support to SHGs.

The target groups of SHG-Bank Linkage Programme are poorest of the poor. Homogeneous groups of the same socio-economic background are preferred to avoid conflicting interests. However, mixed groups can be formed and no discrimination is allowed on the basis of gender, caste or religion. SHGs are formed and nourished by self-help promoting institutions (SHPIs), financed by MFIs for undertaking micro entrepreneurial activities.

It has been observed that small groups of 10-20 members are more participative and active as they are well-acquainted with each other and a good interaction is possible among them. Group meetings at regular intervals give opportunity to the members to express their views on financial and non-financial matters. Transparency at all levels of activities promotes trust and mutual understanding among the members of the group.

The SHG may discuss and finalize a set of by-laws, indicating rules and regulations for the SHGs functioning and also roles and responsibilities of members. It is better to have a written set of byelaws. The self-help promoting institution (SHPI) and bank may guide the SHGs in this regard.

The habit of thrift (small savings) is fundamental to the SHG and helps in building up a strong common fund. Once an SHG has accumulated sizeable amount in the form of savings, say for a period of about 3-6 months, the members may be allowed to avail loans against their savings for emergent consumption and supplementary income generating credit needs.

As soon as the SHG is formed and a couple of group meetings are held, an SHG can open a savings bank account with the nearest commercial or regional rural bank or a co-operative bank. This is essential to keep the thrift and other funds of the SHG safely and also to improve the transparency levels of SHGs transactions. Opening of savings account in fact, is the beginning of relationship between the bank and the SHG.

The Reserve Bank of India (RBI) has issued instructions to all banks permitting them to open savings bank accounts in the name of registered or unregistered SHGs. By initially managing their own common fund for some time, SHG members not only take care of the financing needs of each other, but develop their skills of financial management and intermediation as well. Lending to members also enhances the knowledge of SHG members in setting the interest rate and periodic loan instalments. In order to have participation of cooperative societies in micro finance programme, various State Governments have amended their respective cooperative acts for the promotion of mutually-aided co-operative societies (MACS) based on thrift and self-help.

9.2.3 SHG-Bank Linkage Programme: This is the bank-led micro finance channel which was initiated by NABARD in 1992. Under the SHG model the members, usually women in villages, are encouraged to form groups of around 10-15. The members contribute their savings in the group periodically and from these savings small loans are provided to the members. In the later period, these SHGs are provided with bank loans generally for income generation purpose. Members of the group meet periodically when the new savings come in, recovery of past loans are made from the members and also new loans are disbursed. This model has been very much successful in the past and with time it is becoming more popular. The SHGs are self-sustaining and once the group becomes stable it starts working on its own with some support from NGOs and institutions like NABARD and SIDBI.

Many self-help groups, especially in India, under NABARD's SHG-Bank Linkage Programme, borrow from banks once they have accumulated a base of their own capital and have established a track record of regular repayments.

This model has attracted attention as a possible way of delivering micro finance services to poor people that have been difficult to reach directly through banks or other institutions. By aggregating their individual savings into a single deposit, self-help groups minimize the bank's transaction costs and generate an attractive volume of deposits. Through self-help groups the bank can serve small rural depositors while paying them a market rate of interest.

The SHG-Bank Linkage Programme since its beginning has been predominant in certain states, showing spatial preferences especially for the southern region–Andhra Pradesh, Tamil Nadu, Kerala and Karnataka—with a share of 53 percent as on March 31, 2014 . Total number of SHGs with outstanding bank loans stood at 41,97,338 at the end of March 31, 2014.

9.2.4 Problems of SHGs: SHG programme is not without difficulties and challenges. Some of these are mentioned below.

A. Lack of Support from Family Members: Lack of support from family members discourage woman to join the SHG. In case of mixed groups, male members do not extend support to female members. So, the essential objective of SHGs programme is defeated.

B. Low Income Generating Activities: Economic activities undertaken by the members are traditional. Obviously, the activities generate lower income. Therefore, the micro finance movement is losing its main objective of empowering poor people.

C. Political Interference: Political affiliations of group members disturb group activities. Actually, the concept of self-help group is based on the principle of co-operation, i.e. equality, mutual help, democracy and thrift. It has been observed that political leaders are taking interest in the formation of SHGs to add to their vote bank. Political interference might have adverse impact on the progress of self-help group movement.

The micro finance initiative of NABARD, i.e. SHG-Bank Linkage Programme has passed through various phases over the last two decades, *viz.* pilot testing during 1992 to 1995, mainstreaming during 1996 to 1998 and expansion from 1998 onwards. A self-help group is a group of about 15 to 20 people from a homogenous class who join together to address common issues. They involve voluntary thrift activities on a regular basis, and use of the pooled resource to make interest-bearing loans to the members of the group. In the course of this process, they imbibe the essentials of financial intermediation and also the basics of account keeping. The members also learn to handle resources of size, much beyond their individual capacities. They begin to appreciate the fact that the resources are limited and have a cost.

To sum up, micro credit programme has made rapid strides in India exhibiting considerable democratic functioning and group dynamism. The micro credit programme in India is now the largest in the world. Since Independence, the Government of India and the RBI have made concerted efforts to provide the poor with access to credit. Despite the phenomenal increase in the physical outreach of formal credit institutions in the past several decades, the rural poor continue to depend on informal sources of credit. Institutions have also faced difficulties in dealing effectively with a large number of small borrowers, whose credit needs are small and frequent and their ability to offer collaterals is limited. Besides, cumbersome procedures and risk perceptions of the banks left a gap in serving the credit needs of the rural poor.

10

Mutual Funds

Mutual funds pool together the investments of small investors for participation in the stock market. Mutual funds are very popular all over the world and they play an important role in the financial system of many countries. Mutual funds are an ideal medium for investment by small investors in the stock market. Being institutional investors, mutual funds can afford market analysis generally not available to individual investors. Furthermore, mutual funds can diversify the portfolio in a better way as compared with individual investors due to the expertise and availability of funds.

10.1 Legal and Regulatory Framework

In general, the mutual fund regulatory framework in India is much more extensive and developed than in many other countries. Indian mutual funds are unit trusts, formed under the Indian Trusts Act of 1882. Their operation is governed by mutual fund regulations, totalling 78, promulgated by SEBI in exercise of the powers conferred by Section 30, read with clause (c) of sub-section (2) of Section 11 of the Securities and Exchange Board of India, Act 1992. The first set of mutual fund regulations was originally promulgated in 1996, and has since been amended from time to time. In order to remove any difficulties in the application or interpretation of these regulations, Regulation 77 of the mutual funds regulations additionally authorises SEBI to issue "clarifications and guidelines in the form of notes or circulars which shall be binding upon the sponsor, mutual funds, trustees, asset management companies and custodians".

10.2 History of Mutual Funds

Mutual funds in India were first created in 1963 when the Unit Trust of India (UTI), a state-sponsored entity, came into being. Until 1987, UTI was the only mutual fund in the country. Between 1987 and 1993 other entities belonging to the public sector were permitted to offer mutual funds—basically state-controlled banks and insurers. As part of financial sector reforms, the mutual fund industry was opened to the private sector in 1993. Thus, from 1993 onwards, private sector organisations were permitted to enter the market and the first mutual fund regulations were promulgated, which were subsequently replaced by the SEBI (Mutual Fund) Regulations of 1996. These private sector organisations comprised both Indian and foreign joint ventures as well as purely Indian firms.

Since then, the expansion of mutual fund business has intensified competition and led to product innovation. Mutual funds presently offer a variety of options to investors such as income funds, balanced funds, liquid funds, gift funds, index funds, exchange traded funds, sectoral funds etc. The deceleration in the growth of mutual funds in the 1990s could be attributed partly to the relatively poor performance of the stock markets and partly due to withdrawal of tax benefits under Section 80M of the Indian Income Tax Act, 1961. Some of the mutual funds had offered assured return schemes enabling them to mobilise large resources. A number of mutual funds faced difficulties in meeting their redemption obligations relating to such schemes. In several cases, the sponsors of mutual funds had to infuse additional funds to meet the shortfall. As a result, mutual funds, by and large, discontinued the floatation of assured return schemes, which had some dampening effect on the resource mobilisation by mutual funds.

10.2.1 Bifurcation of UTI: While most of the mutual funds were somehow able to meet their commitments on account of assured return schemes, UTI faced a somewhat different problem on two different occasions between October 1998 and July 2001. US-64, which was the flagship scheme of UTI and enjoyed the investors' faith, first faced problem in December 1998 when the reserves under the scheme were reported negative. In order to restore investors' confidence, several measures were initiated by the Government/UTI. While these measures helped the US-64 to make a turnaround, the problem resurfaced again in July 2001 when UTI slashed down the dividend rates for the year 2000-01 and suspended sales and repurchases of US-64 for a period of 6 months from July 2001 to December 2001. This created a crisis of confidence and to restore investors' confidence various measures were initiated again, which culminated in splitting the UTI into two parts.

On October 28, 2002, an ordinance was promulgated which repealed the UTI Act, and bifurcated UTI into two separate entities. One is the Specified Undertaking of the Unit Trust of India. The Specified Undertaking of Unit Trust of India, functioning under an administrator and under the rules framed by Government of India and does not come under the purview of the mutual fund regulations. It has US-64 and the assured returns schemes. The second is the UTI Mutual Fund Ltd, sponsored by State Bank of India (SBI), Bank of Baroda (BoB), Punjab National Bank (PNB) and Life Insurance Corporation of India (LIC). It is registered with SEBI and functions under the mutual fund regulations. It is an unencumbered mutual fund, with only NAV-based schemes.

The problem with US-64 scheme of UTI adversely affected the resource mobilisation by mutual funds in general and UTI in particular. On both the occasions, when UTI faced difficulties and while resource mobilisation by UTI declined sharply, private sector mutual funds were able to fill the gap created by UTI only partially as overall mobilisation by all mutual funds on both the occasions declined sharply after the occurrence of the problem.

In March 2002, guidelines were issued to enable mutual funds to invest in rated securities in countries with fully convertible currencies. This marked an important milestone, through which mutual funds will be able to deliver better risk/return tradeoffs through international diversification.

10.3 Features of Mutual Fund Industry in India

1. Mutual funds are popular mainly with the middle and high-income groups.
2. Investors are largely based in the urban centres, particularly the metropolitan cities.
3. Penetration of mutual funds in the rural areas remains small.
4. UTI and other state-owned asset management companies have lost market share, while private sector funds have grown rapidly.
5. Asset management companies are divided into those that are predominantly owned by the state (UTI, bank sponsored and institutions) and those that are in the private sector.
6. Mutual fund industry has to compete with attractive assured returns from Government schemes and this is possibly the single most important impediment to the growth of the industry.

Thus, if mutual funds have to grow fast, they would need to devise appropriate schemes to attract the saving of low-income groups, especially in rural areas. This is the only way to ensure participation of all categories of investors into the capital market, which is so crucial for its long-term development.

10.4 Problems of Mutual Funds

India has a high household savings ratio. Indians, like most people anywhere, are conservative in their habits, and it would take many years to change this behaviour, particularly when it comes to the use of their savings. As in most countries, investment in physical assets (mainly housing and gold) accounts for the most important percentage of household assets. Owning a home is usually a first priority once a family has any disposable income at all.

10.4.1 Competition with Government Schemes: Mutual funds compete against a host of high yielding government-backed savings schemes such as public provident fund (PPF), national savings scheme (NSS), RBI bonds, and so on, as well as against life insurance products and, in the future, against the new pension schemes for the unorganised sector. [1] The political and social reasons for keeping yields higher than the market for small savers, particularly retired savers, is understandable. The market is distorted by such a policy. Government should have the strategic aim of discontinuing over time or at least reducing the availability of the unrealistically high yielding avenues for small savings. The objective of widening and deepening ownership of mutual funds is unlikely to be met until this happens.

Fixed income and balanced mutual funds have offered a reasonably competitive rate of return but they are not guaranteed, a key attraction to Indian investors. The net result is that mutual funds fail to attract much money from retail investors, who prefer to invest in a no-risk, high return product, i.e. government saving schemes or provident funds or keep their money safely in the bank.

Government-sponsored instruments *crowd out* mutual funds since for the majority of Indians buying mutual funds, before they have their full complement of government-backed savings instruments, would be both wrong and foolish.

In most countries government guaranteed financial instruments offer returns that are likely to be significantly lower than private sector investments available from mutual funds or insurance companies. This is the penalty that investors are prepared to pay for little or no risk. However, Indian retail investors are not being asked to sacrifice any substantial amount of return in exchange for a government guarantee. Conversely, returns on government assured investments are often better than those available elsewhere. While conventional government bonds do give lower returns than equivalent private sector corporate bonds, the retail government assured products give higher returns for almost no risk. It is thus hardly surprising that an investor of modest means would choose to invest in, for instance, national savings certificates, since he can thus obtain a better return for a much lower risk. Any investor would be well advised to invest the maximum permitted in the various government assured schemes before considering other forms of investment.

The reasons why the government is prepared to pay above market rates of interest on certain financial products is understandable. At a time when interest rates have fallen substantially from their previous levels, savers who had counted on the interest on their savings to provide an income, particularly in retirement, are being subsidised. Given that pension arrangements, particularly in the unorganised sector, are not widespread, such an approach is reasonable and indeed most small savers are acting rationally when they choose the low risk option. However, this approach conflicts with a desire to widen and deepen participation in capital markets through mutual funds or other non-governmental savings products by the less well-off sectors of the population.

10.4.2 Competition from Insurance: The take up life assurance is growing rapidly and may be pre-empting some of the market that mutual funds could aim at. Life assurance is an easier product to sell, since in the mind of the investor the payment of a premium is often linked to a specific outcome, a lump sum payment on death or a guaranteed minimum sum on maturity. It also pays higher commissions to sales agents (typically the amount of the first 5 to 6 months premium). Thus a sales agent will usually prefer to sell a life policy since it will reward him better.

10.4.3 Volatility of Mutual Fund Performance: There is a perception that mutual funds have somehow let down their investors and given them poor returns. In July 2001 when UTI slashed down the dividend rates for the year 2000-01 and suspended sales and repurchases of US-64 for a period of 6 months from July 2001 to December 2001, it created a crisis of confidence among the investors with long-term effects.

10.4.4 Tax System Encourages Short-term Objectives: Mutual funds are regarded in most countries as a diversified, professionally managed and well-regulated vehicle for mobilising household savings and are often accorded tax privileges specifically in pursuit of a government policy goal to encourage long-term savings, notably for retirement. [2] It is unusual for such tax privileges to impel mutual funds towards short-term goals, which is what seems to be the case in India. True, Indian unit trusts are diversified, professionally managed and well-regulated, but they are certainly not serving long-term objectives.

10.5 Mutual Funds and the Stock Market

Mutual funds in India, because of their small size and slower growth in the recent past, have tended to play only a limited role in the stock market. In view of small size of their operations, mutual funds in normal times hardly exert any influence on the stock market. Mutual funds with large funds at their disposal are expected by the government to act as a counterweight to foreign institutional investors (FIIs), which generally exert a significant influence on the stock market. Some leading asset management companies and mutual funds in India are listed in Table 10.1.

To sum up, the mutual fund industry in India is quite sophisticated and successful. It is dominated by good and reputable institutions, both Indian and international. Nevertheless improvements are always possible and desirable in order to enhance the ability of the mutual fund industry to mobilise savings on a wider scale and to contribute to the further development of capital market.

Table 10.1: Leading Asset Management Companies and Mutual Funds in India

Name of Asset Management Company	Mutual Fund
Sponsored by Banks	
Bank of Baroda Asset Management Company	BoB Mutual Fund
Canbank Investment Services Ltd.	Canara Bank
PNB Asset Management Company Ltd.	PNB Mutual Fund
SBI Funds Management Ltd.	SBI Mutual Fund
UTI Asset Management Company Pvt. Ltd.	UTI Mutual Fund
Sponsored by Institutions	
GIC Asset Management Company Ltd.	GIC Mutual Fund
IL & FS Asset Management Company Ltd.	IL & FS Mutual Fund
Jeevan Bima Sahayog Asset Management Company	LIC Mutual Fund
Private Sector Companies	
Benchmark Asset Management Co Pvt. Ltd.	Benchmark Mutual Fund
Cholamandalam AMC Ltd.	Cholamandalam Mutual Fund
Escorts Asset Management Ltd.	Escorts Mutual Fund
First India Asset Management Pvt. Ltd.	First India Mutual Fund
JM Capital Management Pvt. Ltd.	JM Mutual Fund
Kotak Mahindra Asset Management Company Ltd.	Kotak Mahindra Mutual Fund
Reliance Capital Asset Management Ltd.	Reliance Capital Mutual Fund
Sundaram Newton Asset Management Company	Sundaram Mutual Fund
Birla Sunlife Asset Management Company Ltd.	Birla Sunlife Mutual Fund
Credit Capital Asset Management Company Ltd.	Taurus Mutual Fund
DSP Merrill Lynch Fund Managers Ltd.	DSP Merrill Lynch Mutual Fund
HDFC Asset Management Company Ltd.	HDFC Mutual Fund
Tata TD Waterhouse Asset Management Pvt. Ltd.	Tata TD Mutual Fund
Joint Venture Companies	
Alliance Capital Asset Management (India) Pvt. Ltd.	Alliance Capital Mutual Fund
Deutsche Asset Management (India) Pvt. Ltd.	Deutsche Mutual Fund
HSBC Asset Management (India) Pvt. Ltd.	HSBC Mutual Fund
ING Investment Management (India) Pvt Ltd.	ING Vyasa Mutual Fund
Morgan Stanley Investment Management Pvt. Ltd.	Morgan Stanley Mutual Fund
Prudential ICICI Asset Management Company Ltd.	Prudential ICICI Mutual Fund
Standard Chartered Asset Management Company Pvt. Ltd.	Standard Chartered Mutual Fund
Sun F&C Asset Management (India) Pvt. Ltd.	Sun F&C Mutual Fund
Templeton Asset Management (India) Pvt. Ltd.	Templeton India Mutual Fund
Foreign Company	
Principal Asset Management Company Ltd.	Principal Mutual Fund

Table 10.2 presents the assets under management of mutual funds in India.

Table 10.2: Assets under Management of Mutual Funds: 2000-2015

S. No.	**Year** (ending March 31)	**Amount** (in ₹ crore)
1.	2000	1,07,946
2.	2001	90,587
3.	2002	1,00,954
4.	2003	1,09,229
5.	2004	1,39,616
6.	2005	1,49,600
7.	2006	2,31,862
8.	2007	3,26,292
9.	2008	5,05,152
10.	2009	4,17,300
11.	2010	6,13,979
12.	2011	5,92,250
13.	2012	5,87,217
14.	2013	7,01,443
15.	2014	8,25,240
16.	2015	10,82,757
17.	**April 30, 2015**	**11,86,364**

Sources: www.rbi.org and www.amfiindia.com

Endnotes

1. Many of the government assured schemes are probably not fulfilling their original purpose. For example the Public Provident Fund (PPP) was set up in 1968-69 with the objective of providing unorganised sector workers with a facility to accumulate savings for old age income security. As a result of premature withdrawal facilities and tax breaks, individuals largely misuse this scheme for legitimised tax evasion and it does not serve the intended purpose of old age income security.
2. There is no perfect system for taxing the income and gains of mutual funds and their investors. The main principle that almost all regimes follow is that there should be broadly equality of treatment between all mutual fund investors and between mutual fund investors and direct investors in securities. In other words, an investor purchasing assets indirectly through a mutual fund should be no worse off tax-wise than if that same investor bought those assets directly on their own behalf. This is the principle of *fiscal neutrality*.

   The taxation of funds is a key issue for funds and their management companies. Taxation affects both the attractiveness of funds compared with other investments, and also the systems that may have to be designed and implemented in order for funds to operate efficiently and cost effectively. Fund managers in virtually every market in the world lobby governments hard either to remove tax disadvantages or to achieve favourable treatment, so that their product can become more competitive in the market and more attractive to potential buyers.

11

Pension Funds

Noting that only about 12-13 percent of the total workforce was covered by any formal social security system, pension sector reforms were initiated in India to establish a robust and sustainable social security arrangement in the country.

11.1 New Pension System (NPS)

NPS reflects Government's effort to find sustainable solutions to the problem of providing adequate retirement income. As a first step towards instituting pensionary reforms, Government of India moved from a defined benefit pension to a defined contribution-based pension system by making it mandatory for its new recruits (except armed forces) with effect from January 1, 2004.

Since April 1, 2008, the pension contributions of Central Government employees covered by NPS are being invested by professional pension fund managers (PFMs) in line with investment guidelines of Government applicable to non-Government provident funds.

NPS has been made available to every citizen from April 1, 2009 on a voluntary basis. With the extension of NPS to all citizens, every citizen in the country now has the opportunity to participate in a regulated pension market. This will contribute significantly to old age income security in the country.

Features of the NPS design are self-sustainability, portability and scalability. Based on individual choice, it is envisaged as a low-cost and efficient pension system backed by sound regulation. As a pure *defined contribution* product with no defined benefit element, returns are totally market-related. NPS provides various investment options and choices to individuals to switch over from one option to another or from one fund manager to another, subject to certain regulatory restrictions.

NPS architecture is transparent and web-enabled. It allows a subscriber to monitor his/her investments and returns under NPS, the choice of PFM and the investment option also rest with the subscriber. The design allows the subscriber to switch his/her investment options as well as pension funds. The facility for seamless portability and switch between PFMs is designed to enable subscribers to maintain a single pension account throughout their saving period.

Full NPS architecture—comprising a central recordkeeping agency (CRA), point of presence and aggregators, pension fund managers (PFMs), trustee bank, custodian and NPS Trust—has been put in place and is fully operational. National Securities Depository Limited (NSDL) has been selected as the CRA.

NPS has been designed to enable the subscriber to make optimum decisions regarding his/her future and provide for his/her old-age through systemic savings from the day he/she starts his/her employment. It seeks to inculcate the habit of saving for retirement amongst the citizens.

Efforts are under way to extend the reach of the NPS to new segments like Central and State autonomous bodies and the organized sector and introduce micro-pension initiatives focusing on a low cost model of the NPS to be implemented through self-help groups (SHGs) and similar bodies.

11.1.1 Swavalamban Scheme: The Government is extremely concerned about the old age income security of the working poor and is focused on encouraging and enabling them to join the NPS. To encourage workers in the unorganized sector to save voluntarily for their old age, an initiative called the Swavalamban Scheme was launched on September 26, 2010. It is a co-contributory pension scheme whereby the Central Government would contribute a sum of ₹ 1,000 per annum in each NPS account opened having a saving of ₹ 1,000 to ₹ 12,000 per annum. The Swavalamban Scheme was initially announced for 3 years for beneficiaries who enrolled themselves in 2010-11. It was extended to 5 years for beneficiaries enrolled in 2010-11 and 2011-12. For the Swavalamban accounts opened during 2013-2014 to 2016-2017, the benefits will extend till 2016-2017.

Although the NPS is perhaps one of the cheapest financial products available in the country, Swavalamban Scheme enables groups of people to join the NPS at a substantially reduced cost. As per existing scheme under NPS, Swavalamban can be availed either in unorganized sector or in NPS Lite. NPS Lite is a model specifically designed to bring NPS within easy reach of the economically disadvantaged sections of the society. NPS Lite is extremely affordable and viable due to its optimized functionalities available at reduced charges.

11.1.2 NPS Corporate Sector Model: A customized version of the core NPS model, known as the NPS Corporate Sector Model was also introduced from December 2011 to enable organized-sector entities to move their existing and prospective employees to the NPS under its Corporate Model. All the public sector banks have been asked to provide a link on their website to enable individual subscribers to open online NPS Accounts. Several State Governments, autonomous bodies, and undertakings are in dialogue with PFRDA for extending the NPS to their employees. In the non-government NPS segment, clearly NPSLite/Swavalamban has emerged as the vehicle of choice.

11.1.3 Atal Pension Yojana (APY): Budget for the year 2015-16 unleashed the announcement of a universal social security scheme in the insurance and pension sector for all Indians, named as Atal Pension Yojana (APY), meant primarily for the poor and the under-privileged. Under the scheme, a defined pension would be provided, depending on the contribution and its period. The APY will be focussed on all citizens in the unorganised sector, who join the National Pension System (NPS) administered by the Pension Fund Regulatory and Development Authority (PFRDA).

Under the APY, the subscribers would receive the fixed minimum pension of ₹ 1,000 per month, ₹ 2,000 per month, ₹ 3,000 per month, ₹ 4,000 per month and ₹ 5,000 per month, at the age of 60 years, depending on their contributions, which itself would be based on the age of joining the APY. The minimum age of joining APY is 18 years and maximum age is 40 years. Therefore, minimum period of contribution by any subscriber under APY would be 20 years or more. The benefit of fixed minimum pension would be guaranteed by the Government. The APY would be introduced from June 1, 2015.

The Central Government would co-contribute 50 percent of the total contribution or ₹ 1,000 per annum, whichever is lower, to each eligible subscriber account, for a period of 5 years, i.e., from financial year 2015-16 to 2019-20, who join the NPS between the period June 1, 2015 and December 31, 2015 and are not members of any statutory social security scheme and are not income tax payers. However the scheme will continue after this date but Government co-contribution will not be available.

11.2 Pension Fund Regulatory and Development Authority (PFRDA)

PFRDA was established by Government of India on August 23, 2003. The Government has, through an executive order dated October 10, 2003, mandated PFRDA to act as a regulator for the pension sector. The mandate of PFRDA is development and regulation of pension sector in India.

PFRDA, set up as a regulatory body for the pension sector, is engaged in consolidating the initiatives taken so far regarding the full NPS architecture and expanding the reach of the NPS distribution network.

As on January 5, 2015 PFRDA has appointed the following 8 pension fund managers (PFM) for government and private sector NPS:

1. LIC Pension Fund Ltd.
2. SBI Pension Funds Pvt. Ltd.
3. UTI Retirement Solutions Ltd.
4. HDFC Pension Management Company Ltd.
5. ICICI Prudential Pension Fund Management Company Ltd.

6. Reliance Capital Pension Fund Ltd.
7. Kotak Mahindra Pension Fund Ltd.
8. *PF to be incorporated by* Birla Sunlife Insurance Co. Ltd.

PFMs manage three separate schemes consisting of three asset classes, namely: (i) equity, (ii) Government securities, and (iii) credit risk-bearing fixed income instruments, with the investment in equity subject to a cap of 50 percent. The fund managers will invest only in index funds that replicate either the BSE sensitive index or NSE Nifty 50 index. The subscriber will have the option to decide the investment mix of his pension wealth. In case the subscriber is unable/unwilling to exercise any choice regarding asset allocation, his contribution will be invested in accordance with the *auto choice* option with a predefined portfolio.

PFRDA has set up a Trust under the Indian Trusts Act, 1882 to oversee the functions of the PFMs. The NPS Trust is composed of members representing diverse fields and brings wide range of talent to the regulatory framework. PFRDA also intends to intensify its effort towards financial education and awareness as a part of its strategy to protect the interest of the subscribers. PFRDA's efforts are an important milestone in the development of a sustainable and efficient voluntary defined contribution based pension system in India.

PFRDA has also enhanced the maximum entry age into NPS from 55 years to 60 years. These initiatives are expected to help realize the full potential of the NPS in terms of economies of scale and benefit the subscribers in terms of lower fees and charges and higher returns.

Table 11.1: New Pension System (NPS) at a Glance (as on April 7, 2015)

S. No.	Employer/Sector	No. of Subscribers	Assets Under Management (₹ crore)
1.	Central Government	15,12,373	36,921
2.	State Government	26,32,824	37,976
3.	Private Sector	4,61,524	6,361
4.	NPS-Lite	42,37,766	1,629
5.	Total	88,44,487	82,887

Source: Pension Fund Regulatory Development Authority (PFRDA), *Monthly Pension Bulletin, April 2015.*

12

Pradhan Mantri Jan-Dhan Yojana (PMJDY), 2014

Exclusion from the banking system excludes people from all benefits that come from a modern financial system. Thus, financial inclusion is a national priority of the Government of India as it is an enabler for inclusive growth. Financial inclusion is important as it provides an avenue to the poor for bringing their savings into the formal financial system, a means to remit money to their families in villages besides taking them out of the clutches of the usurious money lenders.

12.1 Background

The efforts to include the financially excluded segments of the society in India are not new. The concept was first mooted by the Reserve Bank of India in 2005 and branchless banking through banking agents called *Bank Mitras* [Business Correspondents (BCs)] was started in the year 2006. In the year 2011, banks covered 74,351 villages, with population of more than 2,000 (as per 2011 Census), with banking facilities under the *Swabhimaan* campaign. However, the programme had a very limited reach and impact.

This campaign was limited in its approach in terms of reach and coverage. Convergence of various aspects of comprehensive financial inclusion like opening of bank accounts, access to digital money, availing of micro credit, insurance and pension was lacking.

The campaign focused only on the supply side by providing banking facility in villages of population greater than 2,000 but the entire geography was not targeted. There was no focus on the households. Also, some technology issues hampered further scalability of the campaign. Consequently, the desired benefits could not be achieved and a large number of bank accounts remained dormant. A comprehensive plan was felt necessary to keep the accounts active and use them as an instrument of some economic activity leading to livelihoods.

In order to provide the much needed thrust, a flagship programme called the Pradhan Mantri Jan-Dhan Yojana (PMJDY) was announced by the Prime Minister Narendra Modi in his Independence Day address to the nation on August 15, 2014. PMJDY was launched on August 28, 2014, across the country simultaneously. PMJDY lies at the core of development philosophy of *Sab Ka Sath Sab Ka Vikas* (inclusive growth).

12.2 PMJDY: Brief Introduction

PMJDY is a National Mission on financial inclusion. This Mission would enable all households—urban and rural—to gain easy and universal access to financial services. In this Mission, households will not only have bank accounts with indigenous RuPay debit cards but will also gain access to credit for economic activity and to insurance and pension services for their social security. The Mission has a strong focus on the use of technology and incorporates lessons learnt from earlier efforts.

PMJDY encompasses an integrated approach to bring about comprehensive financial inclusion of all the households in the country. The Plan envisages universal access to banking facilities with at least one basic banking account for every household, financial literacy, access to credit, insurance and pension facility. In addition, the beneficiaries would get RuPay Debit card having in-built accident insurance cover of ₹ 1 lakh. The plan also envisages channelling all Government benefits (from Centre/State/Local Body) to the beneficiaries' accounts and pushing the direct benefits transfer (DBT) scheme of the Union Government. The technological issues like poor connectivity, online transactions would also be addressed. Mobile transactions through telecom operators and their established centres as Cash Out Points are also planned to be used for financial inclusion under the Scheme. Also, an effort is being made to reach out to the youth of the country to participate in this Mission Mode Programme.

PMJDY aims to provide bank account to every household in the country and make available the following basic banking services facilities:

- Opening of bank account with RuPay debit card and mobile banking facility.
- Cash withdrawal and deposits.
- Transfer.
- Balance enquiry.
- Mini statement.

Other services are also to be provided in due course in a time-bound manner apart from financial literacy which is to be disseminated side by side to make citizens capable to use optimum utilization of available financial services. To provide these banking services, banking outlets are to be provided within 5 kilometres distance of every village. Necessary infrastructure also needs to be placed to enable e-KYC for account opening and AEPS for withdrawal of cash-based biometric authentication from UIDAI data base.

12.3 Six Pillars of PMJDY

PMJDY, to be executed in the Mission Mode, envisages provision of affordable financial services to all citizens within a reasonable distance. It comprises of the following six pillars:

1. **Universal Access to Banking Facilities:** Mapping of each district into sub service area (SSA) catering between 1,000-1,500 households in a manner that every habitation has access to banking services within a reasonable distance, say 5 km. by August 14, 2015. Coverage of parts of J&K, Himachal Pradesh, Uttarakhand, North East and the Left Wing Extremism affected districts which have telecom connectivity and infrastructure constraints would spill over to the Phase II of the programme (August 15, 2015 to August 15, 2018).
2. **Providing Basic Banking Accounts with Overdraft Facility and RuPay Debit Card to all Households:** The effort would be to first cover all uncovered households with banking facilities by August 2015, by opening basic bank accounts. Account holder would be provided a RuPay debit card. Facility of an overdraft to every basic banking account holder would be considered after satisfactory operation/credit history of six months.
3. **Financial Literacy Programme:** Financial literacy would be an integral part of the Mission in order to let the beneficiaries make best use of the financial services being made available to them.
4. **Creation of Credit Guarantee Fund:** Creation of a Credit Guarantee Fund would be to cover the defaults in overdraft accounts.
5. **Micro Insurance:** To provide micro insurance to all willing and eligible persons by August 14, 2018, and then on an ongoing basis.
6. **Unorganized Sector Pension Schemes like Swavalamban:** By August 14, 2018 and then on an ongoing basis.

Under the Mission, the first three pillars would be given thrust in the first year.

12.4 Timeline for Financial Inclusion Plan

Comprehensive financial inclusion of the excluded sections is proposed to be achieved by August 14, 2018 in two phases as under:

Phase I-(August 15, 2014 to August 14, 2015):

- Universal access to banking facilities in all areas except areas with infrastructure and connectivity constrains like parts of North East, Himachal Pradesh, Uttarakhand, J&K and 82 Left Wing Extremism (LE) districts.
- Providing basic banking accounts and RuPay debit card which has an in-built accident insurance cover of ₹ 1 lakh. Aadhaar number will be seeded to make account ready for DBT payment.
- Financial Literacy Programme.

Phase II-(August 15, 2015 to August 14, 2018):

- Overdraft facility up to ₹ 5,000 after six months of satisfactory operation/history.
- Creation of Credit Guarantee Fund for coverage of defaults in accounts with overdraft limit up to ₹ 5,000.
- Micro insurance.
- Unorganized sector pension schemes like Swavalamban.

Some of the Phase II activities would also be carried out in Phase I. In addition, in this phase, coverage of households in hilly, tribal and difficult areas would be carried out. Moreover, this phase would focus on coverage of remaining adults in the households and students.

12.5 Strategy for Achievement of Objectives

1. In order to achieve the above objectives, a broad collaborative strategy with all stakeholders is proposed. It is proposed to encourage public-private partnership (PPP). Moreover, inter-department convergence and synergies will be gainfully utilised. The existing rural infrastructure of post offices having *Gramin Dak Sewaks* would be optimally utilized to become *Bank Mitras* [Business Correspondents (BCs)] of the banks. One of the key strategies will be deployment of online fixed point BCs to deliver basic banking services near to the customer doorstep. There are 1.26 lakh common service centres, out of which only 12,000 are BCs of the banks.
2. The strategy is to take forward the BC model for expansion of banking services by modifying it to ensure both operational flexibility and viability of the BC. Technological innovations like RuPay card and mobile banking would be made use of. Banks will use the RBI's scheme for subsidy on rural ATMs and UIDAI's scheme for subsidy on micro ATMs to augment their resources at the village level.
3. Convergence with the National Rural Livelihood Mission (NRLM) in rural areas and National Urban Livelihood Mission (NULM) in urban areas would be sought for in covering each household with bank accounts. The expansion plans of the Department of Telecom to provide telecom connectivity in difficult areas would be effectively utilized for the provision of banking facilities in these areas. Department of Telecom has been requested to ensure that problems of poor and no connectivity are resolved on priority basis.

12.6 Implementation of PMJDY

12.6.1 Reaching Out: Network Expansion and Geographical Coverage of the Banks: The first and basic pillar of PMJDY is the expansion of banking network of the country to reach out to the financially excluded segments of the population.

A. Bank Branches and ATMs: In the year 2013-14, the public sector banks (PSBs) set up 7,840 branches across the country of which about 25 percent were in rural areas. More than 40,000 ATMs were also set up pursuant to the Budget announcement of 2013-14 of providing an ATM at every branch.

The banking network of the country (as on March 31, 2014) comprised of a bank branch network of 1,15,082 and an ATM network of 1,60,055 (no. of ATMs rose to 1,76,410 in December 2014). Of these, 43,962 branches (38.2 percent) and 23,334 ATMs (14.58 percent) were in rural areas and the remaining in semi-urban and metropolitan areas. In the year 2014-15, the public sector banks propose to set up 7,332 branches and 20,130 new ATMs. However, given the staff constraints of banks and the viability of opening full-fledged branches in rural areas, the demands for branch expansion far exceed the supply. The efficient and cost-effective method to cover rural areas is by way of mapping the entire country through sub-service area (SSA) approach and deploying fully enabled online fixed point *Bank Mitra* (Business Correspondent) outlets. Public-private-partnership in this area shall facilitate the process and promote efficiency and pace of coverage.

B. Swabhiman Villages: In the year 2011-12, banks covered more than 74,000 villages, with a population more than 2,000 (as per 2011 Census), with banking facilities under the *Swabhimaan* campaign. Looking to viability of each centre, banks would strive to set up a brick and mortar branch with minimum staff strength of 1+1 or 1+2 in 74,351 villages having population of 2000 or more which were covered by BCs in the earlier campaign. This can be done in a phased manner over a period of 3-5 years.

C. Mapping Sub-Service Areas (SSAs): Under the present plan, all the 6 lakh villages across the entire country are to be mapped according to the service area of each bank and to have at least one fixed point banking outlet catering to 1,000 to 1,500 households, called as sub-service area (SSA). Villages with panchayat offices can be made the nodal point. This approach was tried in 121 DBT districts and the entire mapping resulted in creation of 30,855 SSAs. Of these, 30,751 SSAs were saturated with banking facilities. It is estimated that across the country there would be about 1.3 lakh SSAs, of which under the present campaign, about 0.8 lakh would already be covered by banking facilities and about 50,000 new SSAs would need to be covered. Moreover, there are more than 1.40 lakh BCs of public sector banks and regional rural banks in the rural areas. Public sector banks have estimated to set up about 31,846 SSAs in order to cover the entire geography of the country. In addition, the regional rural banks have estimated to set up another 14,216 SSAs to complete the SSA coverage. This translates to a target of coverage of 46,162 SSAs. Considering the possibility of some field level data mismatches, a conservative estimate of coverage of 50,000 SSAs is being planned for, under the present campaign. However, actual field experience suggests that many of these are not functional. It is estimated that 75,000 replacements of non-functional BCs would be required. There are around 1.26 lakh common service centres (CSCs) in the country, out of which 12,284 centres are working as banking BC outlets. All the remaining CSCs are proposed to be enabled as BC outlets for banks.

D. Coverage of SSAs: It is proposed that SSAs shall be covered through a combination of banking outlets, i.e. branch banking and branchless banking. Branch banking means traditional brick and mortar branches. These branches are manned by bank staff and offer complete banking services including third party payments and processing of loan applications. Branchless banking comprises of fixed point *Bank Mitra* (Business Correspondent), who act as representatives of banks to provide basic banking services, i.e. opening of bank accounts, cash deposit, cash withdrawal, transfer of funds, balance enquiries and mini statement facility. Besides, they also provide value added additional services to the bank. Villages without brick and mortar branches of banks would be covered by fixed location BCs outlets preferably at the *panchayat* office/bus station/local market. The *Bank Mitra* (Business Correspondent) may cater to the neighbouring villages in his area on pre-defined time and days. The working and visit timing would be prominently displayed at his place of working. Every habitation will have access to banking services within 5 km. by August 2015, except parts of J&K, Himachal Pradesh, Uttarakhand, North East and the 82 Left Wing extremism affected districts which have telecom connectivity and infrastructure constraints. RBI had directed banks to cover all villages by March 2016. This task would now need to be pre-poned to August 2015, except in the hilly, tribal, desert and difficult areas having challenges of telecom connectivity.

E. Urban Financial Inclusion: As per Census 2011, there were 7.89 crore urban households out of which 5.34 crore households were availing banking services. As on March 31, 2014, the banking network had 71,120 branches and 1,36,721 ATMs in urban, semi-urban and metropolitan areas. In urban areas too, the banks would engage *Bank Mitra* (Business Correspondent) wherever required. The exact number of uncovered households at present is not available with banks but is estimated to be about 1.5 crore. In the urban centres of the district, the lead district managers (LDMs) would be responsible to co-ordinate with all available banks in the centre to cover all the households. The urban centre saturation would be measured by opening at least 150 percent accounts of the urban households in that centre as per Census 2011.

F. Working of *Bank Mitra* (Business Correspondent): The *Bank Mitra* (Business Correspondent) outlets (in both rural and urban areas) would be fully equipped with the required infrastructure including the computers and other peripherals like micro ATMs, bio-metric scanners, printer, web cam and internet connectivity. *Bank Mitra* (Business Correspondent) needs to carry out online transactions for which internet connectivity is essential. However, as per the present status, there may be certain connectivity related issues particularly in hilly and tribal areas of the country which need to be addressed immediately. Hence, there would be a committee consisting of various stakeholders including BSNL to sort out technology-related issues. Each *Bank Mitra* (Business Correspondent) would be given proper training about basic banking, insurance and pension products and customer handling. Adequate compensation to the *Bank Mitra* (Business Correspondent) would be ensured for enabling him to provide uninterrupted services particularly in the difficult rural and remote areas. The suggested remuneration to reach the last mile *Bank Mitra* (Business Correspondent) would be at least ₹ 5,000 per month comprising of fixed amount and additional transaction/activity-based variable component. While deciding upon the remuneration structure, it would be ensured that the costs on rent, electricity, internet, travelling etc. are also accounted for.

G. Eligibility for Bank Mitra (Business Correspondent): Following entities may be engaged as BCs from time to time:

- Individuals like unemployed youth and entities like retired bank employees, retired teachers, retired government/military personnel.
- *Kirana* shops.
- Fair price shops under public distribution system (PDS).
- Public call offices (PCOs).
- Non-governmental organizations (NGOs).
- Mutual fund institutions (MFIs).
- Self-help groups (SHGs).
- Civil society organizations.
- Agents of small saving schemes of the Government of India.
- Individual petrol pump owners.
- Non-deposit taking non-banking financial companies (NBFCs).
- Post office/postman/*Gramin Dak Sewak.*
- Common service centres (CSCs).
- Co-operative societies.
- Other eligible individuals/entities allowed by RBI from time to time.

Unemployed youth in villages should be encouraged to work as *Bank Mitra*

(Business Correspondent), subject to fulfilling other eligibility conditions.

There would be a dress code with a specified colour for the *Bank Mitra* (Business Correspondent). The dress of *Bank Mitra* (Business Correspondent) will constitute jacket, cap and bag. The dresses would carry the Mission logo as well as the logo of the bank. Regular and timely payment to the *Bank Mitra* (Business Correspondent) for the services rendered by them would be a key factor in ensuring their continuance at the village level.

All banks to put in place a scheme of finance to the *Bank Mitra* (Business Correspondent) with a minimum amount of ₹ 50,000 for equipment, ₹ 25,000 for working capital and ₹ 50,000 for a vehicle loan.

Suggested variants of the *Bank Mitra* (Business Correspondent) structure could be: (a) individual *Bank Mitra* (Business Correspondent) deployed directly by the banks, (b) utilising the network of common service centres (CSCs), (c) through corporate BC companies, i.e. through private participation. While this system has advantages of administration and centralised control for the banks and also insulates them against several threats, but many times these players turn up in exploitation of the last mile delivery agents (*Bank Mitra*), and (d) while engaging the corporate BC companies, the remuneration structure for the agents deployed by them and time line for their payment would be ensured by the respective banks.

I. Mobile Banking: The Inter-Ministerial group on delivery of basic financial services through a comprehensive framework envisaged the creation of "Mobile and Aadhaar linked accounts" by banks. The basic financial transactions on these accounts can be executed through a mobile-based PIN system using "Mobile Banking PoS". Mobile banking through mobile wallet was launched in 2012. Under this service, RBI has authorized 3 telcos and 5 non-telcos to launch this service. Three telcos viz., Airtel under the brand name 'Airtel Money', Vodafone under brand name 'Vodafone m-pesa' and Idea vide 'Idea Money' are active in the space. They control over 80,000, 70,000 and 8,000 agents respectively. Around 60 percent of these *Bank Mitras* (Business Correspondents) are in rural areas. Mobile wallet service is provided by commercial banks e.g., ICICI in case of m-pesa service used for money transfer, bill payment and cash withdrawals. The customer base of customers availing such services is around 70 lakh. Mobile telephony and prepaid wallets would also be utilized for coverage of households under financial inclusion campaign.

J. National Unified USSD Platform (NUUP): USSD-based mobile banking can work on all GSM handsets (93 percent of current 900 million). Through USSD, mobile banking services like balance inquiry, mini statement and fund transfer will be provided. NPCI is to provide Gateway for all the banks with single short code—*99#. Currently, all smart cell phones are already enabled to use mobile banking application and basic cell phones are being enabled now under this platform. The services will be provided by 40 banks initially and will be joined by 100 banks. Agreement has already been done with 11 telecom service providers.

12.6.2 Opening of Basic Saving Bank Account of Every Adult Citizen: The second pillar of this plan envisages providing basic bank accounts [Basic Saving Bank Deposit Account (BSBDA) with zero balance] to all adult citizens starting with coverage of all households. The financial inclusion campaign in the past has targeted opening of basic savings accounts. As per RBI estimates, by March 2014, 242 million basic savings accounts were opened.

Census 2011 estimated that out of 24.67 crore households in the country, 14.48 crore households had access to banking services. Public sector banks (PSBs) have estimated that by May 31, 2014, out of the 9.17 crore rural households which were allocated to them, about 5.23 crore households have been covered.

This leaves about 3.94 crore rural households to be covered by PSBs. In addition, the regional rural banks (RRBs) have also covered about 1.99 crore households out of the 3.97 crore households allocated to them, which leaves 1.98 crore households to be covered by them.

Putting the PSBs and RRBs numbers together implies that about 5.92 crore rural households are yet to be covered. Considering field level data mismatches in some instances, it is estimated that there are about 6 crore uncovered households which would need to be covered in the rural areas.

In addition, account opening of uncovered households in urban areas would also be required. At a conservative estimate, about 1.5 crore uncovered households, would need to be covered in urban areas.

As per Nandan Nilekani Report of the Task Force on Aadhaar-enabled Unified Payment Infrastructure, February 2014, "Another class of customers (largely rural, low-income and uneducated) have been issued smart cards that are operated through *Bank Mitras* (Business Correspondents). This innovation through the use of technology made it possible to bring banking services to un-served areas and un-served population for the very first time. However, this innovation has also created proprietary technology islands, where consumers cannot access their bank account through other channels. The inconvenience of the channel often leads customer to withdraw all the money in their account". In order to ensure that this does not happen in the present Mission, interoperability of the payments will be ensured both through the debit card and through Aadhaar-enabled Payments at the *Bank Mitra* (Business Correspondent) outlets as and when the reach of Aadhaar extends to a substantial part of the country.

In the past, it was seen, that many of the accounts opened did not have sufficient number of transactions for banks to find them viable. This was because these accounts were being opened in isolation without proper linkages. Under the present plan, this anomaly is proposed to be removed by its six pillar approach. Moreover, the accounts will also be ATM-enabled to get the benefits of flexibility. The approach under this pillar of the campaign would be as follows:

A. Opening of SB Account with Zero Balance (BSBDA): For ease of opening of accounts, banks would be advised to take benefit of e-KYC approach. Those banks who have not activated the e-KYC facilities would need to incorporate the same up to the BC level.

B. One Page Account Opening Form: In order to cut down time on account opening, under the campaign, a one page account opening form has been designed. All banks will make suitable amendments in their account opening forms immediately. The network of co-operative/urban co-operative banks which are on CBS would also be used for account opening of uncovered households. This account would be linked with the Aadhaar number of the account holder and would become the single point for receipt of all direct benefit transfers (DBT) from the Central Government/State Government/Local Bodies.

C. ATM/Debit (RuPay) Card: Each SB account holder would be given ATM/debit (RuPay) card. In the country, there are estimated 13.8 crore agriculture landholders, out of which KCC has been provided to 10.2 crore land owners/agriculturists. In the present campaign, endeavour shall be made to provide all KCC holders with RuPay KCC card and non-agriculturists may be provided with RuPay debit card. The card will have in-built accident insurance of ₹ 1 lakh. It has been ascertained from National Payments Corporation of India (NPCI) that the RuPay cards to be issued do not have a production/operationalization constraint and the manufacturing capacity is estimated to be about 18 lakh per day. The personalization capacity available is also 7.75 lakh per day.

D. Financial Literacy: Each account holder would be provided financial literacy sessions on how to manage his/her money and credit facilities.

E. Camp Mode to Open Account: The accounts would be opened in camp mode to ensure that account may be opened for all eligible residents in a time bound manner and thereafter on an ongoing basis. The dates/day of the camp would be announced in advance through adequate and effective publicity locally available. The camps would be organised in coordination with the Government and bank officials. In each of the camp, *Bank Mitra* (Business Correspondent) and bank official/s would ensure availability of sufficient account opening forms and other stationary for opening of account.

F. Overdraft Facility: Overdraft (OD) up to ₹ 5,000 would be provided to the customers after six months of satisfactory performance of saving/credit history. This OD facility would be covered by the Credit Guarantee Fund proposed to be created by the Government.

The rate of interest on these accounts is proposed @ base rate +2 percent or 12 percent whichever is lower (including the fees to be paid to Credit Guarantee Fund). All Government benefits to flow into this account, facilitating servicing of interest and reducing the chances of account becoming dormant.

12.6.3 Financial Literacy and Credit Counselling (FLCC): This important pillar focuses on preparing the people for financial planning and availing credit. It has been seen from the experience of microfinance firms as well as self-help groups (SHGs) that before availing credit, people need to be made aware of the advantages of access to formal financial system, savings, credit, importance of timely repayments and building up a good credit history.

One of the major modes for disseminating financial literacy is the establishment of financial literacy centres (FLCs) which provides free financial literacy/education and credit counselling. As per RBI, 718 financial literacy centres (FLCs) had been set up as at end of March, 2013. A total of 2.2 million people were made aware through awareness camps/choupals, seminars and lectures during 2012-13.

However, most of these FLCs have not been set up in rural areas. The present plan aims to expand the FLCs to the block level. The focus would be on availing credit and coming out of the exploitation by informal financial system.

A. Need for Financial Literacy: Financial literacy is a prerequisite for effective financial inclusion, which will ensure that financial services reach the unreached and under-reached sections of the society.

Financial markets now offer complex choices to consumers, but literacy is essential for consumers to make informed choices. Informed choices will help in demand generation of the financial services.

In countries with diverse social and economic profile like India, financial literacy is particularly relevant for people who are resource-poor, who operate at the margins and are vulnerable to persistent downward financial pressures. With no established financial awareness, the unbanked poor are pushed towards expensive alternatives. India is among the world's most efficient financial markets in terms of technology, regulation and systems. Financial literacy is most important for India as it is a developing country with problem of poverty in addition to illiteracy and population. Financial literacy is considered an important adjunct for promoting financial inclusion and ultimately financial stability of the global economy. In India, the need for financial literacy is even greater considering the low levels of literacy and the large section of the population, remaining out of the formal financial set-up. While savings as a percentage of GDP in India is fairly good, where the savings are invested is a cause for concern. Further, only a minority of Indians are covered by mandated, and/or government financed social security schemes and social safety nets. A country of savers needs to be converted into a nation of investors. Everyone saves money for future needs but the approach most of the time is to save surplus money without preparing household budgets and without prioritizing personal needs.

B. Impact of Financial Illiteracy: Recent experiences in the microfinance arena have shown that poor people take loans that they have no capacity to service. Farmers have also taken loans that they have not been able to repay. Many have been driven to suicide because of debt problems. Unless financial literacy goes hand-in-hand with financial inclusion, instead of helping the poor, they may be put into more trouble.

12.6.4 Credit Guarantee Fund: The fourth pillar of this Plan is the creation of a Credit Guarantee Fund. It is proposed to be housed in National Credit Guarantee Corporation (NCGC).

Provision of overdraft up to ₹ 5,000 is projected to have the following multi-dimensional benefits:

- This exigency fund shall be a great support for poor borrowers in meeting out their basic needs like health, farming etc. The idea is to bring out people from the clutches of money lenders in both rural and urban areas.
- Learning to manage this account shall be the first step to a larger dosage of credit by creating their credit history. It shall help the banks also in credit appraisal for his/her future needs.
- Provision of up to ₹ 5,000 as overdraft is provided after 6 months of satisfactory operation/saving/credit history (it is a credit and not a grant).
- Banks can consider customers having good credit history for more than one year to be eligible for higher credit limits.

The present Plan proposes to create a credit guarantee fund with a corpus of ₹ 1,000 crore to start with, to provide guarantee against defaults in overdrafts in basic banking accounts. As per 2013 estimates, there were 18.2 crore basic banking accounts and it is estimated that by the end of the campaign another 7.5 crore accounts would get added. Out of about 25 crore households, 12 crore are KCC holders. Therefore, for the remaining 13 crore households, an overdraft of up to ₹ 5,000 in each of these would translate to a total of ₹ 65,000 crore. Assuming ⅔rd of the households avail overdraft, the amount would total to ₹ 43,000 crore. Using a 1:10 leverage ratio, we would need ₹ 4,300 crore over a period of time. Hence, to begin with, it is proposed to start with a corpus of ₹ 1,000 crore. This corpus would be budget neutral for the Government of India and would be funded by the Financial

Inclusion Fund (FIF) being maintained by NABARD.

12.6.5 Micro Insurance: The fifth pillar of this Plan is to provide micro insurance to the people. Insurance Regulatory and Development Authority (IRDA) has created a special category of insurance policies called micro insurance policies to promote insurance coverage among economically vulnerable sections of the society. The IRDA Micro insurance Regulations, 2005 defines and enables micro insurance. A micro insurance policy can be a general or life insurance policy with a sum assured of ₹ 50,000 or less.

A general micro insurance product could be:

- Health insurance contract.
- Any contract covering belongings such as: (a) hut, (b) livestock, (c) tools or instruments, and (d) any personal accident contract.

These can be on an individual or group basis.

A life micro insurance product is:

- A term insurance contract with or without return of premium.
- Any endowment insurance contract.
- A health insurance contract.

These can be with or without an accident benefit rider and either on an individual or group basis.

There is flexibility in the regulations for insurers to offer composite coverage or package products that include life and general insurance covers together. Micro insurance business is done through the following intermediaries:

- Non-governmental organisations.
- Self-help groups.
- Micro finance institutions.

Most of the entities appointed as BCAs, including companies registered under Companies Act, have also been permitted by IRDA for appointment as micro insurance Agents to sell micro insurance.

Micro insurance portfolio has made steady progress. More and more life insurers have commenced their micro insurance operations and many new products are being launched every year. The distribution network has also been considerably strengthened and the new business has shown a decent growth, although the volume is still small. Micro insurance business is procured largely under the group portfolio. Life Insurance Corporation of India (LIC) contributes the most, both in terms of policies sold and number of micro insurance agents.

With the notification of the IRDA (Micro Insurance) Regulations, 2005, by the Authority, there has been a steady growth in the design of products catering to the needs of the poor. The flexibilities provided in the regulations allow the insurers to offer composite coverage or package products.

Bank Mitra (Business Correspondent) mechanism would be enabled to offer micro insurance products and full coverage of schemes like *Aam Admi Bima Yojana*.

12.6.6 Unorganized Sector Pension Scheme (Swavalamban): The sixth and final pillar of this Plan relates to old age income security. Almost 400 million people (more than 85 percent of the working population in India) work in the unorganized sector. Of these, at least 120 million are women and a majority have no access to any formal old age income security scheme. Tenuous labour market attachment, intermittent incomes and poor access to social security, renders the unorganized workers highly vulnerable to economic shocks during their working lives.

The Swavalamban scheme is a historic initiative launched by the Government of India in October 2010 to address the old age income protection need of the hitherto unaddressed unorganized/informal sector workers. The objective of the scheme is to encourage the informal sector workers to save small amounts during their working years to enable them to draw a pension in their old age. The Swavalamban scheme uses co-contributions from the Government of India to incentivize and mobilize savings.

A. Benefits under the Swavalamban Scheme:

- The scheme is open to any citizen of India in the unorganized sector, aged between 18 to 60 years. A person is deemed to be in the unorganized sector if he/she is not in regular employment of the Central/State government or an autonomous body/CPSU having employer-assisted retirement scheme, or is not covered by any social security scheme.
- Government of India contributes ₹ 1,000 p.a. for a stipulated period to all eligible NPS Swavalamban accounts where the subscriber deposits a minimum of ₹ 1,000 to a maximum of ₹ 12,000 p.a. The benefit of the Government of India co-contribution is presently available up to 2016-17.
- Subscribers can exit at the specified age, at which point the built up corpus is given to the subscriber partly as a lump sum and partly as an annuity.
- The Scheme is regulated and managed by the PFRDA (Pension Fund Regulatory and Development Authority) which is a statutory body set up by an Act of the Parliament.
- Swavalamban is a low-cost, feature optimized model which works on the sophisticated architecture of the National Pension System and is completely IT-enabled, has professional fund managers for investment of funds and follows prudential investment guidelines to safeguard the interests of the subscribers.

- A number of state government entities in states like Andhra Pradesh, Karnataka, Jharkhand, Haryana, Chhattisgarh, Government of NCT of Delhi, Assam, Bihar and Rajasthan have adopted the scheme for different subscriber groups and some of these are also making additional co-contributions to the beneficiaries of Swavalamban accounts.

B. How to Join Swavalamban?:

- NPS/Swavalamban is operated through grassroots level intermediaries called 'Aggregators' who provide the interface between the subscribers and the NPS architecture. They are responsible for providing services to the subscribers on the ground as per the PFRDA regulations. The 79 aggregators include *inter alia* all public sector banks, several state governments entities, MFIs etc. with over 80,000 registered points of contact called NLCCs.
- PFRDA registers these Aggregators after a stringent due diligence procedure.
- The incentive for providing services under NPS/Swavalamban is borne by the Government of India.

C. Performance of Swavalamban Scheme:

- The scheme has met with an overwhelming response, showing a CAGR of 75 percent since the four years of operation.
- Aanganwadi workers, ASHA workers, construction workers, women SHGs etc. have joined the scheme in large numbers.
- Total number of unique subscribers to the scheme has crossed 2.7 million.
- Almost 1.6 million subscribers received the Swavalamban co-contribution during the year 2013-14.
- More than 50 percent of the eligible subscribers are below the age of 40, and over 70 percent are women, hence, the scheme has managed to target the appropriate subscriber base for a long-term defined contribution pension scheme.
- As against a total government co-contribution of ₹ 363 crore till March 2014, subscribers' own contribution has been ₹ 564 crore, i.e. the scheme has managed a multiple of 1.6 times the government investment in aggregating the small savings of the unorganized sector and directing it to old age income security.
- A total of 3,01,980 subscribers during 2010-11, 6,43,979 subscribers during 2011-12 and 11,01,079 subscribers during 2012-13 have been benefited. During the financial year 2013-14, 15,94,790 subscribers were benefited.
- *Bank Mitras* (Business Correspondents) have been used to expand the coverage.

12.7 Monitoring Mechanism

A web portal shall be created by DFS at "financial services.gov.in" for online monitoring of the creation of *Bank Mitras* (Business Correspondents). In the field, it shall be a tool to ensure proper coverage of the villages.

The reports to be generated would be district-wise/state-wise and would include the following:

- Covered villages with uncovered households needing opening of fresh account.
- Covered villages with uncovered households needing at least one fully enabled account per family or reactivation of earlier account.
- Uncovered villages with households needing fresh accounts to be opened.
- Urban areas with uncovered households needing fresh account/account reactivation.
- Number of new *Bank Mitras* (Business Correspondents) set up in rural and urban areas.

Each bank would have a structured system generated MIS system to monitor the function of *Bank Mitra* (Business Correspondent) in the field. The format would be standardised across the system for ease and uniformity purposes. This shall be uploaded regularly on the portal created by DFS for this purpose.

This MIS would have a linkage with the portal for DFS, i.e. "financial services.gov.in". All banks have already been provided with the necessary ID and password to access the portal.

The MIS reports to be collected for monitoring during the campaign will have two parts: one would be the reports generated by the banks from the CBS which shall be weekly and the second part will have reports from the SLBCs which will also involve surveys of the ground level position. The ground level survey should be completed within 3 months of the start of the campaign.

It has been decided to link the lady of the house as head of the household with the other members in the CBS so that the number the households that are covered during the campaign can be ascertained.

IBA will have a monitoring committee which shall review the progress on weekly basis. The information for monitoring shall be extracted from the DFS portal.

A project management group would be set up in DFS, comprising of sector experts for day-to-day monitoring.

SLBCs will have a toll free number connected to a call centre. Citizens facing difficulty in opening of account may call on this number where his/her complaint shall be registered. The same shall then be forwarded to the person concerned for necessary action within 15 days.

12.8 Challenges Identified in the Implementation of the Mission

12.8.1 Telecom Connectivity: The feedback from the banks is that in tribal and hilly areas of the country, the telecom network is not reliable and therefore setting up *Bank Mitra* (Business Correspondent) in these areas and ensuring opening of bank accounts is going to be difficult. A meeting was held with representatives of the Department of Telecom (DoT) and BSNL in this regard and it was assured that the ongoing telecom connectivity problems would be resolved by mutual consultation. It was also informed that DoT is separately seeking the Government approval to cover all villages in the North-East and difficult areas with telecom connectivity. Banks would also work to utilize the National Optical Fibre Network (NOFN) when it reaches the Panchayat level.

12.8.2 Keeping the Accounts "Live": It is essential that all Government benefits—Central, State or local—should flow to these accounts as it has been observed that a lot of duplicity exists in this area and sometimes States have not followed the services area approach and allocated areas to some banks other than service area banks, creating avoidable confusion. The DBT schemes especially MNREGA needs to be pushed and DBT in LPG needs to be restarted.

12.8.3 Brand Awareness and Sensitization: In order to achieve a "demand" side pull effect, it would be essential that there is branding and awareness on *Bank Mitra* (Business Correspondent) model for providing basic banking services, banking products available at *Bank Mitra* (Business Correspondent) outlets and RuPay cards. Customers should be made aware that overdraft of up to ₹ 5,000 to be provided in their account is a credit facility which needs to be repaid in order to get fresh limits and it is not a grant.

12.8.4 Commission to Bank on Direct Benefit Transfer (DBT): A task force on Aadhaar-enabled Unified Payment infrastructure headed by Sh. Nandan Nilekani in its report in February 2012 recommended that last mile transaction cost of 3.14 percent with a cap of ₹ 20 per transaction be budgeted for various EBT, DTS and last mile payments through micro ATMs and ATMs. The commission applicable for DBT should also cover DBTL (DBT of LPG). MGNREGA may also be included in the direct benefit transfer.

12.8.5 Coverage of Difficult Areas: Parts of North-East, Himachal Pradesh, Uttarakhand, J&K and 82 Left Wing Extremism (LWE) districts face challenges of infrastructure besides telecom connectivity. All households in such areas may not be fully covered under the campaign.

Coverage of some of the areas might, therefore, spill over to Phase-II.

12.9 Roles of Major Stakeholders

12.9.1 Department of Financial Services:

- Overall ownership of the Mission Mode Project on Financial Inclusion.

- Overall monitoring and implementation of the Mission.

12.9.2 Other Central Government Departments:

- In order to achieve the complete financial inclusion and transfer of social benefits in the accounts of the beneficiaries, the concerned departments of Central Government would coordinate with the stake holders.
- Presently, 26 centrally social benefits scheme under DBT and sponsored by 8 departments of the Central Government are as under:

1. Ministry of Social Justice and Empowerment.
2. Ministry of Human Resources Development, D/o Higher Education.
3. Ministry of Human Resources Development, D/o School Education and Literacy.
4. Ministry of Tribal Affairs.
5. Ministry of Minority Affairs.
6. Ministry of Women and Child Development.
7. Ministry of Health and Family Welfare.
8. Ministry of Labour and Employment.

- MGNREGA is sponsored by the Ministry of Rural Development (MoRD, GoI), and is likely to be included in the direct benefit transfer.
- Departments like Department of Posts for using the rural post offices/*Gramin Dak Sewak*, Department of Telecommunications for telecom connectivity, Ministry of Information and Broadcasting and DAVP to assist in media campaign, DEITY in development of logistic support for monitoring like creation of portal for data updating, development of electronic reporting system, MoRD for convergence with NRLM, HUPA for convergence with NULM etc.

12.9.3 Reserve Bank of India (RBI):

- To align their directions to the banks on financial inclusion with the mission mode.
- FIF fund allocation support.
- Depositor Education and Awareness Fund Scheme 2014 support.
- To guide and support banks in financial literacy campaign and revamping and expansion of FLCCs up to the block level.

12.9.4 Commercial Banks: As defined in the Mission Mode Document.

12.9.5 Indian Banks' Association (IBA):

- Coordination in financial inclusion effort with all banks.
- Key monitoring role in financial literacy campaign.
- Coordination in publicity and campaign.
- Coordination in centralised handling of customer grievances/issues through toll-free numbers in coordination with banks.

- A dedicated desk to be set up for monitoring of implementation of FI. Coordinate with SLBC for grievance redressal.

12.9.6 National Bank for Agriculture and Rural Development (NABARD):

- Coordination in publicity and campaign.
- Monitoring of implementation of financial inclusion in respect of organisations working under NABARD.
- Allocation of funds from Financial Inclusion Fund (FIF).
- Financial literacy by SHG/JLG beneficiaries.

12.9.7 State Governments:

- Appointment of Mission director at State level.
- Monitoring of financial inclusion campaign in coordination with SLBC and all the stake holders.
- Direct benefit transfer of the statc schemes in the bank accounts of the beneficiaries.
- One officer of the State Government on deputation to oversee the implementation issue.

12.9.8 State Level Bankers Committee (SLBC):

- SLBC Convenor GM to act as secretary to state implementation committee.
- Coordination with all the banks for financial inclusion activity.
- Monitoring and follow up of different activities of financial inclusion.

12.9.9 District Administration:

- Key role in implementation of FI in the districts.
- District collector (DC) to act as chairman of district level implementation committee.

12.9.10 Lead District Manager (LDM):

- Lead district manager (LDM) to act as secretary to the district implementation committee.
- LDM to coordinate with all the banks in financial inclusion implementation in the district.

12.9.11 Local Bodies:

- Representatives of local bodies (*panchayats* in rural areas and municipalities in urban areas) to assist in implementation of financial inclusion in various ways like in organising camps in opening of accounts, identification of persons for opening of account, in financial literacy campaign etc.

12.9.12 National Payment Corporation of India (NPCI):

- Coordination and necessary guidance and support to banks for proper operations of RuPay cards.

- To facilitate inter-operability among *Bank Mitras* (Business Correspondents).
- Necessary supports to banks in making available USSD-based mobile banking with low-end mobile phones so that customer can avail basic banking services like deposit, withdrawal, fund transfer, balance enquiry etc. across the banks. This product may be enabled at *Bank Mitra* (Business Correspondent) outlets also.

12.9.13 Unique Identification Authority of India (UIDAI):

- Convergence of Aadhaar enrolment with bank account opening.
- Facilitating the subsidy scheme on procurement of Aadhaar-enabled Payment System (AEPS) machines by banks.
- Fast conversion of EID to UID to ensure faster credit to bank accounts.
- Mapping multiple accounts with a single Aadhaar number.

To sum up, PMJDY is a national mission on financial inclusion to provide all households in the country with financial services, with particular focus to empower the weaker sections of society, including women, small and marginal farmers and labourers, both rural and urban. The necessity of launching such a mission was felt in view of the fact that less than two-thirds of the households in the country have access to banking facilities even after 67 years of Independence. The Mission seeks to provide all households in the country, both rural and urban, with access to the financial services, like bank account with RuPay debit card, access to credit, remittance, insurance and pension. Thus, the Mission not only brings the excluded sections into the financial mainstream but makes the transfer of benefits of various subsidy schemes of the government more efficient.

See also section 13.5 of chapter 13 of this book.

Access to formal banking system is affected by several implementation and policy barriers such as culture, financial literacy, gender, income and assets, proof of identity, remoteness of residence etc. Over a period of time, several measures have been taken by the banks in India to improve access to affordable financial services through financial education, awareness generation, business communication networking and leveraging technology. The lack of awareness, low incomes and assets, social exclusion and illiteracy are the barriers from demand side. The distance from bank branch, branch timings, cumbersome banking procedure and requirements of documents for opening bank accounts, unsuitable banking products or schemes, language, high transaction costs and attitudes of bank officials are the barriers from supply side. Hence, there is a need for financial inclusion to build uniform economic development through greater accessibility and transparency in fund-flow regime for ushering in greater economic and social equity.

13

Role of Technology in Financial Inclusion

Information technology (IT) provides a great opportunity to innovate at a much faster pace and to create new financial products; along with accessibility of financial services, that are closely linked to the needs of the consumer. There is a need to create an enabling working ecosystem which is conducive to foster innovation by leveraging the best available technological platforms.

Information technology (IT) has transformed the functioning of businesses the world over. It has bridged the gaps in terms of the reach and the coverage of systems and enabled better decision-making based on latest and accurate information, reduced costs and overall improvement in efficiency. In the Indian context, the financial sector, especially the banking sector, has been a major beneficiary from the inroads made by IT. Many new processes, products and services offered by banks and other financial intermediaries are now IT-centred. Effective integration of technology with sound business practices requires business process re-engineering and banks in India need to follow up on the beginnings made in this regard.

Newer delivery channels to customers—automated teller machines (ATMs), networking of ATMs in the form of shared payment networks, internet banking—and implementation of core banking solutions by most banks are some examples. Reserve Bank of India (RBI) has played a proactive role in the implementation of IT in the banking sector. IT-based initiatives are focused on meeting the three-pronged objective of better house keeping, improved customer service and overall systemic efficiency.

13.1 Information Technology (IT) and Modern Banking

The financial structure in a country is influenced and shaped also by non-financial developments. Changes in the field of telecommunications, computers, non-financial sector policies, and economic growth itself influence the structure of the financial system. Technological improvements lower transaction costs and affect financial arrangements. Many of the standard arguments which are advocated in the case of *public goods* also can be extended to technology and hence the emphasis on technology. For banks, technology has a critical role to play in reducing transaction and operation cost component for the banks in providing financial services to its poorest customers. Reducing these costs shall lead to a reduction in lending costs, which would definitely help in improving the viability of rural businesses. For addressing the problem of long distances and poor transport linkages in rural areas, communications technology could play an important role by bridging the last mile between the customer and the provider and thus facilitating transactions.

Banks in India have been able to achieve a substantial level of computerization in their operations, however, tremendous scope still exists for them to learn from mobile operators to optimize back-end technologies and leverage volume to significantly reduce the back-end costs. Post-liberalization, the use of ATMs has helped to reduce front-end costs, which continue to be the dominant costs for banks. Banks need to promote low cost indigenous ATM technologies, especially for rural areas. No doubt internet banking transactions have zero front-end costs for the banks but still efforts have to be made to make this a preferred mode of transaction for large corporations.

13.2 Technological Solutions for Financial Services

Most of the initiatives regarding technology are aimed at providing better and more efficient customer service by offering multiple options to the customer. The death of distance, which is a by-product of technology, has become a reality in the banking sector. Technology is also playing a key role in banks' strategy for gaining a competitive edge.

Many banks have commenced the process of setting up core banking solutions, which are at various stages of implementation. While such systems are already in place in respect of new private sector banks, a few old private sector banks and public sector banks are also quickly moving to set up such processes. This would benefit the customer in the banking sector. Computerisation of the business of banks has been receiving high importance. The public sector banks have already crossed the 70 percent level of computerisation of their business. The directive from the Central Vigilance Commission (CVC) to achieve 100 percent computerisation has resulted in renewed vigour towards computerisation of branches.

Networking has been receiving focused attention by banks. This activity is also being monitored by the RBI. Most banks have their own corporate networks to facilitate inter-branch and branch-controlling office communication in an electronic mode. Inter-bank and inter-city communication takes place through the Indian Financial Network (INFINET). As part of the INFINET, the terrestrial lines have been augmented to provide for increased data transfer capabilities. All these have resulted in the dependence of banks on network-based computing which has benefited the customer.

INFINET also provides for safe and secure transmission of electronic messages with the use of public key infrastructure (PKI) which has the legal backing of Information Technology Act, 2000. It also provides for messages to flow in a structured environment, using the structured financial messaging solutions (SFMS), which provides for inter-operability of messages so that straight through processing (STP) is achieved.

Another major development witnessed in recent years is the growth in multiple delivery channels to customers such as internet-based banking, mobile banking and anywhere banking. This has benefited the customers and the banks alike. While customers have now a wide variety of options to choose from, banks have been able to reduce costs which have had a positive impact on their profitability.

These developments have, however, also posed certain challenges. In a world where geographical barriers are losing significance, it is essential that security is given prime importance in a trans-national scenario where large sums of money are at stake. While the challenges relating to physical security could be confronted with relative ease, the position is much more complicated in respect of IT security. The RBI has, therefore, provided guidelines on information system (IS) security as also IS audit which banks can use for their benefit. These are generic in nature and do not have any prescriptive tones.

13.3 Technological Channels for the Delivery of Financial Services

As is well-known, the financial sector has witnessed a quantum jump in the availability of technological solutions for delivery of financial services, and the RBI too has launched several payment system products for improving the efficiency of the payment system. [1]

13.3.1 National Electronic Funds Transfer (NEFT): The NEFT was launched by the RBI in November 2005 as a more secure, nation-wide retail electronic payment system to facilitate funds transfer by the bank customers, between the networked bank branches in the country. It has, however, been observed that the public sector banks are not the most active users of this product and the majority of NEFT outward transactions are originated by a few new-generation private sector banks and foreign banks.

In order to popularise the e-payments in the country, the RBI, on its part, waived the service charges to be levied on the member banks, till March 31, 2009, in respect of the real time gross settlement (RTGS) and NEFT transactions. The RBI also provides, free of charge, intra-day liquidity to the banks for the RTGS transactions. The service charges to be levied by banks from their customers for RTGS and NEFT have, however, been deregulated and left to the discretion of the individual banks. While some of the banks have rationalised their service charges and a few have made it even cost-free to the customers, there are also certain banks that have fixed unreasonably high service charges for providing these services to their customers—even though the RBI provides these services to the banks free of charge.

13.3.2 ATM Networks: The National Financial Switch (NFS) network started its operations on August 27, 2004. As in March 2015, a total of 1,92,857 ATMs existed in NFS.

NFS is one of the several shared ATM networks which inter-connect the ATM switches of the banks together and thus enable inter-operability of the ATM cards issued by any bank across the entire network. The Board for Regulation and Supervision of Payment and Settlement systems (BPSS) approved in-principle to issue authorisation to National Payments Corporation of India (NPCI) for operating various retail payment systems in the country.

Reserve Bank of India also issued authorisation to NPCI to take over the operations of National Financial Switch (NFS) from the Institute of Development and Research in Banking Technology (IDRBT) on October 15, 2009. NPCI took over NFS operations from December 14, 2009. Use of the ATMs connected through any of the ATM networks in the country became cost free for the customers from April 1, 2009. As at end-December 2014, the number of on-site ATMs in the country stood at 93,119 and the number of off-site ATMs in the country stood at 83,291.

13.3.3 Credit Cards: There has been phenomenal increase in the number of credit cards issued by the banks in India during the last few years. The number of outstanding credit cards at end-December 2014 stood at 2.03 crore. While the increasing usage of the credit cards is a welcome development in as much as it reduces reliance on currency for settlement of transactions, it also entails certain additional elements of operational risk and can be a potential source of customer complaints.

In order to ensure orderly growth of the card segment of consumer credit and protect the interests of banks/non-banking financial companies (NBFCs) and their customers, the RBI constituted a Working Group on Regulatory Mechanism for Cards (Chairman: R. Gandhi). Based of the recommendations of the Working Group, draft guidelines on credit cards were framed by the RBI in June 2005 for all commercial banks/NBFCs with regard to their credit card operations.

The draft guidelines delineated the broad parameters that banks/NBFCs should, at the minimum, take into account with regard to the following:

1. Issue of cards with respect to clear mentioning of most important terms and

conditions (MITCs).
2. Interest rates and other charges on customers.
3. Corrective mechanism on account of wrongful billing.
4. Use of direct sale agents and other agents for outsourcing various credit card operations.
5. Protection of customer rights especially in respect of right to privacy, customer confidentiality and fair practices in debt collection.
6. Redressal avenues of customer grievances.
7. Internal control and monitoring systems of the banks/NBFCs for such card operations.

The draft guidelines further stipulated that each bank/NBFC must have a well-documented policy and a *fair practices code* for credit card operations. The *fair practices code* for credit card operations released by the IBA in March 2005 could also be used by banks/NBFCs. The bank/NBFCs code should, at the minimum, however, incorporate the relevant guidelines contained in the draft guidelines released by the RBI.

13.3.4 Satellite Banking: Having regard to much greater reliability of a satellite-based communication link for interconnecting the branches of the banks, particularly in the hilly areas and difficult terrain where terrestrial communication link is difficult to provide, the RBI had constituted a Technical Group to examine the proposal for providing satellite connectivity to the bank branches in such areas.

The objective is to enable greater penetration of the electronic payment products in the hinterland areas also, by facilitating the integration of the rural and remote branches with the core banking solution platform of the banks and help them providing efficient banking services to their customers.

Under the proposal, the RBI would be bearing a part of the leased rentals for the satellite connectivity, provided the banks use it for connecting their branches in the North Eastern States and in the under-banked districts in the rest of the country. Thus, the RBI would be providing an incentive to the banks for adopting the satellite communication technology for networking their branches in the remote areas. A discussion paper on this scheme was placed on RBI website in June 2008 for public comments.

13.4 Technology for Financial Inclusion

Technology and financial inclusion are the popular coinage in banking parlance in the country. Main hurdle in financial inclusion so far has been large numbers and low volumes, translating into unaffordable costs. The only way to bring down the cost to an affordable level and to improve the reach to the farthest/remotest corner of the country is by effectively leveraging the technology. In order to make available the banking facilities across the length and breadth of the country, latest technological products like e-KYC, IMPS, AEPS, mobile banking etc. have the potential to emerge as a game changer in terms of costs, convenience, and speed of reach business models of banks, telecom operators and other stakeholders need to converge.

Under the guidance of RBI various organisations like National Payments Corporation of India (NPCI), Institute for Development and Research in Banking Technology (IDRBT) etc. are contributing significantly in bringing new technology based products.

RBI has, thus, been actively involved in harnessing technology for the development of the Indian banking sector over the years. A major technological development in banking sector is the adoption of the core banking solutions (CBS). CBS is a step towards enhancing, customer convenience through anywhere, anytime banking. It is important to leverage this technological advancement to look at areas beyond CBS that can help in not just delivering quality and efficient services to customers but also generating and managing information effectively. The adoption of CBS led to various technological products like NEFT, RTGS, mobile banking, Internet banking, ATMs etc. Some of the technological-based products that have made significant changes in the banking outreach to the masses are appended below:

- Adopting core banking solution (CBS) by the banks, including regional rural banks (RRBs).
- Use of multi-channel branchless approach using hand-held devices, mobiles, cards, micro-ATMs and kiosks.
- Transactions put through such front-end devices are seamlessly integrated with the CBS of banks.
- Implementation of the electronic payment system such as RTGS (real time gross settlement).
- Electronic clearing service (ECS).
- National electronic funds transfer (NEFT).
- Cheque truncation system (CTS).
- Banking transaction by using mobile phones etc.

13.5 Use of Technology for Pradhan Mantri Jan-Dhan Yojana (PMJDY), 2014

PMJDY, under National Mission on Financial Inclusion, proposes to use the technology in a big way to achieve the goal in a time-bound manner. [2] Some of the major products are explained hereunder.

13.5.1 Electronically Know Your Customer (e-KYC): In the year 2013, RBI permitted e-KYC as a valid process for KYC verification under Prevention of Money Laundering (Maintenance of Records) Rules, 2005. In order to reduce the risk of identity fraud, documentary forgery and have paperless KYC verification, UIDAI has launched its e-KYC services. Under the e-KYC process—and after the explicit consent of the customer and after his or her biometric authentication from UIDAI database—individual basic data comprising name, age, gender and photograph can be shared electronically with authorised users like banks, which is a valid process for KYC.

The aforesaid process is paperless and has made the account opening of customers having Aadhaar number much easier. Almost all the banks have either adopted this process or are in the advanced stage of putting the system live. The e-KYC process would be used in large scale for opening accounts in future.

13.5.2 Transaction through Mobile Banking: The mobile phone revolution that is transforming the country could also turn into a banking revolution in terms of reach and transaction. The reach of mobile to the remote village and its usage by the common man has become order of the day and it is estimated that around 1/4th of mobile users are residing in villages/small towns. The coverage of mobile phones and the use of such instruments by all sections of the population can be exploited for extending financial services to the excluded population. It enables the subscribers to manage their financial transactions (funds transfer) independent of place and time. The subscriber can approach a retailer of mobile network for withdrawal/deposit of money and the transaction takes place using SMS messages.

The mobile banking services are generally available through a java application on Blackberry, Android, iPhones and Windows mobile phones. Various banking services like funds transfer, immediate payment services, enquiry services (balance enquiry/mini statement), demat account services, requests for cheque book, bill payments etc. may be carried out through mobile banking. There are transaction limits for mobile banking and these services are free of charge. The mobile banking services are also available over SMS.

The basic financial transactions from the bank accounts can be executed through a mobile based PIN system using "mobile banking". Mobile banking through mobile wallet was also launched in 2012. Mobile telephony and pre-paid wallets can also be utilized for coverage of households under the financial inclusion campaign.

13.5.3 Immediate Payment System (IMPS): IMPS was launched by NPCI on November 22, 2010. It offers an instant, 24x7, inter-bank electronic funds transfer service through mobile phones as well as internet banking and ATMs. In the process of remittances across the bank there are four stakeholders, i.e. (a) remitter (sender), (b) beneficiary (receiver), (c) banks, and (d) National Financial Switch.

In order to remit fund through IMPS, the sender should use mobile banking to send money, the receiver mobile number should be registered with his bank and the money is credited to receivers account instantly. For registration the remitter must register for mobile banking and get mobile money identifier (MMID) and mobile banking PIN (MPIN) for initiation of a transaction. MMID is a 7-digit number, to be issued by the bank to the customer upon registration and the beneficiary must register his/her mobile number with the bank account and get MMID. A remitter can initiate an IMPS transaction by sending an SMS to his bank typing the beneficiary mobile number, beneficiary MMID and amount. The receiver will get an SMS confirmation for the credit of his account. National Payments Corporation of India (NPCI) is facilitating the Inter-bank Mobile Payment Service (IMPS).

13.5.4 Micro ATMs: Micro ATMs are biometric authentication enabled hand-held devices. In order to make the ATMs viable at rural/semi-urban centres, low cost micro ATMs can be deployed at each of the *Bank Mitra* (Business Correspondent) location. This would enable a person to instantly deposit or withdraw funds regardless of the bank associated with a particular *Bank Mitra*. This device can be based on a mobile phone connection and made available to every *Bank Mitra* (Business Correspondent). Customers would have to get their identity authenticated and withdraw or put money into their bank accounts. This money will come from the cash drawer of the *Bank Mitra*. Essentially, *Bank Mitras* will act as bank for the customers and all they need to do is verify the authenticity of customer using customer's UID. The basic transaction types to be supported by micro ATM are deposit, withdrawal, fund transfer and balance enquiry. Micro ATM offers one of the most promising options for providing financial services to the unbanked population. Micro ATMs would have various options of authentication like biometric, PIN-based etc. and they can also be used as mobile ATMs to enable transactions near the door step of the customers.

Micro ATMs offer an online interoperable, low-cost payments platform to everyone in the country.

13.5.5 National Unified USSD Platform (NUUP): Mobile banking is one of the most potent modes for increasing reach of banking facilities to the masses. Today, mobile phones have become a household device in India.

Mobile banking service can be initiated using SMS—an unencrypted service, considered unsafe—or using mobile banking app. Though very interactive, the major problem with mobile banking apps is that these need to be downloaded and installed on the mobile phone. Less than 40 percent of Indian users have compatible J2ME handsets and GPRS connection on their mobile phone, as required by this system.

To resolve aforesaid issues, an alternative solution on USSD platform is available. Customers can avail USSD solution through any mobile phone on GSM network, irrespective of make and model of the phone. This does not require any application to be downloaded on customer's mobile phone and need for GPRS connectivity. USSD is user-friendly so it is easy to communicate and educate customers as well. USSD alleviates the need for application download and is more secure than SMS channel.

Banking customers can use this service by dialling *99#, a common number across all telecom service providers, (TSPs), on their mobile and transact through an interactive menu displayed on the mobile screen.

Using *99#, a customer will be able to access both financial services (like fund transfer) and non-financial services (like balance enquiry and mini statement of bank account), at his/her own convenience. Key services that NUUP will offer include inter-bank account to account fund transfer, balance enquiry, mini statement besides a host of other services. A notable inclusion in the NUUP service is a new addition in the form of Query Service on Aadhaar Mapper (QSAM). Under this feature, a user can come to know about his/her Aadhaar seeding status with the banks, a service that will find tremendous utility for the government's direct subsidy disbursals programme.

13.5.6 RuPay Debit Cards: RuPay is a new card payment scheme launched by the National Payments Corporation of India (NPCI), to offer a domestic, open-loop, multilateral system which will allow all Indian banks and financial institutions in India to participate in electronic payments. "RuPay", the word itself has a sense of nationality in it. RuPay is the coinage of two terms Rupee and payment. RuPay cards address the needs of Indian consumers, merchants and banks. The benefits of RuPay debit card are the flexibility of the product platform, high levels of acceptance and the strength of the RuPay brand, all of which will contribute to an increased product experience. The main features are: (a) lower cost and affordability, (b) customized product offering, (c) protection of information related to Indian consumers, and (d) provision of electronic product options to untapped/unexplored consumer segment.

13.5.7 Aadhaar-enabled Payment System (AEPS): AEPS is a banking product which allows online interoperable financial inclusion transaction at PoS (micro ATM) or kiosk banking through the Business Correspondent of any bank using the Aadhaar authentication. Presently, four Aadhaar-enabled basic types of banking transactions are available, i.e.: (a) balance enquiry, (b) cash withdrawal,

(c) cash deposit, and (d) Aadhaar to Aadhaar funds transfer. For undertaking AEPS transaction by customer, two inputs, i.e. IIN (Identifying the Bank to which the customer is associated) and Aadhaar number are required.

13.5.8 Aadhaar Payments Bridge System (APBS): APBS enables the transfer of payments from Government and Government Institutions to Aadhaar-enabled accounts of beneficiaries at banks and post offices. Every Government department or institution that sends EBT and DBT/DBTL payments to individuals simply needs to prepare a file containing the Aadhaar number and amount and submit it to their accredited bank. The accredited bank then processes the file through an interoperable Aadhaar payments bridge and funds are credited into the accounts of beneficiaries. Upon receiving incoming funds, the beneficiary's bank will notify him or her through an SMS or any other communication channel that is established between the bank and the customer.

Endnotes

1. It is, however, the general perception that the awareness of these products in the system has remained rather limited. This lack of awareness is not confined to only to the members of public at large. It is not uncommon to find that even the branch staff, having direct interface with the banking customers, is not aware of these products and services offered by the bank. This has, therefore, resulted in the continued reliance of the members of public on the traditional methods for availing of various banking services and the benefits of technology have not fully percolated to the level of the customers. There is thus the need to take appropriate measures to increase the awareness of the electronic payment products—not only among the clientele of the banks but also among the own staff of banks so that the members of public can be properly guided and efficient and hassle-free customer service is rendered to them.
2. See chapter 12 of this book for details of PMJDY.

Appendix

Appendix

Main Findings and Recommendations of the Committee on Financial Inclusion (Chairman: C. Rangarajan), January 2008

The Government of India vide order no. 6/5/2006/AC dated June 22, 2006 constituted a Committee on Financial Inclusion under the chairmanship of Dr. C. Rangarajan with the following terms of reference:

1. To study the pattern of exclusion from access to financial services disaggregated by region, gender and occupational structure.
2. To identify the barriers confronted by vulnerable groups in accessing credit and financial services, including supply, demand and institutional constraints.
3. To review the international experience in implementing policies for financial inclusion and examine their relevance/applicability to India.
4. To suggest:

- a strategy to extend financial services to small and marginal farmers and other vulnerable groups, including measures to streamline and simplify procedures, reduce transaction costs and make the operations transparent;
- measures including institutional changes to be undertaken by the financial sector to implement the proposed strategy of financial inclusion;
- a monitoring mechanism to assess the quality and quantum of financial inclusion including indicators for assessing progress.

The Committee submitted its report in January 2008. Main findings and recommendations of the Report are as under.

Financial Inclusion Defined

The recent developments in banking technology have transformed banking from the traditional brick-and-mortar infrastructure like staffed branches to a system supplemented by other channels like automated teller machines (ATMs), credit/debit cards, internet banking, online money transfers, etc. The moot point, however, is that access to such technology is restricted only to certain segments of the society. Indeed, some trends, such as increasingly sophisticated customer segmentation technology—allowing, for example, more accurate targeting of sections of the market—have led to restricted access to financial services for some groups. There is a growing divide, with an increased range of personal finance options for a segment of high and upper middle income population and a significantly large section of the population who lack access to even the most basic banking services. This is termed "financial exclusion". These people, particularly, those living on low incomes, cannot access mainstream financial products such as bank accounts, credit, remittances and payment services, financial advisory services, insurance facilities etc.

Deliberations on the subject of Financial Inclusion contributed to a consensus that merely having a bank account may not be a good indicator of financial inclusion. Further, indebtedness as quantified in the NSSO 59th round (2003) may not also be a reflective indicator. The ideal definition should look at people who want to access financial services but are denied the same. If genuine claimants for credit and financial services are denied the same, then that is a case of exclusion. As this aspect would raise the issue of credit worthiness or bankability, it is also necessary to dwell upon what could be done to make the claimants of institutional credit bankable or creditworthy. This would require re-engineering of existing financial products or delivery systems and making them more in tune with the expectations and absorptive capacity of the intended clientele. Based on the above consideration, a broad working definition of financial inclusion could be as under:

"Financial inclusion may be defined as the process of ensuring access to financial services and timely and adequate credit where needed by vulnerable groups such as weaker sections and low income groups at an affordable cost".

The essence of financial inclusion is in trying to ensure that a range of appropriate financial services is available to every individual and enabling them to understand and access those services. Apart from the regular form of financial intermediation, it may include a basic no frills banking account for making and receiving payments, a savings product suited to the pattern of cash flows of a poor household, money transfer facilities, small loans and overdrafts for productive, personal and other purposes, insurance (life and non-life), etc. While financial inclusion, in the narrow sense, may be achieved to some extent by offering any one of these services, the objective of "Comprehensive Financial Inclusion" would be to provide a holistic set of services encompassing all of the above.

With a view to understanding the extent of exclusion, the Committee perused data put out by various sources. The summary of conclusions is indicated below.

Extent of Exclusion: NSSO Survey 59th Round

(a) General:

- 51.4 percent of farmer households are financially excluded from both formal/informal sources.

- Of the total farmer households, only 27 percent access formal sources of credit; one-third of this group also borrows from non-formal sources.
- Overall, 73 percent of farmer households have no access to formal sources of credit.

(b) Region-wise:

- Exclusion is most acute in Central, Eastern and North-Eastern regions– having a concentration of 64 percent of all financially excluded farmer households in the country.
- Overall indebtedness to formal sources of finance alone is only 19.66 percent in these three regions.

(c) Occupational Groups:

- Marginal farmer households constitute 66 percent of total farm households. Only 45 percent of these households are indebted to either formal or non formal sources of finance.
- About 20 percent of indebted marginal farmer households have access to formal sources of credit.
- Among non-cultivator households nearly 80 percent do not access credit from any source.

(d) Social Groups:

- Only 36 percent of ST farmer households are indebted [SCs and other backward classes (OBCs) 51 percent] mostly to informal sources.

Analysis of the data provided by RBI through its Basic Statistical Returns reveal that critical exclusion (in terms of credit) is manifest in 256 districts, spread across 17 States and 1 UT, with a credit gap of 95 percent and above. This is in respect of commercial banks and RRBs.

As per CMIE (March 2006), there are 11.56 crore land holdings. 5.91 crore KCCs have been issued as at the end of March 2006, which translated into a credit coverage of more than 51 percent of land holdings by formal sources. Further data with NABARD on the doubling of agricultural credit indicates that agricultural loan disbursements during 2006-07 covered 3.97 crore accounts.

Thus, there are different estimates of the extent of inclusion thru' formal sources, as the reference period of the data is not uniform. Consequently, this has had an impact on quantifying the extent of levels of exclusion.

Strategy for Building an Inclusive Financial Sector

Overall strategy for building an inclusive financial sector may be based on:

- Effecting improvements within the existing formal credit delivery mechanism;
- Suggesting measures for improving credit absorption capacity especially

amongst marginal and sub marginal farmers and poor non-cultivator households;

- Evolving new models for effective outreach, and
- Leveraging on technology based solutions.

National Rural Financial Inclusion Plan (NRFIP)

Looking at the enormity of the task involved, financial inclusion must be taken up in a mission mode as a Financial Inclusion Plan at the national level.

The target for NRFIP could be to provide access to comprehensive financial services to at least 50 percent (55.77 million) of the excluded rural cultivator and non-cultivator households, across different States by 2012 through rural/semi urban branches of CBs and RRBs. The remaining households, with such shifts as may occur in the rural/urban population, have to be covered by 2015.

Semi-urban and rural branches of commercial banks and RRBs may set for themselves a minimum target of covering 250 new cultivator and non-cultivator households per branch per annum, aggregating 11.15 million households per annum, with clear emphasis on financing marginal farmers, tenant cultivators and poor non-cultivator households.

The national targets would have to be disaggregated State-wise with adequate focus on districts having a large percentage of population not accessing bank credit.

Since per branch annual coverage under the Plan would be quite high in some of the North-Eastern, Eastern and Central States, needed support including financial assistance may be provided to banks operating in the above regions.

To operationalise the NRFIP, DLCCs at district level shall draw up block-wise/village-wise maps of rural households not having access to formal credit sources. This information should be disseminated widely. District administration and Lead Banks will extend appropriate help to DLCC for completing the exercise in a time bound manner. This should to be dovetailed with the work being done by the monitoring mechanism set up at the district level for implementation of the recommendations of the CD Ratio Committee.

Thereafter, a State Level Rural Financial Inclusion Plan (SLRFIP) shall be prepared jointly by the State Level Bankers' Committee (SLBC) and NABARD for arriving at a conclusive Financial Inclusion Plan for the State. With a minimum target coverage of 50 percent of currently excluded by the year 2012, States will be free to set for themselves higher targets.

The Plan so prepared will thereafter be allocated institution-wise, among commercial banks and RRBs. Other institutions like cooperative banks, NBFCs, MFIs may also be asked to join in the task of financial inclusion with self-set targets.

The progress in implementation shall be reported to and monitored at the DLCC.

With a view to firming up the implementation of the recommendations of the Committee, it is proposed that Government of India may consider constituting a National Mission on Financial Inclusion (NaMFI) comprising representatives of all stakeholders. The purpose of the Mission shall be to aim at achieving universal financial inclusion within a specific time frame. The Mission should be responsible for suggesting the overall policy changes required for achieving the desired level of financial inclusion, and for supporting a range of stakeholders—in the domain of public, private and NGO sectors—in undertaking promotional initiatives. Govt. may decide on appropriate representation from all stakeholders in the Mission.

Commercial Banks

Specific recommendations for achieving the targets under NRFIP by leveraging the existing commercial bank branch network in rural areas would include the following:

Targets for Rural/Semi-urban Branches: Given the existing staff strength, it should be possible for commercial banks (including RRBs) to provide access to credit to at least 250 hitherto excluded rural households at each of their existing rural and semi-urban branches. For this, banks will have to strengthen their staff and use a variety of delivery mechanisms.

Targeted Branch Expansion in Identified Districts: In districts where population per rural and semi urban branch office is much higher than the national average, the DLCCs may identify centres for opening branches by commercial banks and RRBs in the next three years. For the North-Eastern Region, the Committee on Financial Sector Plan has already identified such centres and branch expansion plan as indicated therein may be implemented.

Product Innovation: The excluded segments of the population require products which are customized, taking into consideration their varied needs. The products and services offered at present do not effectively meet these needs.

(a) Savings: Savings products to meet the specific requirements of the poor need to be evolved. SHGs may be utilized for tapping the small savings by providing incentives to SHGs with suitable back-end technology support. Banks can develop medium and long term savings instruments by issue of pre-printed deposit receipts to SHGs which in turn can be sold to SHG members. Banks could be given the freedom to develop their own products, suited to local requirements and felt needs of the poor.

(b) Credit: A savings-linked financing model can be adopted for these segments. The approach should be kept simple which should guarantee the beneficiaries a credit limit, subject to adherence to simple terms and conditions.

Credit within a specified limit can be made available in 2-3 tranches, with the second and subsequent tranches disbursed based on repayment behaviour of the first tranche. This is to ensure that the vulnerable groups do not get into a debt trap; it would also ensure good credit dispensation.

(c) Insurance: Banks can play a vital role in this regard—by distributing suitable micro insurance products.

Incentivising Human Resource: Measurable Performance Indicators: Lending to low income groups and providing inclusive financial services need motivated bank staff. Such motivation is a function of attitudes and beliefs as also a system of incentives/disincentives put in place by the bank's management for special efforts/failures to achieve desired levels of financial inclusion.

The existing staff posted to rural branches can be incentivised within a framework of performance parameters including covering of new households through deposit and loan accounts, increase in business in existing and new small loan/deposit accounts, increase in number of SHGs/joint liability groups (JLGs) formed and credit linked, efforts put in for promotion of asset management skills and developing linkages to promote credit absorption.

Funding: There is a cost involved in providing credit plus services and adopting technology applications. Commercial banks are expected to meet a part of the costs. In the initial stages some funding support may be extended through specially constituted Funds.

Financial Inclusion Funds

Two funds may be constituted: (a) Financial Inclusion Promotion and Development Fund, with NABARD, for meeting the cost of developmental and promotional interventions and (b) Financial Inclusion Technology Fund, with NABARD to meet the costs of technology adoption. Each Fund will have an initial corpus of ₹ 500 crore, with a start up funding of ₹ 250 crore each, to be contributed equally by GoI/RBI/NABARD and annual accretions thereto. Banks will be eligible for support from the Funds on a matching contribution of 50 percent from the Fund in regard to districts other than tribal districts and 75 percent in case of branches located in tribal districts identified under the Tribal Sub Plan.

Financial Inclusion Promotion and Development Fund: The Financial Inclusion Promotion and Development Fund will focus on financing the following interventions:

Farmers' Service Centres (FSC): The Centres will network on the technology front with Agricultural Universities/KVKs, farmers clubs, the formal extension machinery of the State Governments, technical staff of banks, portals of national level Commodity Exchanges, etc. Such FSCs can be financed by the banks on the pattern of agri clinics. In the initial stages, some support by way of viability gap funding may be provided.

Promoting Rural Entrepreneurship: Commercial banks may consider setting up institutions like farmer training centres and Rural Development and Self Employment Training Institutes (RUDSETI) for developing skills among farmers and rural entrepreneurs for effectively managing the assets financed.

Self-Help Groups: The SHG movement is yet to catch up on a big scale in regions manifesting high levels of exclusion (Central, Eastern and North-Eastern Regions). Funding support for promotion, nurturing and credit-linking of SHGs can be extended.

Developing HR**:** Lending to the poor raises, inter alia, issues of attitudes towards the poor as viable and profitable customers. The Committee has observed that there is a positive correlation between training received by the branch managers and their overall attitudes. The training module developed and tested for commercial banks and RRBs in the College of Agricultural Banking, Pune may be used/adopted by banks for bringing about the right mindset among branch staff.

Resource Centres: Resource Centres, apart from facilitating members of mature SHGs to graduate to micro-enterprises, also helps in ensuring long-term sustainability of SHGs. The cost of setting up such centres can be met out of this Fund and / or the MFDEF. This is discussed in detail later in the Report.

Federations: As indicated later in the Report, funding support may also be extended from this Fund and/or MFDEF for voluntary establishment of federations.

Capacity Building of BFs/BCs**:** Funding support, on priority basis, to be extended to specialized institutions which provide capacity building inputs to BFs/BCs, as discussed later in the Report.

Financial Inclusion Technology Fund: Extending outreach on a scale envisaged under NRFIP would require the application of low-cost technology solutions, which call for certain levels of funding support for rolling out such IT-based and inclusive financial sector plan.

Funds Guidelines: NABARD, in consultation with RBI, may prepare detailed guidelines for operationalising the funds.

Procedural Changes:

- Simplifying Mortgage Requirements.
- Enabling legislation has been passed in some States for acceptance of a simple declaratory charge as equitable mortgage. This may be done by all the State Governments.
- Stamp duty may be waived in respect of loans for small/marginal farmers, tenant

cultivators and oral lessees.

- Saral documentation for agricultural loans.
- NABARD, in cooperation with a core group of bankers, has prepared a one page document for agricultural loans up to ₹ 1 lakh. This may be adopted by all banks.

Nodal Branches (ADB Model): One branch of the lead bank at the block/taluka level may be identified as the nodal branch to address the issue of exclusion. Lead banks may strengthen these nodal branches with technical staff to provide agricultural/business development services in farm and non-farm sectors respectively, comprising technical inputs and extension services. The services of the nodal branch technical staff may be made available to all other branches in the block, under an appropriate cost sharing arrangement.

In some districts, where RRBs have dominant presence, sponsor banks may assist the RRBs in putting in place arrangements for technical staff for providing credit plus services. NABARD may defray the cost of such technical staff, particularly, in the North-Eastern Region.

Business Facilitators/Business Correspondents (BFs/BCs)

RBI has permitted banks to use the services of NGOs/SHGs, MFIs and other civil society organisations as intermediaries in providing financial and banking services through the use of BF and BC Models. The response of the banking system has been of low key and the model is yet to be fully grounded.

Following recommendations in respect of the BF/BC Model are made:

Business Facilitators (BFs): Originally, only individuals who were insurance agents could act as BFs while no individuals could be placed as BC. This was later on widened to include retired officials, viz., Government servants like postmasters, school teachers and headmasters, who were considered by RBI as eligible to act as BF. Banks may make use of this relaxation and use individuals as indicated above as BF.

- Banks may appoint ex-servicemen/retired bank staff as their BFs.
- Banks should ensure that the banking awareness created by BFs get converted to business potential by providing suitable banking services like mobile outlets.
- Banks may facilitate easy roll-out of this mobile banking model through simplification and rationalization of back-end processes and front-end procedures so that banking operations are made more customer-friendly.

Business Correspondents (BCs): In addition to the institutions presently allowed by RBI to function as BCs, individuals like locally settled retired Government servants like postmasters, school teachers, ex-servicemen and ex-bank staff, whose relationship with the banking system through a pension account has already been established, may be permitted to act as BCs.

Further, MF-NBFCs may be allowed to act as limited BCs of banks for only providing savings and remittance services.

Technology has to be an integral part in sustaining outreach efforts through the BC model. Ultimately, banks should endeavour to have a BC touch point in each of the six lakh villages in the country.

In order to sustain and encourage the arrangements, banks may formulate suitable incentive mechanism for BCs linked to the number of accounts opened/transactions put through by them. Further, banks may consider placing BCs even in areas having their own branches.

To begin with, the BC model envisaged by RBI could be implemented widely. In due course, when the BCs reach a higher level of turnover, they should bear commensurate financial responsibilities.

Banks may appoint any individual/institution of their choice as BCs, after exercising due diligence. This will facilitate greater acceptance of the BC Model by banks.

Funds may be provided to specialized institutions which provide capacity building inputs to BCs. Such funding support could be extended on priority basis to most excluded areas/sectors of the society.

SLBC convener banks may initiate discussion with their respective State Governments regarding routing government payments through BCs using the smart card or other relevant technology on a pilot basis.

SLBCs may undertake a study to identify organisations having the capacity to serve as customer service points and BC. In States like Andhra Pradesh and Kerala, the VOs and Kudumbashree structures already exist and these can be used as customer service points.

Training modules for BFs/BCs may be prepared in vernacular and in culture sensitive pictorial forms.

Role of Microfinance

Deepening the outreach of the microfinance programme is an effective way in reaching out to the excluded segments. Commercial Banks have played a very important role in the SHG-Bank Linkage Programme having linked 15.95 lakh SHGs, forming more than 54 percent of the total SHGs credit-linked in the country. This programme should be strengthened and carried further, playing a key role in financial inclusion.

Financing Poor Farmers: Joint liability groups (JLGs) of the poor such as landless, share croppers and tenant farmers is another innovative mechanism towards ensuring greater financial inclusion. Commercial banks can actively promote such groups for effectively purveying credit and other facilities to such clients. RBI may encourage banks to adopt the JLG model for lending to SF/MF, tenant cultivators, share croppers and oral lessees.

Making Marginal Farm Holdings Viable and Enabling their Financial Inclusion

The following recommendations are made:

- Government programmes aimed at enhancing agricultural productivity should be effectively linked with bank credit (e.g. Banking Plan in post-watershed projects).
- A massive programme for financing minor irrigation structures (wherever ground water levels are safe or where surface irrigation potential is available) may be undertaken specifically targeting marginal farm households.
- Supplementary activities like dairy, small poultry, sheep-rearing etc. have to be specifically targeted for marginal farmers, tenants and non-cultivator households.
- A National Dairy Plan (NDP) has been prepared to target production enhancement in 323 potential districts. Similar initiatives may be considered for other sectors also like poultry, horticulture, etc.
- Farm aggregation models including contract farming fully protecting the interests of farmers could be an option. Credit-marketing linkage can also be effected.

Regional Rural Banks

Post-merger, RRBs with 14,494 branches, represent a powerful instrument for financial inclusion. Their role and relevance in financial inclusion is crucial as:

- In rural areas, they account for 37 percent of total offices of all scheduled commercial banks.
- 91 percent of the total workforce in RRBs is posted in rural and semi-urban areas as compared to 38 percent for other scheduled commercial banks.
- In rural areas, RRBs account for 31 percent of deposit accounts and 19 percent of deposit amount of all scheduled commercial banks. Lower average deposit amount per account in RRBs as compared with commercial banks implies their better reach to small depositors.
- Share of RRBs in loan accounts is an impressive 37 percent in rural areas.
- Of all the scheduled commercial banks, RRBs account for 34 percent of branches in NE, 30 percent in Eastern and 32 percent in Central regions. Incidentally, these regions manifest financial exclusion of a high order.
- Of the total 29.25 lakh SHGs credit linked by the banking system (as on 31 March 2007), 31 percent linkage is done by RRBs. More significantly, the more backward a region, greater is the share of RRBs. In North Eastern

Region, it is 56 percent, Central region 48 percent and Eastern region 40 percent.

- RRBs have also played a significant role as self-help promoting institutions (SHPIs). As many as 104 RRBs (March 31, 2006) are functioning as SHPIs with grant assistance from NABARD.

Recommendations: Keeping the above in view, the following recommendations are made for RRBs:

RRBs should extend their services to unbanked areas and increase their credit to deposit (CD) ratio. The post-merger scenario of RRBs poses a series of challenges for them and these are to be addressed. The following areas would require attention from the point of view of financial inclusion:

- Setting exclusive targets for microfinance and financial inclusion.
- Providing funding support.
- Providing technology support.

No Further Merger of RRBs: Further merger of all RRBs at State-level across sponsor banks is not required. It may not also be desirable if there has to be a firm reinforcement of their rural orientation with a specific mandate on financial inclusion. Therefore, the process of merger should not proceed beyond the level of sponsor bank in each State.

***Recapitalisation of RRBs with Negative Net Worth*:** Recapitalisation of RRBs with negative net worth has to be given a serious consideration as it would facilitate their growth, provide lenders a level of comfort and enable their achieving standard capital adequacy ratio.

***Widening Network and Expanding Coverage*:** As on April 1, 2007, RRBs are covering 535 districts. They may be directed to cover all unbanked areas in these districts, taking the village as a unit, either by opening a branch (wherever feasible) or through the BF/BC model in a time bound manner. 87 districts in the country were not covered by RRBs as on April 1, 2007 and their area of operation may be extended to cover these districts.

***Strategic Microfinance Plan with NABARD Support*:** RRBs have the potential and capability to emerge as niche operators in microfinance. They are playing a major role in the SHG-Bank Linkage Programme especially also as SHPIs. Their dual role has special meaning in areas which face severe financial exclusion and which do not have a sufficient presence of well performing NGOs. However, to upscale the programme to a level where it can really make a visible impact, RRBs need handholding particularly in the areas of training, promotion and development. NABARD may provide required assistance.

NABARD should prepare a strategic action plan RRB-wise, for promotion and credit linkage of SHGs. RRBs may be asked to form, nurture and credit link at least 3,000 SHGs in districts covered by them in North-Eastern, Eastern and Central Regions. A memorandum of understanding (MoU) may be signed by RRBs with NABARD for a period of 5 years—with NABARD providing the promotional and development assistance out of the "Financial Inclusion Promotion and Development Fund" and RRBs forming, nurturing and providing financial services to SHGs. RRBs may accomplish the task with the support of individual rural volunteers, BFs, their staff members, etc. NABARD may closely monitor the programme with focus on qualitative aspects.

NRFIP for RRBs: The strategy recommended for NRFIP for commercial banks would be equally applicable for RRBs. They would require promotional, funding and technology support in different areas as outlined below. RRBs may endeavour to cover a large part of their incremental lending through the group mode (SHGs/JLGs) as it will enhance their outreach to financially excluded. Lending through group mode would also keep NPAs at low level.

Pilot testing of BF/BC Model by RRBs: RRBs should adopt the BF and BC models as a major strategy of financial inclusion. NABARD should extend the required support including running pilots in selected banks. The proposal for a technology based intervention under the BC model would be equally relevant for RRBs. However, RRBs would require some handholding in implementing the proposal. NABARD may identify 10 RRBs across the country, giving greater weightage to regions manifesting higher levels of financial exclusion and work in strategic alliance with these RRBs and their sponsor banks in implementing the proposal. The RRBs identified by NABARD for the project will require to develop a core banking software for proper integration of the technology model proposed. NABARD should enter into a MoU with identified sponsor banks and RRBs and provide initial funding and technology support.

Separate Credit Plan for Excluded Regions: The RRBs operating in predominantly tribal areas and having high levels of exclusion may prepare annual credit plans having a separate component for excluded groups, which would integrate credit provision with promotional assistance. Refinance and promotional support may be provided by NABARD to RRBs on a large scale for implementation of these credit plans.

Computerisation: With a view to facilitating the seamless integration of RRBs with the main payments system, there is a need to provide computerisation support to them. Banks will be eligible for support from the Financial Inclusion Funds on a matching contribution of 50 percent in regard to districts other than tribal districts and 75 percent in case of branches located in tribal districts under the Tribal Sub Plan.

***Strengthening Boards of Management*:** Post-merger, it is necessary that Boards of Management of RRBs are strengthened and powers delegated to them on policy and business operations, viz. introduction of new liability and credit products, investment decisions, improving market orientation in raising and deployment of resources, non-fund based business, career progression, transfer policy etc.

***Tax Incentives*:** From 2006-07, RRBs are liable to pay income tax. To further strengthen the RRBs, profits transferred to reserves could be exempted from tax till they achieve standard capital adequacy ratios. Alternately, RRBs may be allowed tax concessions to the extent of 40 percent of their profits, as per provisions under Section 36 (1)(viii) of the Income Tax Act.

***NABARD to Support HR Development in RRBs*:** NABARD may continue to give special priority to RRBs to train their staff through its training institutions. NABARD may design suitable training programmes to enable RRBs to meet the challenges in the post merger environment. This training may also cover members of the Board of RRBs.

***Implementation of RBI Initiatives for Financial Inclusion*:** All the recent circulars relating to financial inclusion, viz. no frills accounts, GCC, one time settlement (OTS) for loans up to ₹ 25,000, use of intermediaries, etc., should be implemented by RRBs.

***Local Area Banks (LABs)*:** RBI may allow new LABs to come into operation, especially in districts/regions manifesting high levels of exclusion, without compromising on regulatory prescriptions. LABs can integrate well with local financial markets and offer a host of financial services including savings, credit, remittances, insurance etc.

Cooperative Credit Institutions

Rural credit cooperatives, in India, have a very long history. Democratic in features, the cooperative movement was envisaged as a mechanism for pooling the resources of people with small means and providing them with access to different financial services. In the backdrop of the reform process underway for cooperative banks, they have a very significant role to play in facilitating greater inclusion.

Early Implementation of Vaidyanathan Committee Revival Package: All necessary steps should be taken for the early implementation of the STCCS revival package in all States.

Cooperatives in SHG-Bank Linkage: Need for Enabling Legislation: In certain States, legislation has been enacted, admitting SHGs as members of PACS. Similar legislation in other States would require to be enacted to enable the emergence of cooperatives as effective SHPIs. Federations of SHGs may be registered in all the States under the Cooperative Societies Act or the parallel Self Reliant Cooperatives Act and availability of funds to these cooperatives for advancing loans may be considered by NABARD, based on objective rating criteria. NABARD may also set aside requisite funds for sensitising the cooperative movement in this regard.

Use of PACS and other Primary Cooperatives as Business Correspondents: There are a large number of PACS and primary cooperatives under the parallel Acts located in rural areas where there are no other financial services outlets. Many of these cooperatives are in districts where the DCCBs are defunct or moribund. Such PACS could provide valuable services to their members if they get access to a commercial bank. RBI has already listed Cooperatives as eligible institutions under the BF/BC Model.

In the circumstances, Cooperatives may make use of this opportunity at least in States which have accepted the Vaidyanathan Committee recommendations. NABARD may be asked to suggest appropriate guidelines for the purpose, subject to the approval of RBI.

Cooperatives Adopting Group Approach for Financing Excluded Groups: Micro enterprises, in order to be successful, require larger funding which NGOs cannot provide. It will, therefore, be necessary to develop/test a new form of community based organisation other than SHGs which may be more appropriate to support members who engage in micro-enterprises. Those members of SHG who opt to graduate to micro-enterprises could be formed into JLGs or some similar organisation.

The relations of mutual trust and support which is described as affinity in a SHG tend to be weaker in a JLG. Therefore, new forms of collateral or guarantee may have to be worked out. Guidelines circulated by NABARD may be adopted by banks.

Further, the use of the BF model could be thought of to organize vulnerable segments of the population into JLGs. The pilot project presently under implementation by NABARD should be sufficiently broad based to cover the role of facilitators in formation and linkage of JLGs.

Risk Mitigation: Setting up of Credit Guarantee Fund: A Credit Guarantee Fund may be set up as a risk mitigation mechanism and also for providing comfort to the banks for lending to such JLGs [akin to the Credit Guarantee Fund Scheme of SIDBI for Small/Micro Enterprises Industries (CGFSI) available for small-scale industries (SSIs) at present].

Self-help Group (SHG)–Bank Linkage Model

The SHG-Bank Linkage Programme is a major plank of the strategy for delivering financial services to the poor in a sustainable manner. As at the end of March 2007, as many as 29.25 lakh SHGs have been credit-linked with banks, benefiting more than 400 lakh poor families. There is a need for further deepening and upscaling of microfinance interventions.

Encouraging SHGs in Excluded Regions: Funding Support: If the SHG-Bank Linkage Programme has to reach a critical scale, the Department of Women and Child Development at State-level should be actively involved in promoting and nurturing of SHGs. The State Governments and NABARD may, therefore, set aside specific funds out of budgetary support and the Micro Finance Development and Equity Fund (MFDEF) respectively for the purpose of promoting SHGs in regions with high levels of exclusion. The spread of SHGs in hilly regions, particularly in the North-Eastern Region, is poor. One of the reasons for this is the low population density in hilly areas and weak banking network. There is a need to evolve SHG models suited to the local context.

Capacity Building of Government Functionaries: Certain deficiencies like poor follow up, ineffective monitoring and inadequate training and capacity building efforts have been observed in the past. Adequate safeguards may, therefore, be devised and built in future programme implementation strategies. NABARD can also facilitate this process by providing support for capacity building of Government functionaries from grass root level upwards within the SHG framework.

Legal Status for SHGs: As of now, SHGs are operating as thrift and credit groups. They may, in future, evolve to a higher level of commercial enterprise. The question of providing a simplified legal status to the SHGs may have to be examined in full, in this context. This would also facilitate their becoming members of PACS.

Maintenance of Participatory Character of SHG Movement: A movement of such large scale involving people's participation could lead to attempts towards politicization. This must be avoided. Sufficient care has to be taken to ensure that the SHG movement retains its participatory and self-help character.

NABARD to Open 'Project Offices' in Identified Priority States: NABARD is managing the MFDEF with a corpus of ₹ 200 crore. One major focus of the Fund should be promoting the SHG-Bank Linkage Programme in States where it has been comparatively slow moving. NABARD has already identified States with large population of the poor, but exhibiting low performance in implementation of the programme. The ongoing efforts of NABARD to upscale the programme in the identified States need to be given a fresh impetus. NABARD can open dedicated project offices in the 13 States for upscaling the SHG-Bank Linkage Programme by strategizing interventions such as stronger involvement of State Governments, capacity building of NGOs, broadening the range of SHPI, etc.

Incentive Package for NGOs: Many of the NGOs have played a commendable role in promoting SHGs and linking them with banks. NGOs, being local initiators with their low resources are finding it difficult to expand in other areas and regions. There is, therefore, a need to evolve an incentive package which should motivate these NGOs to diversify into other backward areas. Incentive package could be in the form of expeditious and hassle-free grant support.

RBI/NABARD to Study the Issue of 'Evergreening': A certain element of "evergreening" of loans is reportedly taking place among credit linked SHGs. This, if established, is a matter of concern. RBI/NABARD may expeditiously study this aspect and come out with suggestions for reversing this unsettling trend.

Transparency in Maintenance of Records: In order to ensure sustainability of the SHGs, their activities and linkages, there should be better transparency in the books of accounts maintained at the group level. These books should reflect the position of deposits in members' accounts, interest paid on savings, distribution of corpus or operating surplus among members, evergreening of loan accounts, etc. Banks, with the help of NABARD, should evolve a checklist for concurrent monitoring of SHGs.

SHGs to Evolve Norms for Distribution of Surplus: Many of the SHGs do not have the practice of distributing the surplus generated from their business activities within the group and the awareness on this issue among the SHG members is very low. There is a need to evolve norms for distribution of surplus (akin to dividend) especially at the time when a member drops out of the group.

Need to Restructure Design and Direction of SGSY Subsidy: Subsidies provided under SGSY need to be restructured. Linking credit with subsidy is not an effective approach for reaching out to the poor. There is a need to formulate a single programme synergising the positive features of SGSY such as specific targeting of below poverty line (BPL) families, etc. and those of the SHG-Bank Linkage Programme such as group cohesiveness, discipline etc. While recognizing that individual subsidies are distortionary, the Government may consider redirecting subsidy in the SGSY Programme for the following purposes:

- Capacity building of NGOs and other field based agencies such as *Krishi Vigyan Kendras*, to form and strengthen SHGs.
- Exposure visits to successful models by bankers, government officials and SHG leaders etc.

- For strengthening input supply and marketing arrangements.

Some of the State Governments like West Bengal and Andhra Pradesh have initiated efforts in this direction. Further, it is understood that the proposals are awaiting approval of the GoI. The approaches adopted by these States for bringing synergy between SGSY groups and the SHGs of the linkage programme can be studied so that the same can be replicated in other States. The broad features of the proposed convergence model are indicated in Annexure V of the main report. The need for technology adoption for effective disbursal of Govt. subsidy should be recognized. The existing dispensation of subsidy under SGSY and payouts under NREGP could be routed through bank accounts, with suitable technology support.

Interest Rate Subsidy: Certain States are reportedly providing a subsidy on interest rates being charged by banks to the SHGs. The margin available to SHGs is sufficient to take care of operational costs, even after considering the small amounts of loan provided to members. Thus, a subsidy on interest rates cuts at the very root of the self help character of SHGs. The subsidy could be re-directed towards capacity building efforts or in providing input supplies and marketing support to the SHGs.

Resource Centres: For ensuring the long term sustainability of SHGs and for helping the members of mature SHGs to graduate from microfinance to micro enterprises, resource centres on the lines of the Andhra Pradesh Mahila Abhivruddhi Society (APMAS) can be set up in different parts of the country.

There are a large number of SHGs which are well established in their savings and credit operations. Their members want to expand and diversify their activities with a view to attain economies of scale. Many of the groups are organizing themselves into federations and other higher level structures. To achieve this effectively, resource centres can play a vital role.

Resource centres can be set up by various stakeholders such as NGOs, banks, Government departments, NABARD at the State/district level to play an important role in preparing training modules, developing a cadre of trainers, conduct of field studies and in promoting interface between SHG members and service providers. The specific role of resource centres would be:

- To work towards a comprehensive capacity building of SHGs.
- Share innovative ideas and models that can be replicated elsewhere.
- Enhance functional literacy among SHG members.
- Support livelihood interventions among SHG members.
- Facilitate availability of all services to SHG members under one roof.

The cost for setting up resource centres can be met out of the Financial

Inclusion Fund and/or the MFDEF.

SHGs to Provide Alternative Savings Products: Most of the SHGs encourage compulsory savings with equal small amounts by members on a regular basis. SHGs need to offer a wide range of savings products so as to capture the huge potential of savings that remains untapped. Groups should be free to design savings products suiting to members' requirements. Certain level of experimentation could be attempted by the Resource Centres in designing new saving products and NABARD should encourage and support such experiments.

Adoption of JLG Model to Cover Marginalized Groups: A scheme for financing JLGs of tenant farmers and oral lessees has been evolved by NABARD for implementation by all the commercial banks, RRBs and Cooperatives. The adoption of the concept of JLGs, if properly grounded, could be another effective method for purveying credit to mid-segment clients such as small farmers, marginal farmers, tenant farmers, etc. and thereby reduce their dependence on informal sources of credit.

From Micro Credit to Micro Enterprise: Challenges: The present challenge is to induce SHGs and their members to graduate into matured levels of enterprise, factor in livelihood diversification, increase their access to the supply chain, linkages to the capital market and appropriate production and processing technologies. A spin off of this challenge is how to address the investment capital requirements of matured SHGs, which have initially met members' consumption needs and are now on the threshold of taking off into "enterprise". There is evidence in MYRADA experience where lending for productive purposes has already been given greater emphasis by SHGs. The community managed resource centres (CMRCs) organized by MYRADA provide a variety of linkage services to SHGs and individual entrepreneurs among SHG members. This model requires to be studied.

The SHG-Bank Linkage Programme needs to introspect whether it is sufficient for SHGs to only meet the financial needs of their members, or whether there is also a further obligation on their part to meet the non-financial requirements necessary for setting up business and enterprises. Ideally, it must meet both.

Greater Role for NABARD: While greater emphasis is needed for growth and spread of SHGs across the country, the quality in terms of outreach of financial services, capacity building, sustainability etc., needs to be reemphasized. NABARD shall play a pro-active role and identify new initiatives that will contribute to effectively improving outreach to the poor through SHGs, MFIs etc.

Federations: Federations, if they emerge voluntarily from amongst SHGs, can be encouraged. However, the Committee feels that they cannot be entrusted with the financial intermediation function. In Andhra Pradesh, federations are registered as societies under the MACS Act. The SHG members (as individuals) are permitted to be members in the federation. In Uttarakhand, SHGs are permitted to become members of PACS directly. Other States may adopt similar enabling legislation.

Voluntary establishment of federations could be supported out of the Financial Inclusion Fund and the MFDEF. While extending support, it should be ensured that:

- Federations emerge voluntarily, on the felt need of the SHGs,
- Federations provide other value added services to member SHGs. Based on a study of Federations operating across the country, a broad list of such services and the modus operandi of federations in providing such services can be prepared and circulated by NABARD.
- Federations, in terms of distance, operate in close proximity to members.

Urban Microfinance: There are no clear estimates of the number of people in urban areas with no access to organized financial services. This may be attributed, in part at least, to the migratory nature of the urban poor, comprising mostly of migrants from the rural areas. Even money lenders often shy away from lending to urban poor. There have been a few instances of MFIs venturing into this area of lending to urban poor who are undertaking micro-enterprises and small business activities. Urban branches of banks, even though having manpower and technology support, are not attuned to SHG lending or micro finance.

Opening of specialised microfinance branches/cells in potential urban centres exclusively catering for microfinance and SHG-Bank Linkage could be thought of, to address the requirements of the urban poor. BFs/BCs could be the mechanism to reach the target clientele in these areas. Banks can also consider associating with MFIs undertaking urban micro lending as a viable option.

Amendment to NABARD Act: At present, NABARD is permitted, as per its Act and Mandate, to support micro finance activities in rural and semi-urban areas only. An enabling provision be made in the NABARD Act, 1981 permitting NABARD to provide micro finance services to the urban poor.

Micro Finance Institutions: Introduction

Firm data regarding the number of MFIs operating under different forms is not available. However, it is roughly estimated that there are about 1,000 NGO-MFIs and more than 20 company MFIs. Further, in Andhra Pradesh, nearly 30,000 cooperative organizations are engaged in mF activities. However, the company MFIs are major players accounting for over 80 percent of the micro finance loan portfolio.

Definition of MFI: The proposed Microfinance Services Regulation Bill defines microfinance services as "providing financial assistance to an individual or an eligible client, either directly or through a group mechanism for an amount, not exceeding rupees fifty thousand in aggregate (₹ 1,50,000 if for housing purposes). Greater legitimacy, accountability and transparency will not only enable MFIs to source adequate debt and equity funds, but could eventually enable MFIs to take and use savings as a low cost source for on-lending.

Recognising MF-NBFCs: There is a need to recognize a separate category of Micro finance–Non-banking Finance Companies (MF-NBFCs), without any relaxation on start-up capital and subject to the regulatory prescriptions applicable for NBFCs. Such MF-NBFCs could be defined as companies that provide thrift, credit, micro-insurance, remittances and other financial services up to a specified amount to the poor in rural, semi-urban and urban areas.

At least 80 percent of the assets of MF-NBFCs should be in the form of micro credit of up to ₹ 50,000 for agriculture, allied and non-farm activities and in case of housing, loans up to ₹ 1,50,000 per individual borrower, whether given through a group mechanism or directly.

MF-NBFCs as BCs: To enable the poor to have access to savings services, MF-NBFCs may be recognized as Business Correspondents of banks for only providing savings and remittance services.

Relaxation in FIPB guidelines: Current guidelines used by FIPB (Foreign Investment Promotion Board) require a minimum of US$ 500,000 equity investment from a foreign entity. MFNBFCs' initial capital needs may not be very large and the Committee is of the view that the minimum amount of foreign equity for MF-NBFCs may be reduced to a level of US$ 100,000.

NABARD may extend equity support out of its MFDEF to such MF-NBFCs based on objective rating/criteria. NABARD may accord priority in providing equity support to those MF-NBFCs operating in regions featuring high levels of exclusion. The SEBI Venture Capital Guidelines may permit Venture Capital Funds to invest in MF-NBFCs.

Tax Concessions: MF-NBFCs may be allowed tax concessions to the extent of 40 percent of their profits, as a proportion to their business portfolio in excluded districts as identified by NABARD without attracting tax. For this, MF-NBFCs may be included as eligible institutions under Section 36(1)(viii) of the Income Tax Act.

MF-NBFCs as Micro insurance Agents: The IRDA Micro insurance Guidelines, 2005 may permit MF-NBFCs to offer micro insurance services as agents of regulated life and non-life insurance companies.

Code of Conduct: A voluntary mutual code of conduct, already prepared, covering aspects including mission, governance, transparency, interest rates, handling of customer grievances, staff conduct, recovery practices, etc., may be made mandatory for MFIs.

Accounting and Disclosure Norms: The Institute of Chartered Accountants of India (ICAI) may be involved in formulating appropriate accounting and disclosure norms for MFIs. Banks lending to MFIs may undertake studies on the cost of funds of MFIs, risk premium, etc. and exercise a lender's discipline in enforcing reasonable rates of interest and acceptable modes of recovery.

Unifying Regulatory Oversight: RBI may consider bringing all regulatory aspects of microfinance under a single mechanism. Further, supervision of MF-NBFCs could be delegated to NABARD by RBI.

Micro Finance Bill: While Section 25 Companies could be covered by the Micro Financial Sector (Development and Regulation) Bill, 2007, cooperatives can be taken out of the purview of the proposed Bill.

Technology Applications

Technological developments in the recent past have provided the perfect launch pad for extending banking outposts to remote locations without having to open bank branches. This could be achieved by leveraging technology to open up channels beyond branch network and create the required banking footprints to reach the unbanked so as to extend banking services similar to those dispensed from branches.

The Committee, while concurring with the RBI's advisory group for IT-enabled financial inclusion, is of the view that nearly all pilot models converge on certain essential components and processes to be followed in technology application. The essence of a majority of the models under consideration features the issue of a smart card to the farmer on which all his transactions are recorded, a hand-held terminal with the BC at the village level and a central processor unit (CPU) linking the smart cards and BC terminals with the banks. There are also other models where smart cards are dispensed with and mobile telephones, etc., are used. The fundamental outlines of the existing technology-based models may be examined for application in such manner and to such extent as may be deemed fit. The operating costs of the various models are expected to be minimal and can be easily absorbed by banks as the increase in business volumes will justify the incremental operating costs. Also, the costs are substantially lowered if the infrastructure is shared. It is, therefore, recommended that shared infrastructure among different banks enabling nationwide financial inclusion would confer large scale benefits and also enable effortless transfer of funds between the card holders of various banks.

Essentially, the start up costs are the initial investment costs comprising cost of the smart card, terminals with the BC and the CPU. The Committee is of the view that the Financial Inclusion Technology Fund can provide the necessary support for defraying part of the costs.

Optimisation of Existing Infrastructure: The Committee is of the opinion that the existing banking infra-structure and NGOs which have already made extensive inroads in rural areas should be made optimal use of for enabling outreach of banking services. The BF/BC models backed by technology applications should encourage a role for the small players and integrate them with the national system. The Committee is of the opinion that the State Governments should make payments under National Rural Employment Guarantee Scheme and Social Security Payments thru' such technology based solutions.

Building Database: The creation of a national database, sectoral, geographic and demographic reports, and also a payment system benefiting the card holders from the underprivileged/unbanked population will not be possible without the extensive use of IT. This alone can bring down the costs of the small ticket transactions of the poor and make nationwide financial inclusion a reality. The technology suppliers and banks should evolve common minimum standards for ensuring inter-operability between their systems.

Remittance Needs of the Poor

Ahmednagar DCCB has implemented a system of low cost anywhere banking solution which has a facility of card to card transfer. Savings/current account holders at all its 280 branches have a choice to keep their savings bank account or a part thereof in a separate account at the bank's head office. Customers can have access to this account from all the bank branches. It was learnt that the customer is charged only ₹ 4 per transaction. Such experiments may be studied for replication.

A low value card linked to a bank account, which can be encashed at PoS and which allow transfer of small amounts from one card to another would alleviate remittance problems. This would substantially increase banking outreach as at present there are about 3 lakh PoS as compared to around 70,000 scheduled commercial bank branches and 22,000 ATMs. However, a majority of PoS machines are now located in urban and semi-urban areas. It is expected that as the system takes roots, more PoS will come in rural areas, facilitating such transfers.

The e-kiosks in villages could be yet another source of operating a remittance system that is accessible to the poor.

Other Recommendations

The following suggestions would substantially address the remittance needs of the poor in the country:

- The combined network of nearly 70000 branches of scheduled commercial banks (including RRBs) and a network of more than 1.50 lakh post offices can ideally provide the institutional mechanism for extending remittance facilities in remote areas. With adoption of appropriate technology, it may be possible to bring down the transaction costs which would encourage and enable the poor to make use of such remittance facilities. A committee may be set up with representatives from RBI, Department of Posts, NABARD and commercial banks for exploring the feasibility of integrating postal network with the banking system and developing a nation wide remittance system.
- The remittance product could be an electronic product similar to "Instacash" where a 16-digit code is given to the originator of the transaction, and the beneficiary can take the amount from select post offices by giving the code, and identity proof. This product should be available across banks, post offices and other institutions and be affordable. Another option could be to credit the remitted amount to a central server at the originating point and at every touch point should be able to withdraw it.
- Banks should endeavour to have a BC touch point in each of the six lakh villages in the country. There should be a micro-bank in every village.
- Banks should introduce card-based remittance products which can be encashed all over the country. This may be card to card transfer, or simply a scratch card type remittance card.

Micro Insurance

Helping the rural poor systematically manage financial risks to their livelihoods and lives through micro-insurance offers innovative ways to combat poverty in India. Micro insurance should provide greater economic and psychological security to the poor as it reduces exposure to multiple risks and cushions the impact of a disaster. Micro insurance in conjunction with micro savings and micro credit could go a long way in keeping this segment away from the poverty trap and would truly be an integral component of financial inclusion. In 2003, GoI constituted a Consultative Group on Micro Insurance to examine existing insurance schemes for rural and urban poor. The report of the consultative group has brought out the following key issues:

- Micro insurance is not viable as a standalone insurance product.
- Micro insurance has not penetrated rural markets. Traditional insurers have

not made much headway in bringing micro insurance products to the rural poor. (In addition, the Committee feels that micro insurance has not penetrated even among the urban poor).

- Partnership between an insurer and a social organisation like NGO would be desirable to promote micro insurance by drawing on their mutual strengths.
- Design of micro insurance products must have the features of simplicity, availability, affordability, accessibility and flexibility.

The Committee studied four different models for delivering micro insurance services to the targeted clientele, viz., the partner-agent model, full service model, community-based model and provider model.

Recommendations

***Leveraging the Existing Network for Micro Insurance*:** To economise on costs and to increase the outreach of micro insurance to the poor, the insurers need to utilize existing Government organisations and NGOs, having greater acceptability among the financially excluded. The partner-agent model for delivery where the insurer underwrites the risk and the distribution is handled by an existing intermediary, seems apt in this scenario.

***Linking Micro Credit with Micro Insurance*:** The Committee concurs with the view that offering micro credit without micro-insurance is financial behaviour fraught with risk. There is, therefore, a need to emphasise linking of micro credit with micro insurance. Further, as it helps in bringing down the inherent risk cost of lending, the Committee feels that NABARD should be regularly involved in issues relating to rural and micro insurance to leverage on its experience of being a catalyst in the field of micro credit.

***Implementation Strategy for Micro Insurance*:** The Committee has identified major areas for formulation of strategies for effective implementation of micro insurance programmes as explained in the following paragraphs:

***Human Resources Requirement and Training*:** To tap the huge micro insurance potential, IRDA may consider putting in place an appropriate institutional structure for deciding on service packages including premia and formulating strategies for effective promotion of micro insurance. There is also a felt need for development, of both full-time and part-time staff, through effective training in insurance marketing and servicing concepts.

***Operations and Systems*:** To address the requirements of the huge market potential available, appropriate systems should be evolved for tracking client information, either manually or using technology. While a technology platform may take time for setting up, in the long-run, the same will be cost-effective and reliable. Similarly, the procedures for claims, premium payments/renewals and other services should be formalized along with increased customization of products to stimulate demand.

***Development of Adequate Feedback Mechanism*:** Keeping in view the diverse nature of market requirements, suitable mechanisms to collect market intelligence, collating and interpretation of the same in a formally structured manner, is important for product development and process refinement.

***Development of Data Base*:** High costs of penetration and acquisition often leads to higher pricing of products, thereby impacting client outreach and market depth. Building up historical data base on risk profiles, claims, settlement ratios, etc., will facilitate in better pricing of products, based on actual rather than presumed risks. Besides enabling cost reduction, warehousing of such data will make the market more transparent for entry of more operators.

***Consumer Education, Marketing and Grievance Handling*:** The micro insurance sector is unique in the sense that there is an ongoing challenge to explain the concept and benefits to the insured. Creating awareness through use of pictorial posters, local folk arts and street theatres might be useful to explain the mechanisms of insurance. Local community-based organisations could organize premium collections, as they have better access to the local people. To make it more acceptable to the people, micro insurance products, apart from covering only risks, should also provide an opportunity for long-term savings (endowment).

***Product Development/Process Re-engineering*:** Customised product development to suit the varying requirements of the local populace is a pre-requisite. The processes/procedures are to be streamlined and simplified, to facilitate easier access for the rural poor. Information should be made available in vernacular for easy understanding of the terms on offer.

***Using Existing Infrastructure*:** Micro-insurance service providers can use the existing banking infrastructure and also adopt the agency-mode (NGOs, SHGs, NBFCs, etc.) for providing services, thereby leveraging on the existing physical branch network and reducing costs.

***Use of Technology*:** The technology platforms being envisioned to facilitate financial inclusion should enable micro insurance transactions also. Towards this end, there is a need to integrate the various modules—savings, credit, insurance, etc.—into the technology framework so that holistic inclusive efforts are possible in the rural areas.

***Review of Existing Schemes*:** There are a large number of group life and health insurance schemes which are run by various central ministries and State Governments. The level of actual coverage in terms of claims preferred and settled in such schemes is disturbingly low. These schemes should be reviewed by an expert group set up by the IRDA.

Life Insurance

A wide range of products are available but penetration is really limited in rural areas. The procedural requirements at the time of entry and in case of claims settlement are cumbersome. The commission structure for agents is also heavily weighed in favour of getting new policies with very little incentive to service existing policies. In this regard, Micro Insurance Guidelines (MIG), 2005 issued by IRDA has provided for equal commission throughout the life of a policy and this will now remove the disincentive in servicing existing policy holders.

Health Insurance

In case of health insurance, penetration level is even much lower than Life Insurance. The two categories viz., critical illness and hospitalisation are the main product segments. Some State Governments have developed health insurance schemes which are still in very early stages.

The Committee has observed that the mutual health insurance models have advantages of its members performing a number of roles such as awareness creation, marketing, enrolment, premium collection, claims processing, monitoring, etc. Under this arrangement, the costs of offering small-ticket health insurance gets significantly reduced. The high co-variant risks such as epidemics will have to be taken care of by a mutual entity taking re-insurance for such risks.

IRDA has also suggested that the capital requirements for stand-alone health insurance companies be reduced to ₹ 50 crore as against ₹ 100 crore for Life Insurance Companies and the Committee endorses the same.

Crop Insurance

This is a very important risk mitigation arrangement for small and marginal farmers. However, leaving the discretion to notify crops/regions to state governments has contributed to adverse selection. Further, claims settlement based on yield estimation has been cumbersome and the sampling area for crop cutting experiments is very large. An alternative model based on weather insurance has been attempted. To make it more effective, there is a need for having a large number of smaller weather stations. The Committee recommends that policies be evolved to make crop insurance universal, viz., applicable to all crops/regions and pricing actuarial.

Livestock Insurance

As in life insurance, the problem lies in the process of enrolment and claims settlement. Several pilots indicate that the involvement of local organisations like SHGs, dairy co-operatives, NGOs and MFIs improves the quality of service, reduces false claims and expedites claims settlement. The Committee recommends that these experiences be studied and adopted by insurance companies.

Asset Insurance

This could cover a wide range including residential buildings, farm and non-farm equipments and vehicles. The main constraint seems to be lack of distribution channels appropriate for lower income groups. The Committee again recommends that involving local NGOs, MFIs, SHGs, etc. as distribution channels as well as facilitators of claims settlements would be quite useful.

Demand Side Causes and Solutions for Financial Inclusion

The Committee's Report has so far concentrated on supply side issues of financial inclusion and what can be done to enhance supply of financial services, through increased outreach by existing institutions, enhancing their incentives to serve the excluded and adding new distribution channels. The Committee is of the view that financial exclusion is also caused by demand side issues. Unless some initiatives are taken on the demand side, or in the "real sectors", mere supply side solutions from the financial sector will not work.

Recommendations

***Human Development*:** Regions, segments and sectors financially excluded require substantial investments in human development. In particular, primary health, nutrition, primary education and vocational training need attention. The Twelfth Finance Commission had already taken a lead in this direction by earmarking additional funds for health and education in backward States. The Committee is of the view that this will lead to enhanced economic efficiency and consequent demand for financial inclusion, within a few years.

***Access to Land and Titling*:** The Committee is supportive of various Government programmes under which surplus land is distributed to landless and marginal farmers. The Committee has also noted that the Government has enacted recently The Forest Dwellers and Tribal Land Rights Act, 2006, which will ensure that those who had been cultivating a piece of land for decades in the middle of forests, will now get security of tenure. This will open up the possibility of their accessing credit from banks.

The Committee has noted and endorses the recent move by NABARD to provide refinance for credit extended by banks and co-operatives to oral lessees and tenant farmers. This category of farmers has long been financially excluded due to lack of land titling or recorded tenures. Procedural changes in banks must be brought about to extend credit outreach to all such productive farmers.

Banks hesitate to finance tenant farmers/oral lessees as they do not have documentary proof of their right to till the land for raising crops or for investment purposes. Recording of tenancy and ownership rights on land is an important measure to enable access to credit.

Certificates by revenue officers or a system of land cultivation certificate by the Village Panchayats or local bodies may be made acceptable as documentary proof for cultivating the land.

Computerisation of land records will lead to systematization of land records and overall availability of required information to banks facilitating their loan appraisal process. It is observed that 12 States have already initiated the process and GoI may advise all States to give priority for completing this process within a year. This will reduce cost to farmers in obtaining various documents and recording encumbrance.

Access to Work: NREGA: Given the fact that nearly 80 percent of farmer households in the country are small and marginal farmers, who rarely have work on their own farms for more than 100 days a year, the availability of wage employment in the vicinity of their villages is critical. In this context, the Committee noted the nation-wide roll-out plans supported by the National Rural Employment Guarantee Act (NREGA) which ensures that every household in need can ask for paid wage work for up to 100 days per year.

The Committee endorses the creative use of the NREGP payments through bank accounts to enhance financial inclusion, as practiced in Andhra Pradesh. In Andhra Pradesh, the beneficiaries/depositors will be issued smart cards to enable transactions at several locations besides the bank branch.

Infrastructure Support: The Committee noted the significant progress made for rural connectivity through the Pradhan Mantri Gram Sadak Yojana and the attempt to extend electric power to unconnected villages through the Rajiv Gandhi Gram Vidyutikaran Yojana. In several states the RIDF managed by NABARD has enabled the creation of much needed roads, bridges, irrigation canals, water harvesting structures and other useful infrastructure. The Committee endorses this and recommends a further impetus in the area.

The National Development Council (NDC) has recommended that the normative allocation of RIDF funds among States should be decided by factoring in, *inter alia*, the CD ratio as a relevant criterion. This should be attempted by NABARD to improve equitable distribution of RIDF resources.

Productivity Enhancement: In this connection, the Committee has already recommended the establishment of nodal branches in each block to undertake intensive efforts for agricultural and business development services to farm and non-farm sector borrowers respectively. The Committee also recommends that banks explore tie-ups with government extension agencies, Krishi Vigyan Kendras, reputed NGOs working in this field, agri-business clinics and corporates engaged in agricultural activities, to provide inputs, extension services and market linkages to the bank's borrowers so as to offer credit plus services and enhance the efficiency of credit.

Value Addition: Primary Processing: The Committee recommends that efforts should be made to ensure that all agricultural produce is subjected to primary and if possible secondary value addition locally. This means that post-harvest drying, sorting, grading and packing, can be done at the village level, preferably by women's SHGs. Farmers groups can come together to establish secondary value addition facilities such as groundnut shelling, cotton ginning, dal milling, rice hulling, fruit pulping, milk chilling, etc.

Alternate Market Linkages: Roads, transport, power and water provide critical linkages in support of production-based activities. Social services like health, education, etc. contribute to improvements in the quality of rural life. State Governments should prioritise infrastructure planning, use of funds of the National Rural Employment Guarantee Programme (NREGP) for building critical infrastructure and encourage community participation in creation and maintenance of assets.

Risk Mitigation through Non-financial Channels: A vast majority of poorer households in India are exposed to high levels of risk and considered as not insurable at reasonable levels of premium. Their risk levels need to be mitigated through soil and water conservation measures, watershed development, installing protective irrigation and by using appropriate agronomic practices all the way from ploughing techniques to seed selection and timely farm operations. In the case of livestock rearers, risks can be reduced by proper herd management practices and mass vaccination for example against foot and mouth disease. It is only after these types of investments have reduced the risks in farming that the private expense in buying insurance can be affordable.

Calamity Relief Fund

Repeated natural calamities and consequent rescheduling of bank loans take the debt burden beyond the repaying capacity of farmers. There is a need for the creation of a National Calamity Fund to address the problems of farmers in distress districts. Further, the subsidy on crop insurance may be directed more effectively towards the disadvantaged sectors. Apart from the physical risks which impact crop yields, farmers also suffer from price risks. In bumper years, their harvest fetches low prices. In order to hedge against such price risks the right instrument is commodity derivatives, particularly futures options in which a farmer can be assured of selling his produce at a certain price in future.

The Committee also noted that the Indian farmer is highly attuned to dealing in spot markets, traditionally known as *Mandis*, where the commodity is exchanged for cash. The Committee therefore supports any initiatives towards improving the transactional efficiency of spot markets.

The Committee noted that several multi-commodity exchanges have come up in the last few years and that they are registering a large turn over. This enables farmers to discover the future price and take decisions related to crop selection. The Committee is supportive of such initiatives.

However, the Committee noted the fact that a vast majority of financially excluded farmers have only a small marketable surplus and thus cannot benefit from the vibrant commodity exchanges, where the minimum traded lot is much larger than what the individual farmer has to offer. In order to extend the benefits of derivative exchanges to excluded farmers, aggregation mechanisms such as cooperatives need to come up.

In the interim, financial instruments such as warehouse receipts and post-harvest credit can be offered so that farmers can avoid distress sales. The passage of the Warehousing (Development and Regulation) Bill, 2005 by the Parliament is likely to open up a number of avenues for farmers to mitigate their price risks by encashing stock pledged in a warehouse to meet their cash needs, while waiting for the right price. The Committee is supportive of efforts to establish a chain of authorized warehouses throughout rural India, to provide such services, particularly when such warehouses are linked to PACS.

Cooperative Credit Movement over the Years

Rural credit cooperatives in India were originally envisaged as a mechanism for pooling the resources of people with small means and providing them with access to different financial services. Democratic in features, the movement was also an effective instrument for development of degraded waste lands, increasing productivity, providing food security, generating employment opportunities in rural areas and ensuring social and economic justice to the poor and vulnerable.

The history of the cooperative credit movement in India can be divided in four phases. In the First Phase (1900-30), the Cooperative Societies Act was passed (1904) and "cooperation" became a provincial subject by 1919. The major development during the Second Phase (1930-50) was the pioneering role played by RBI in guiding and supporting the cooperatives. However, even during this phase, signs of sickness in the Indian rural cooperative movement were becoming evident. The 1945 Cooperative Planning Committee had discerned these signs in the movement, finding that a large number of cooperatives were "saddled with the problem of frozen assets because of heavy overdues in repayment". Even so, also in the Third Phase (1950-90), the way forward was seen to lie in cooperative credit societies. The All India Rural Credit Survey was set up which not only recommended state partnership in terms of equity but also partnership in terms of governance and management. NABARD was also created during this phase. The Fourth Phase from 1990s onwards saw an increasing realization of the disruptive effects of intrusive state patronage and politicisation of the cooperatives, especially financial cooperatives, which resulted in poor governance and management and the consequent impairment of their financial health. A number of Committees were therefore set up to suggest reforms in the sector.

Though the network of commercial banks and RRBs has spread rapidly and they now have nearly 50,000 branches, their reach in the countryside both in terms of the number of clients and accessibility to the small and marginal farmers and other poorer segments is far less than that of cooperatives. In terms of number of agricultural credit accounts, the STCCS has 50 percent more accounts than the commercial banks and RRBs put together. Directly or indirectly, it covers nearly half of India's total population.

Health of Rural Credit Cooperatives: Despite the phenomenal outreach and volume of operations, the health of a very large proportion of these rural credit cooperatives has deteriorated significantly. The institutions are beset with problems like low resource base, high dependence on external sources of funding, excessive Governmental control, dual control, huge accumulated losses, imbalances, poor business diversification, low recovery, etc. Around half of the PACS, a fourth of the intermediate tier, viz., the DCCBs, and under a sixth of the State-level apex institutions, viz., the SCBs are loss-making. The accumulated losses of the system aggregate over ₹ 9,100 crore. Non-performing assets (NPAs), as a percentage of loans outstanding at the level of SCBs and DCCBs, at the end of March 2006 were around 16 percent and 20 percent respectively. These institutions do not, therefore, inspire confidence among their existing and potential members, depositors, borrowers and lenders. Thus, there is a need to find ways for strengthening the cooperative movement and making it a well-managed and vibrant medium to serve the credit needs of rural India, especially the small and marginal farmers.

Need for Revival of the Cooperative Credit Institutions: Given the above indicators, there has been considerable debate on whether there is an imperative need for revival of these institutions. Herein, it may be pertinent to reiterate the following points:

In the first place, India is a country with a population of more than 100 crore, of which around 70 crore reside in a little over 6 lakh villages. As there are a little over one lakh PACS in the country, the first fact to be appreciated, therefore, is that every 6th village, on an average, has an existing cooperative credit outlet.

Secondly, although the rural credit system includes about 45,000 rural and semi urban branches of commercial banks and RRBs, if one would net out the cooperatives from the aggregate rural presence of all RFIs, the per outlet population coverage deteriorates from 1:4,393 to 1:14,893. The short point is that on grounds of outreach, cooperatives cannot be ignored.

Thirdly, the outreach is significant not merely in absolute numbers but also in terms of location of outlets. The number of PACS located in hilly terrains, deserts and other areas with poor access far exceed the number of rural branches of commercial banks and RRBs.

The same set of conclusions flow when the system is viewed in the context of its membership. Assuming an artificially low family size of 4, a back of envelope calculation shows that cooperative membership touches the lives of nearly 48 crore rural people which is more than half the aggregate rural population.

As regards number of agricultural credit accounts, the credit cooperatives have 50 percent more accounts than scheduled commercial banks (including RRBs). Of these, 70 percent are estimated to be marginal and sub-marginal farmers.

On the financial side, it is sometimes argued that in terms of deposits, rural and semi-urban branches of commercial banks have nearly six times more deposits than cooperatives. While this is true, it is also true that this is part of a historic policy infirmity which allowed cooperatives to be treated as "refinance windows" instead of incentivising them into becoming genuine thrift and credit institutions.

Coming to the assets side of the balance sheet we find that cooperatives have a 37 percent share in the aggregate crop loans provided by the RFIs. However, in many districts, particularly in remote, hilly and desert areas the share is upwards of 50 percent.

Notwithstanding a larger client base, the share of cooperatives in institutional credit is lower than that provided by the commercial banks. This is because the average loan size of cooperatives is smaller at ₹ 6,637 as compared to ₹ 31,585 of commercial banks which also confirms the claim that nearly 70 percent of the cooperative structure's clients are small and marginal farmers.

A little known fact is that the system has nearly 64,000 godowns. Given an appropriate policy dispensation entailing private partnership, conditions can be created for holding of crops by farmers at the ground level in these godowns while allowing them to negotiate the godown receipts in the market. A specific plan to revitalize these godowns in cooperative sector be drawn to make them the nerve centres of rural economy on a 'kiosk' model providing storage and financial services.

Cooperatives and the Reform Process: In the backdrop of these credentials, a look has to be taken at the reform process and what it means to the cooperative credit institutions. The financial sector reforms have been components of the overall economic reforms undertaken in a phased manner from 1991-92 by the GoI. These reforms also envisaged improving the efficiency and productivity of the rural credit delivery system which in turn would accelerate the requisite credit flow to the productive sectors of the economy.

The major objectives of these reforms in the cooperative sector were:

- To make the institutions competitive by removing external constraints having a bearing on their operations,
- To improve their financial health,
- To ensure transparency in their business operations,
- To improve their profitability, and
- Institutional building and strengthening.

According to the Task Force on Revival of Rural Cooperative Credit Institutions (Vaidyanathan Committee), the STCCS never realized the enormous potential opened up by its vast outreach owing mainly to a "deep impairment of governance". While they were originally visualized as member-driven, democratic, self-governing, self-reliant institutions, cooperatives have, over the years, constantly looked up to the State for several basic functions. The Task Force has described in detail how the State Governments have become the dominant shareholders, managers, regulators, supervisors and auditors of the STCCS. The concept of mutuality (with savings and credit functions going together), that provided strength to cooperatives all over the world, has been missing in India. This "borrower-driven" system is beset with conflict of interest and has led to regulatory arbitrage, recurrent losses, deposit erosion, poor portfolio quality and a loss of competitive edge for the cooperatives. The Task Force Report also recognised that there is an impasse in the laws governing cooperative banking institutions in the country as cooperation is a State subject while banking activities are regulated by a Central Act. Further, the Task Force also took cognizance of the poor quality of internal control systems, house keeping and audit in addition to professionally not qualified human resources manning the CCS.

For the revival of the STCCS, the Vaidyanathan Committee Report has suggested an implementable Action Plan with substantial financial assistance for recapitalisation subject to introduction of strict legal and institutional reforms together with technical assistance for human resource development (HRD), establishment of a common accounting system and computerisation. The implementation of the Revival Package would result in the emergence of strong and robust cooperatives with conducive legal and institutional environment for it to prosper. At the macro level, the Revival Package is expected to promote growth with social justice and greater financial inclusion. In this background, the following observations are noteworthy:

- With 127 million plus membership and 45 million plus borrowing membership, the STCCS already exceeds the combined client base of commercial banks and RRBs. With nearly 1.25 lakh outlets spread throughout the length and breadth of the country, the STCCS after implementation of the recommendations of the Vaidyanathan Committee would be adequately equipped and would be a highly appropriate mechanism to promote financial inclusion.
- Located in rural areas, governed by local community leadership and managed by the staff with roots in rural areas, the STCCS would be oriented for promoting financial inclusion more effectively.
- The CCS with large membership of small and marginal farmers would have necessary ethos to promote and encourage financial inclusion of deprived sections of the rural economy.
- With limited overheads, the CCS outlets will be an appropriate medium for encouraging financial inclusion through "no frills" savings accounts etc.
- The rural populace will be more comfortable and will easily identify culturally with the STCCS.
- Payments under various social welfare schemes of Central and State Governments for instance old age pension, Employment Guarantee Scheme (EGS), scholarships for students, etc. could be made more transparent, safe and foolproof if routed through the STCCS and the recipients could receive the assistance at their doorsteps.
- As envisaged in the Vaidyanathan Committee Report, the membership of PACS should be open to all members of the village without any restrictions. For the purpose, the existing restrictions regarding land holding etc., should be done away with. If need be, PACS could be rechristened as Primary All-purpose Credit Societies instead of Primary Agriculture Credit Societies.
- The STCCS would be an ideal instrument for promoting financial inclusion through SHGs. Many cooperatives could be transformed into SHPIs with

proper sensitisation. Promotion of SHGs could, indeed, become a major component of the Business Development Plan of cooperative organisations of the STCCS.

- As the Vaidyanathan Committee is envisaging application of IT right from PACS to SCBs, the STCCS would be in a position to cope with the additional work load on account of promoting financial inclusion. This, in fact, would go a long way in improving the productivity of the credit cooperatives. With due internal controls and checks in place, PACS could ideally be developed as BCs of DCCBs as well as for commercial banks/RRBs wherever the reform process facilitates this.
- As financial inclusion also envisages delivery of financial services at an affordable cost, the STCCS being accessible at the door step of the financially excluded sections of the society will be in a better position to render these services more effectively.
- Located in the rural areas, the STCCS units will have better knowledge of their existing and potential clients and, as such, KYC will not be a major hindrance.

Bibliography

Bibliography

Ahluwalia, M.S. (2011), *Second Generation Reforms in the Banks: Major Issues*, paper presented at the Bank Economists' Conference, January, New Delhi.

Basu, Priya (2005), "A Financial System for India's Poor", *Economic and Political Weekly*, No. 37.

Basu, Priya (2005), *Rural Finance Access Survey (RFAS)*, World Bank and the National Council of Applied Economic Research (NCAER).

Beatrize, Armendariz and Jonathan Morduch (2007), "Economics of Microfinance", Prentice Hall of India Pvt. Ltd.

Bhatt, Nitin and Y.S.P. Thorat (2001), "India' Regional Rural Banks: The Institutional Dimension of Reforms", *Journal of Microfinance*, Vol. 3, No.1.

Bhavani, T.A. and N.R. Bhanumurthy (2012), "Financial Access in Post-Reform India", Oxford University Press, New Delhi, Chapter 12.

Binswanger, Hans P., Shahidur R. Khandker and Mark R. Rosenzweig (1993), "How Infrastructure and Financial Institutions Affect Agricultural Output and Investment in India", *Journal of Development Economics*, 41: 337-366.

Chattopadhyay, S.K. (2010), RBI Working Paper on Financial Inclusion in India: A Case Study of West Bengal, Working Paper Series 8-10, September, RBI.

European Central Bank, *Report on Electronic Money*, August 1998.

—*Opinion of ECB on e-money*, January 1999.

—*Issues Arising from the Emergence of Electronic Money*, Monthly Bulletin, November 2000.

Fisher, Thomas and M.S. Sriram (2000), "Beyond Micro-credit: Putting Development Back into Micro-finance", Vistaar Publications.

Gopinath, S. (2005), "Recent Development in Forex, Money and Government Securities Markets: Account and Outlook", *RBI Bulletin*, August.

Government of India, *Banking Committee Report*, 1972.

—Planning Commission, *Five Year Plans*.

—Ministry of Finance, *Budget Papers* (various years).

—Ministry of Finance, *Economic Survey* (various issues).

—Ministry of Law, Justice, and Company Affairs, *Constitution of India.*

Greening, H. and Bikki Randhwa (1999), "A Framework for Regulating Microfinance Institutions", World Bank.

International Monetary Fund (IMF), *World Economic Outlook*, April 2015.

—*Global Financial Stability Report,* April 2014.

Jadhav, Narendra (2003), "Central Bank Strategies, Credibility and Independence: Global Evolution and the Indian Experience", *RBI Occasional Papers.*

—"Monetary Policy, Financial Stability and Central Banking in India", New Delhi: Macmillan India Ltd., 2005.

Jadhav, Narendra, Partha Ray, Bose, D. and Indranil Sen Gupta (2003), "The Reserve

Bank of India's Balance Sheet: Analytics and Dynamics of Evolution", *RBI Occasional Papers.*

Jalan, Bimal, "Finance and Development: Which Way Now?", *RBI Bulletin*, January 2001.

—*Strengthening Indian Banking and Finance: Progress and Prospects*, Speech delivered at the Bank Economists' Conference at Bangalore, December 27, 2002.

Johri and Jauhari (1994), "Role of Computers in Banking Operation Systems", Himalaya Publishing House, New Delhi.

Kalpana, K. (2005), "Shifting Trajectories in Micro Finance Discourse", *Economic and Political Weekly*, Vol. XL, No. 51.

Kaveri, V.S. (2001), Loan Default and Profitability of Banks, *IBA Bulletin,* January.

Kohli, S.S. (2001), "Indian Banking Industry: Emerging Challenge", *IBA Bulletin,* March.

Kulkarni, R.V. (2000), "Changing Face of Banking from Brick and Mortar Banking to E-Banking", *IBA Bulletin,* January.

Malhotra, R.N. (1990), *Evolution of Financial System,* Nineteenth Frank Moraes Memorial Lecture, Chennai, September.

Martinez, Jose de Luna and Rose Thomas A. (2003), *International Survey of Integrated Financial Sector Supervision,* World Bank Policy Research Working Paper 3096.

Merton, R.C. (2005), "Financial Innovation and Economic Performance", *Journal of Applied Corporate Finance,* Vol. 4, Issue 4, pp. 12-22.

Metzer, S.R. (2000), "Strategic Planning for Future Bank Growth", *The Banker's Magazine,* July-August.

Mohan, Rakesh, "Transforming Indian Banking: In Search of a Better Tomorrow", *RBI Bulletin,* 2003.

—Agricultural Credit in India: Status, Issues and Future Agenda, *RBI Bulletin,* 2004.

—Indian Banking and e-Security, *RBI Bulletin,* November 2004.

—Ownership and Governance in Private Sector Banks in India, *RBI Bulletin,* 2004.

—Financial Sector Reforms in India: Policies and Performance Analysis, *RBI Bulletin,* October 2004.

Nair, C.K.G. (2012), "Financial Sector Reforms: Refining the Architecture", in R. Malhotra (ed.), *A Critical Decade: Policies for India's Development,* Oxford University Press, New Delhi.

Puhazhendhi, V. and K.J.S. Satyasai (2001), "Microfinance for Rural People: An Impact Study", NABARD, Mumbai.

Rajan, R. and L. Zingales (1998), "Financial Dependence and Growth", *American Economic Review,* Vol. 88.

Rajaraman, Indira (2005), "Financing Rural Infrastructure in Developing Countries", *Applied Econometrics and International Development,* Vol. 5.

Rangarajan, C., *Issues in Monetary Management,* Presidential Address at the Indian Economic Conference, Calcutta, December 1988.

—Report of the Committee (Chairman: C. Rangarajan) of Financial Inclusion, Planning

Commission, Government of India, 2008.

Rao, K.S. (2009), "Micro Credit Engine for Inclusive Growth", *The Indian Banker*, September, Vol. 4, No. 9, pp. 40-43.

Reddy, Y.V., "Financial Sector Reforms and RBI's Balance Sheet Management", *RBI Bulletin*, December 1997.

—"Banking Soundness, Monetary Policy and Macro-economic Management: Random Thoughts", *RBI Bulletin*, February 1998.

—*Financial Stability: Indian Experience*, Speech at Zurich University Zurich. Switzerland, 2004.

Reserve Bank of India, *Functions and Working of RBI,* Fourth Edition (1983).

—*Reserve Bank of India: Fifty Years (1935-85)*, 1985.

—*Report of the Committee on Financial System* (Chairman: M. Narasimham), 1991.

—*Report of the Committee on Banking Sector Reforms* (Chairman: M. Narasimham), 1998.

—*Report of the Working Group on Internet Banking* (Chairman: S.R. Mittal), 2001.

—*Reserve Bank of India: Functions and Working,* Reserve Bank Staff College, Chennai, 2001.

—*Committee on Flow of Credit to Agriculture and Related Activities from the Banking System* (Chairman: V.S. Vyas), 2004.

—*History of the Reserve Bank of India* (Vol. III), 2005.

—*Report on Trend and Progress of Banking in India (2004-05)*, 2005.

—*Report on Currency and Finance* (various years).

—*Handbook of Statistics on Indian Economy* (various years).

—*Bulletins.*

—*Occasional Papers.*

—*Supplement on Finances of State Governments.*

—*Annual Report* (Various Issues).

Sarkar, A.N. and Jagjit Singh (2006), "Savings-led Micro Finance to Bank the Unbankables: Sharing of Global Experience", *Global Economic Review*, July, Vol. 7, No. 2.

Sarma, M. (2008), "Index of Financial Inclusion", ICRIER Working Paper, August.

Sen, Amartya, (2000), "Development as Freedom", Anchor Books, New York.

Shetty, S.L. (2003), "Credit Flows to Rural Poor", mimeo, EPW Research Foundation, Mumbai.

Sinha, Saurabh (1998), "Micro Credit: Impact, Training and Sustainability", *Institute of Development Studies* (IDS), Vol. 29, No. 4, October, University Sussex, U.K.

Stern, Nicholas H. (2001), *Building a Climate for Investment, Growth and Poverty Reduction in India*, 16th Exim Bank Commencement Day Annual Lecture, Mumbai.

Tarapore, S.S., *Domestic Debt Management Policy and Monetary Control*, 18th SEANZA Central Banking Course Lectures, Reserve Bank of India, Mumbai, 1990.

Tara, S. Nair (2005), "The Transforming World of Indian Micro Finance", *Economic and Political Weekly*, April 23.

Thingalaya, N.K. (2000), "The Other Side of Rural Banking", BIRD Publication, Lucknow.

Thorat, U., Keynote address at a panel session on "Setting New Paradigm in Regulation" at the FICCI-IBA Conference on 'Global Banking: Paradigm Shift', 2010.

Trivedi, Pratima (2008), "Financial Inclusion: A Must for Financial Stability", *Vinimaya*, Vol. XXIX (2), pp. 59-64.

UNCDF (2006), "Building Inclusive Financial Sectors for Development", UNCDF, May, available online at bluebook.uncdf.org.

Valpy, FitzGerald (2006), "Financial Development and Economic Growth: A Critical View", Background paper for World Economic and Social Survey, 2006, Oxford University, U.K.

World Bank, "Improving Access to Finance for India's Rural Poor", The World Bank, 2008.

— "Finance for All: Policies and Pitfalls in Expanding Access", World Bank, Washington, 2008.

—"Measuring Financial Inclusion", Policy Research Working Paper, 6025, World Bank, Washington D.C., 2011.

—"Financial Access: The State of Financial Inclusion through the Crisis', Consultative Group to Assist the Poor (CGAP), 2010.

Websites

Ministry of Finance, Government of India
Reserve Bank of India (RBI)
Securities and Exchange Board of India (SEBI)
National Bank for Agriculture and Rural Development (NABARD)

Index

Index